STIRRED BY A NOBLE THEME

Stirred by a Noble Theme

The book of Psalms in the life of the church

Edited by ANDREW G. SHEAD

APOLLOS (an imprint of Inter-Varsity Press)
Norton Street, Nottingham NG7 3HR, England
Email: ivp@ivpbooks.com
Website: www.ivpbooks.com

First published 2013

British Library Cataloguing in Publication Data
A catalogue record for this book is available from the British Library.

UK ISBN: 978-1-78359-011-7

Set in Monotype Garamond 11/13pt
Typeset in Great Britain by CRB Associates, Potterhanworth, Lincolnshire
Printed and bound in Great Britain by Ashford Colour Press Ltd, Gosport,
Hampshire

*Inter-Varsity Press publishes Christian books that are true to the Bible and that communicate
the gospel, develop discipleship and strengthen the church for its mission in the world.*

*Inter-Varsity Press is closely linked with the Universities and Colleges Christian Fellowship,
a student movement connecting Christian Unions in universities and colleges throughout Great
Britain, and a member movement of the International Fellowship of Evangelical Students.
Website: www.uccf.org.uk.*

CONTENTS

TABLES AND FIGURES

Tables

Figures

CONTRIBUTORS

Greg Anderson heads the Mission department at Moore College, after returning from twelve years working with indigenous Australian Christians and churches in the Northern Territory. His research interests include Fourth World missiology and Christian engagement with Islam.

Kit Barker is a lecturer in Old Testament at Sydney Missionary and Bible College, where his teaching focuses on the Psalms and the prophets. He has published an article in *JTI* on speech-act theory and hermeneutics, and has recently completed doctoral research on theological interpretation and the Psalms.

Andrew Cameron lectures in ethics, social ethics and philosophy at Moore Theological College, and chairs the Social Issues Executive of the Anglican Diocese of Sydney. He is the author of *Joined-up Life: A Christian Account of How Ethics Works* (Inter-Varsity Press) and co-editor of *The Trials of Theology* (Christian Focus) and *Still Deadly* (Aquila).

James Hely Hutchinson is Director of the Institut Biblique Belge, in Brussels, where he teaches Old Testament, biblical theology and biblical languages, and where he edits *Le Maillon* (http://www.institutbiblique.be). He is the author of several articles on the book of Psalms.

Seumas Macdonald is a lecturer at Union Bible Theological College, Mongolia, where he teaches New Testament exegesis and theology. He is also completing a doctoral thesis in patristic theology at Macquarie University.

David Peterson is an emeritus faculty member of Moore Theological College, where he continues to teach part time. His most recent publications include *The Acts of the Apostles* (PNTC), *Transformed by God* (Inter-Varsity Press) and *Encountering God Together* (Inter-Varsity Press).

Andrew Shead is the head of the Old Testament department at Moore Theological College, where he teaches Hebrew, textual criticism, Psalms and the prophets. His most recent publication is *A Mouth Full of Fire: The Word of God in the Words of Jeremiah* (Apollos), and he is writing a commentary on Jeremiah and Lamentations (Zondervan).

Andrew Sloane is Senior Lecturer in Old Testament and Christian thought at Morling College, where he teaches Old Testament interpretation, theology, ethics and philosophy. He has published *At Home in a Strange Land: Using the Old Testament in Christian Ethics* (Hendricksen/Baker), and is working on a book on a Christian philosophical theology of medicine (T. & T. Clark).

Tara Stenhouse serves as the Dean of Women at Moore College, where she oversees the pastoral care of the female students. She also teaches within the Ministry department. Previously she served in university ministry, having been ordained as a deacon in the Sydney Anglican Church.

Mark Thompson is the Principal of Moore Theological College, Sydney. He lectures in Christian doctrine and also heads the college's Theology, Philosophy and Ethics department. He has written numerous books and articles with a particular focus on the doctrine of Scripture. His *A Clear and Present Word: The Clarity of Scripture* (Apollos) appeared in 2006. He is researching a book on Christology.

John Woodhouse has retired from serving as Principal of Moore Theological College. He recently published *Looking for a Leader: 1 Samuel* (Preach the Word, Crossway) and *Colossians and Philemon* (Focus on the Bible, Christian Focus). His current writing project is an expository commentary on 2 Samuel (Preach the Word, Crossway).

Dan Wu lectures in biblical studies at Moore Theological College. His doctoral research explores the themes of honour, shame and guilt in the book of Ezekiel. Until recently he worked as the minister of an Anglican congregation in Sydney.

ABBREVIATIONS

4QFlor *Florilegium* (Dead Sea Scrolls)
AASF Annales Academiae scientiarum fennicae
ACW Ancient Christian Writers
AJET *Africa Journal of Evangelical Theology*
ANF A. Roberts (ed.), *Ante-Nicene Fathers* (Peabody:
  Hendricksen, repr. 1995 [1885])
AV Authorized (King James) Version
BCOT Baker Commentary on the Old Testament
BDAG W. Bauer, F. W. Danker, W. F. Arndt and W. F.
  Gingrich, *A Greek–English Lexicon of the New
  Testament and Other Early Christian Literature*, 3rd ed.
  (Chicago: University of Chicago Press, 2000)
BDB F. Brown, S. R. Driver and C. A. Briggs, *A Hebrew
  and English Lexicon of the Old Testament* (Oxford:
  Clarendon, 1907; repr. Peabody: Hendrickson, 2005)
BSac *Bibliotheca sacra*
BST The Bible Speaks Today
BT *The Bible Translator*
BZ *Biblische Zeitschrift*
c. circa
CBQ *Catholic Biblical Quarterly*
CBR *Currents in Biblical Research*
CBSC Cambridge Bible for Schools and Colleges
Chm *Churchman*
CR K. G. Bretschneider, H. E. Bindseil, G. Baum et al.
  (eds.), *Corpus Reformatorum*, 101 vols. (Halle: C. A.
  Schwetschke et Filium, 1834–1907)
CTJ *Calvin Theological Journal*

DPHL   *Dictionary of Paul and His Letters*, ed. G. F. Hawthorne
and R. P. Martin (Downers Grove: InterVarsity Press;
Leicester: Inter-Varsity Press, 1993)

ERT   *Evangelical Review of Theology*

ESV   English Standard Version (2002)

EvQ   *Evangelical Quarterly*

Gk.   Greek

HCSB   Holman Standard Christian Bible (2003)

Hebr.   Hebrew

Int   *Interpretation*

JETS   *Journal of the Evangelical Theological Society*

JPC   *Journal of Psychology and Christianity*

JQRSup   Jewish Quarterly Review, Supplement Series

JSOT   *Journal for the Study of the Old Testament*

JSOTSup   Journal for the Study of the Old Testament,
Supplement Series

JSS   *Journal of Semitic Studies*

JTI   *Journal of Theological Interpretation*

LCL   Loeb Classical Library

LD   Lectio divina

lit.   literally

LXX   the Septuagint

mg.   margin

MS   manuscript

MT   Masoretic Text

NETS   New English Translation of the Septuagint

NIDOTTE   *New International Dictionary of Old Testament Theology
and Exegesis*, ed. W. A. VanGemeren, 5 vols. (Grand
Rapids: Zondervan; Carlisle: Paternoster, 1997)

NIGTC   New International Greek Testament Commentary

NIV   New International Version (2011)

NIVAC   NIV Application Commentary

NRSV   New Revised Standard Version (1995)

NSBT   New Studies in Biblical Theology

OBO   Orbis biblicus et orientalis

OT   Old Testament

PG   Patrologiae, cursus completus, patres ecclesiae, series
graeca, ed. J.-P. Migne, 162 vols. (Paris: Cerf, 1857–86)

PL   Patrologiae, cursus completus, patres ecclesiae, series
      latina, ed. J.-P. Migne, 221 vols. (Paris: Cerf, 1844–64)
PNTC   Pillar New Testament Commentary
Pss Sol.   *Psalms of Solomon*
RB   *Revue biblique*
REB   Revised English Bible (1989)
RSV   Revised Standard Version (1971)
SBLDS   SBL Dissertation Series
SBS   Stuttgarter Bibelstudien
SBT   Studies in Biblical Theology
SubBi   Subsidia biblica
TDNT   *Theological Dictionary of the New Testament*, ed. G. Kittel
      and G. Friedrich, tr. G. W. Bromiley, 10 vols. (Grand
      Rapids: Eerdmans, 1964–76)
TNIV   Today's New International Version (2005)
TOTC   Tyndale Old Testament Commentaries
tr.   translation
TrinJ   *Trinity Journal*
TynB   *Tyndale Bulletin*
VT   *Vetus Testamentum*
WA   *D. Martin Luthers Werke: kritische Gesamtausgabe
      (Weimar Ausgabe)* (Weimar: Hermann Buhlaus
      Nachfolger, 1966–)
WTJ   *Westminster Theological Journal*

INTRODUCTION

Andrew G. Shead

No biblical book has had a richer history in the life of the church than the Psalms. Preached, sung, memorized and prayed for two thousand years, these poems have written themselves into the DNA of Christ's people. They have shaped the way Christians exist in the world, the way they process the pains and joys of life.

This makes it all the more troubling that so many evangelical churches have set the Psalms to one side. With the dominance of contemporary music some of us have stopped singing them; with the loss of traditional liturgy some of us have stopped saying them. The aim of this book is to encourage churches to take up the Psalms, and to use them well – well enough to claim and hold our affections.

One of the reasons many of us are slow to take up the Psalms is that we are not sure how to use them well. This is not simply about the creative challenge of making them a living, breathing part of our gathered worship, but the deeper hermeneutical challenge of reading them well as Christian Scripture.

For the Psalms present us with unique difficulties of reading. They are not like other parts of Scripture. The prophets spoke oracles from God, but the theology of the Psalms arises from the daily lives of his people. The apostles expounded the death and resurrection of Christ through sermon and epistle, but the Christology of the Psalms is expressed in poetry. The Gospels show us Jesus in the flesh, teaching, healing, dying and rising. In the Psalms we are invited to accompany him on his journey of suffering, trust and vindication.

What are we to do with such unique theology? How should we hear it as Christians? How can it shape our life together, and our lives as individuals? The present volume does not provide a single, simple answer, as a singly authored work might do. Instead, it lets us hear a variety of complementary voices, voices that explore these issues with a common seriousness about the text and its application and a common respect for its authority, unity and Christ-centredness, but that offer a range of perspectives on how these principles of evangelical reading should best be expressed.

Perhaps the most basic of these issues is the hermeneutical challenge of reading the Psalms Christologically without doing violence to their initial context and meaning. To what extent may we read each psalm as a prayer of Jesus Christ? How do the psalms in which David confesses his sin foreshadow Jesus? The different insights contributors have offered on this question add up to a conversation aimed at helping readers think more carefully and fruitfully about good reading.

The annual conference from which these chapters derive was for many years published with the subtitle 'Explorations', and the description remains apt. The contributions are not always 'safe'; they aim to provoke and push us perhaps beyond our comfort zones at times. How far can holistic reading of the psalter be taken? How far can Christological reading be taken? How far can translation be taken? How far can corporate lament, or imprecation, be taken? Few readers will agree with every word they read, but our goal as authors is to push people to be better readers of Scripture – more careful, more patient, more honest, more Christian, and more obedient.

The plan of the volume is well conveyed by the table of contents, and requires little elaboration. The opening chapters explore how to read the book of Psalms, with a special focus on 'Christ-shaped reading'. From James Hely Hutchinson's foundational chapter on the shape and message of the psalter as a book, and the implications this shape has for preachers and teachers, we move to three studies of Christ-shaped reading from three different angles. John Woodhouse immerses us in the Psalms to show, through an inductive reading, how psalms principally serve to illuminate the news that *'Jesus* is the Christ', but also guide Christians to take refuge in him. David Peterson provides us with an important study of the use of the Psalms in Acts and Hebrews: in Acts the psalms feature as prophetic literature, applied to Jesus out of an understanding of the role of David in God's plan. Davidic typology also plays a role in Hebrews' confidence that the psalms bear prophetic witness to Christ as Son and Priest. Finally, Mark Thompson demonstrates, through a close reading of Psalm 22, that the poetic form of the Psalms in no way hinders the activity of systematic theological reflection, but actually enriches it by modelling the truth that good theology is 'fit to be addressed to God'. Next, Seumas Macdonald has translated excerpts from sermons by Basil of Caesarea, Chrysostom and Augustine on the same Psalm (Ps. 45) to illustrate both the variety and the consistency of Christological reading of the Psalms in the early church.

The four principal chapters lay the groundwork for the seven that follow Seumas Macdonald's, each of which explores a different facet of the Psalms in the life of the church. (1) Does the poetry of the psalms need to find a fresh voice in the twenty-first century? How should the poetic form of the Psalms shape the way we hear and teach them? (2) How can the Psalms, taken as God's songs for us to sing with Christ, shape the church's life together? How might we tackle the reluctance to use Psalms in churches enamoured with newly written songs? (3) What can we learn from the experiences of suffering Christians who have turned to the psalms of lament in times of trouble? (4) How do imprecations function as the word of God? Can imprecation still be a righteous response for the Christian? (5) Can we move from the psalters' moments of existential crisis to a Christological resolution? How can we hang on to confidence in the midst of perplexity? (6) What does the book of Psalms have to say about God's concern for human social arrangements and the role of God's people in enacting them? How can the Psalms shape political theology and social engagement? (7) If the psalter is about God's universal reign and the way we enthrone him on our praises, what does the mission of God's people look like in the Psalms? Is there an implicit model for mission in the psalter?

In short, our goal is to hear the message of the Psalms – as a story, as prophecy, as theology, as poetry, as praise – and to explore its application for the people of God in every situation, whether in joy or pain, perplexity or persecution, politics or mission.

Thanks go to my colleagues on the Moore College faculty who contributed papers, and especially to guest presenters who came from other Sydney colleges or, in the case of Dr Hely Hutchinson, from across the world, to take part in the conference. Their work has been ushered into print with initial help from my research assistant Matthew Kennedy and, as always, the patient, encouraging and excellent work of Phil Duce and the team at Inter-Varsity Press.

Why do nations riot? Populations
cry and mutter empty imprecations?
Kings of earth stand adamantly steadfast,
dignitaries join in solemn council –
to oppose the LORD and his Anointed!
'Let us tear their manacles asunder,
fling from off ourselves their binding shackles!'

The one who sits in heaven laughs,
the LORD m-m-m-mocks them.
Then speaks to them in burning wrath,
in his fury panics them:
'It's I who have installed my king
on Zion, my holy mountain.'

Let me recount the LORD's decree:
'You are my son,' he said to me,
'I did this day beget you.
Ask it of me and I shall make
nations into your freehold,
earth's ends your estate.
You'll batter them with an iron rod,
like porcelain you'll shatter them.'

Now therefore, O kings, be wise,
be instructed, earthly judges.
Serve the LORD with fearfulness
and rejoice with trembling.
Kiss the Son or he will rage –
and you will drop in your tracks,
for his wrath will flare in a flash.

Lucky for all who hide themselves in him.

(Psalm 2, tr. Andrew G. Shead)

PART 1

READING THE PSALMS
AS CHRISTIAN SCRIPTURE

1. THE PSALTER AS A BOOK

James Hely Hutchinson

Introduction: 'macro' and 'micro'

Since the early 1990s or so, something of a revolution has taken place in the world of Psalms scholarship. This revolution hinges on a concern to interpret the *psalter* – to understand the book of Psalms at the 'macro' level, as opposed to 'merely' understanding the book's individual psalms at the 'micro' level. Many of the key indicators of macro shape have long been recognized and are uncontroversial: the psalter contains five books (each with a concluding doxology), an editorial comment following Book 2 (Ps. 72:20), various groups of psalms (such as the Songs of Ascents [Pss 120 – 134]), twin psalms found side by side (such as Pss 105 – 106), psalms whose collocation reflects concatenation (or linking, such as Pss 134 – 135 – 136). The revolution involves *making sense* of these phenomena – drawing inferences from them – as well as discerning other, less obvious, indicators. Although the last few years have seen the deaths of arguably the three key protagonists of this movement (Brevard Childs, Gerald Wilson, Erich Zenger), yet the legitimacy of macro (or 'canonical') psalter research is now almost universally recognized by Old Testament scholars.[1] We find ourselves, however, in a state of flux: much ink continues to be spilled, but no clear consensus appears to be emerging as to the significance of the arrangement of the canonical psalter. '[I]t is inconceivable that conversations about the shape and shaping of the Psalter will abate', asserts Kenneth Kuntz as he concludes a survey of recent Psalms research.[2]

Yet the effects of the revolution have already been trickling down into the church. Indeed, popular commentaries that reflect a macro concern (in English,[3] German[4] and French[5]), as well as accessible books,[6] have begun to claim the attention of the preacher and the pew. My presupposition is that, against this background, many busy pastor-preachers are liable to feel unsure of their ground as they seek to go about the task of teaching from this important book of the Scriptures. My primary aim in this chapter will be to offer some guidance as to the (macro) shape of the psalter, but I will also touch on the implications of this shape for our approach to appropriating and teaching the various (micro) individual psalms.

---

1. Notable among the exceptions are R. Norman Whybray, *Reading the Psalms as a Book*, JSOTSup 222 (Sheffield: Sheffield Academic Press, 1996), ch. 1, pp. 15–35; and Tremper Longman III, 'Messiah', in Tremper Longman and Peter Enns (eds.), *Dictionary of the Old Testament: Wisdom, Poetry & Writings* (Downers Grove: InterVarsity Press; Nottingham: Inter-Varsity Press, 2008), p. 471: '[O]ne has to seriously question any new insight like this that has not been recognized over the millennia of previous interpretation'.

2. J. Kenneth Kuntz, 'Continuing the Engagement: Psalms Research Since the Early 1990s', *CBR* 10 (2012), p. 364.

3. Michael Wilcock, *The Message of Psalms*, 2 vols., BST (Leicester: Inter-Varsity Press, 2001); Gerald H. Wilson, *Psalms*, vol. 1, NIVAC.

4. Frank-Lothar Hossfeld and Erich Zenger, *Die Psalmen*, 3 vols., Die Neue Echter Bibel (Würzburg: Echter, 1993, 2002, 2012); Beat Weber, *Werkbuch Psalmen*, 2 vols. (Stuttgart: Kohlhammer, 2001, 2003).

5. Jean-Luc Vesco, *Le Psautier de David*, 2 vols., LD (Paris: Cerf, 2006).

6. E.g. Mark D. Futato, *Transformed by Praise: The Purpose and Message of the Psalms* (Phillipsburg: P. & R., 2002); Gordon J. Wenham, *Psalms as Torah: Reading Biblical Song Ethically* (Grand Rapids: Baker Academic, 2012), ch. 2, pp. 27–40.

Flow of the psalter's message

Introduction (Pss 1 – 2): 'Happy are those who meditate on Psalm 2!'

In line with current scholarly consensus, it is appropriate to consider that the first *two* psalms serve as the psalter's introduction, or the gateway into the rest of the book. Several links between Psalms 1 and 2 are sufficiently striking to invite reflection as to how they fit together. In the final verse of both psalms, we read of a 'way' that is associated with 'destruction'. Both psalms pronounce 'happy' (my tr.) those who avoid this way. This idea of being happy corresponds in both psalms to the idea of being wise, Psalm 1 being a wisdom psalm and the last section of Psalm 2 (vv. 10–12) containing wisdom features. In Psalm 1 the idea of being happy or wise is conditional on meditating on 'the *tôrâ* of Yahweh', whereas in Psalm 2 it is conditional on serving Yahweh, kissing the Son and taking refuge 'in him' – probably the Son.

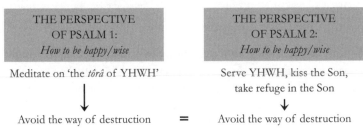

Figure 1.1 Complementary perspectives of Psalms 1 and 2.

Since the idea of being happy frames the two psalms (1:1; 2:12), it is reasonable to suppose that these two means of avoiding the 'way of destruction' are not in conflict with one another. How then do they tie together? The key to answering that question lies with the 'therefore' of 2:10. Serving Yahweh, kissing the Son and taking refuge in the Son are actions that wise people will take in view of the data of Psalm 2 that precede verse 10. To summarize those data, Yahweh's reaction to the nations' rebellion is one of derision and wrath, for he has established his anointed on Zion, his 'holy hill'; this King, the Son, is on a par with Yahweh and is thus *supreme* – indeed, he is ultimately the owner and judge of the nations.

Thus, the logic of the interplay between these two psalms leads us to understand that there are not two independent, or even simply complementary, means of avoiding the 'way of destruction' – one that involves meditating on 'the *tôrâ* of Yahweh' and a second one that involves recognizing the supremacy of the Son. Rather, Psalm 2 unpacks Psalm 1: if one meditates on 'the *tôrâ* of Yahweh', one meditates on the supremacy of the Son (hence the horizontal arrow in this expanded version of the diagram):

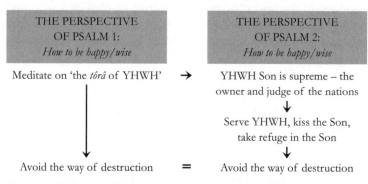

Figure 1.2 Psalm 2 as an 'unpacking' of Psalm 1.

This might seem counterintuitive. Such an understanding might appear to require that the word *tôrâ* here should denote 'instruction', 'revelation', without bearing any connotation of the Law of Moses. But this would be to downplay three related observations. First, as is now widely recognized, a close relationship between the opening psalms and the remainder of the psalter is suggested by the fact that Psalms 1 and 2 are 'recalled' at structurally significant junctures, notably at the beginning and end of books.[7] This is particularly true of Psalm 2. In the following diagram, 'W' means 'wisdom psalm' and 'R/C' 'royal/covenantal psalm', and it is particularly to be noted that the psalms which stand at the end of Books 2, 3, 4 and 5 all reflect the subject matter of Psalm 2:

---

7. Cf. Gerald H. Wilson, *The Editing of the Hebrew Psalter*, SBLDS 76 (Chico: Scholars Press, 1985), pp. 209–228; 'The Use of Royal Psalms at the "Seams" of the Hebrew Psalter', *JSOT* 35 (1986), pp. 85–94; 'The Shape of the Book of Psalms', *Int* 46 (1992), pp. 129–142.

INTRO (1 – 2)	BOOK 1 (3 – 41)	BOOK 2 (42 – 72)	BOOK 3 (73 – 89)	BOOK 4 (90 – 106)	BOOK 5 (107 – 144/145)	CONCL (145/146 –150)
W R/C		R/C	W R/C	(W) R/C	(W) R/C	

Figure 1.3 Royal/covenantal and wisdom psalms featuring at boundaries between books.

As one might expect in view of the introductory role that Psalm 2 plays, it turns out that the psalter as a whole sets forth an extended meditation on Psalm 2. I trust this will become clear from my treatment below. Secondly, in the historical context of the compilation of the psalter, the original recipients of this book – the (potentially) happy, wise people who (potentially) first carry out the meditating – are located after the Babylonian exile and prior to the first coming of the Psalm 2 king.[8] We could usefully have in mind someone like Ezra[9] – or, more familiar to most Bible readers, Joseph (Mary's fiancé), Simeon, Anna or any other righteous individual belonging to the post-exilic period. Their circumstances appear to belie the truths of Psalm 2, and their meditating reflects a standpoint of crisis: during the post-exilic period, the Persians, Greeks and Romans hold sway, but not Yahweh's anointed. Joseph,

---

8. Ps. 137 is certainly post-exilic. We should not, however, allow the data from Qumran to lead us to affirm a first-century AD date for the final form of the psalter (contra Wilson, *Psalms*, p. 30). See Roger Beckwith, 'The Early History of the Psalter', *TynB* 46 (1995), pp. 1–28 ('The eccentric Psalms MSS from Qumran are probably liturgical adaptations,' p. 1); and Leslie McFall, 'The Evidence for a Logical Arrangement of the Psalter', *WTJ* 62 (2000), pp. 223–256 ('Whatever the Qumran sect did with its store of Psalms is probably confined to them,' p. 225). There are good reasons to believe that the psalter had reached its final form before Chronicles – that the chronicler quotes the closing doxology of Book 4 along with Ps. 106 (1 Chr. 16:35–36) and not the other way round. Be that as it may, the LXX reflects the final form of the psalter, implying an early second-century BC date as *terminus ad quem* for the latter (cf. Jean-Marie Auwers, *La Composition littéraire du Psautier: Un état de la question*, Cahiers de la Revue Biblique 46 [Paris: Gabalda, 2000], p. 168, and the bibliography he cites in n. 527).

9. Who has sometimes been credited with the role of compiler-editor of the psalter. While this suggestion fits with Ezra 7:6, 10, it remains speculative.

Simeon and Anna have to wrestle to try to reconcile what they see in Jerusalem with what they perceive by faith, and the psalter may be viewed as the story of their journey of meditation against the backdrop of crisis. Thirdly, the resolution to this crisis lies *precisely* with the Law of Moses, which delivers the theological ammunition that provides for appropriate meditating on Psalm 2 in adverse circumstances. This is made clear by the theological heart of the psalter, Book 4. In short, from the perspective of the psalter as a whole, there is no warrant for driving a wedge between meditating on the Law of Moses and meditating on the person and work of the Christ of Psalm 2. This should become clear as we now accompany Joseph, Simeon and Anna on their journey.

Book 1 (Pss 3 – 41): 'David's a reverse type!'

The meditating begins with David, the first king over all Israel and established as such in Jerusalem. The compiler-editor of the psalter has provided us with the equivalent (in today's terms) of an explanatory footnote following the end of Book 2 that speaks of the end of the 'prayers of David, son of Jesse' (Ps. 72:20). Prior to this point, the psalter is essentially Davidic, and explicitly so in all the psalm titles in Book 1 (there are only two psalms in Book 1 without a title, and these are closely tied to their predecessors). These prayers, uttered by the (historic) David,[10] provide the reader of the psalter with two portraits of this king. In one of them David seems to match the king of Psalm 2. This is the portrait that emerges from Psalms 15 – 24, a section bracketed by the question as to who is fit to live on Yahweh's holy hill (15:1; 24:3).[11] According to Psalm 2, the answer to this question is *Yahweh's Son* (2:6). According to Psalms 15 – 24, the answer to this question is *David*. His righteousness and integrity are particularly highlighted in Psalm 18 (especially vv. 20–24). This psalm echoes many themes from Psalm 2, presenting an 'anointed'

---

10. See the titles of Pss 7 and 18.

11. For the structure of this section, Pierre Auffret's analysis has convinced a large proportion of the scholarly community. See his *La Sagesse a bâti sa maison: Etudes de structures littéraires dans l'Ancien Testament et spécialement dans les Psaumes*, OBO 49 (Fribourg: Editions Universitaires; Göttingen: Vandenhoeck & Ruprecht, 1982), pp. 409–438.

whose supremacy is absolute; David himself, and not merely his offspring, proves to be a beneficiary of God's *ḥesed* or loyalty to the promise to establish his throne:

> He gives his king great victories,
> he shows unfailing love to his anointed,
> to David and to his descendants for ever.
> (Ps. 18:50; cf. 2 Sam. 7:12–16)

The same perspective is found in the twin Psalms 20 – 21, which form the counterpart to Psalm 18 in a concentric structure across this group of psalms. It is true that this section also presents a David who suffers, but these sufferings are a prelude to ultimate victory and the satisfaction of close proximity with Yahweh: David will 'dwell in the house of the LORD for ever' (23:6).

The second portrait in Book 1 is the more dominant one. It depicts a David who is the inverse of the Psalm 2 king. David's problems are presented cumulatively through the other three sections of the book: observing the broad brushstrokes, he is having to face up to enemy opposition (Pss 3 – 14); enemy opposition and personal sin (Pss 25 – 34);[12] enemy opposition and personal sin and personal sickness (Pss 35 – 41). It is not that these psalms are devoid of expressions of confidence that God can deliver from enemies, sin and sickness; but by the end of the book it is clear that these three problems are intertwined (Ps. 39:7–11), and they combine to form a picture of a David who, patently, is not qualified to be the supreme ruler. The suggestion that he could be, or become, the owner of the nations, or their judge, is simply incongruous. Whether he is fleeing from Absalom (as at the start of the book, Ps. 3) or lying on his sickbed (as at the end, Ps. 41), he is not established on Zion, Yahweh's holy hill. Thus, from a macro (psalter) perspective, the David of the main portrait of Book 1 does not fit the bill of the Messiah of Psalm 2.

---

12. This section appears to be bracketed by alphabetic acrostics that feature the same irregularities: Pss 25 and 34 both omit the sixth letter and add an extra line at the end that begins with a form of the verb *pādâ* (redeem).

Joseph, Simeon and Anna are starting to make sense of the history of their nation. They understand that, from one camera angle, David is a type of the Psalm 2 king, and that, from another camera angle, he is a reverse type. David is not *himself* the one appointed 'to dash [the nations] to pieces like pottery' (Ps. 2:9). And so the meditating moves on to Book 2.

Book 2 (Pss 42 – 72): 'Bring on Solomon!'

In one sense the second book provides us with more of the same. As was true for Book 1, the two psalms without a title are closely tied to their predecessors; as was true for Book 1, the historical David is in view, although some Book 2 psalms are authored by his musicians; substantial parts of Book 1 are essentially reproduced in Psalm 53 (which corresponds to Ps. 14) and in Psalm 70 (which corresponds to Ps. 40:13–17), and echoes are not merely of content but also of placement within the respective books. Given such formal pointers of continuity, it comes as no surprise that Book 2 reinforces the message of Book 1 by presenting us with a David who is beleaguered by his enemies and troubled by his sins.

But the meditating by Joseph, Simeon and Anna does develop in Book 2 in three significant ways relative to Book 1. First, the gap between David and the Psalm 2 king widens: in the first psalm 'of David' (Ps. 51), he prays in his capacity as an adulterer and murderer, and, in the last one (Ps. 71),[13] he prays in his capacity as an old man, devoid of strength. Further, the 'holy hill' that is Zion is given some prominence in this book (notably in Pss 46 – 48), but David is conspicuously absent from this location: the historical information in the titles has him on the run, in a cave, in captivity, in the desert – almost anywhere but Jerusalem.

Secondly, and accordingly, the search for the Psalm 2 king is now focused elsewhere. The structure of Book 2 serves to point this up. The beginning of the book sets forth enemy oppression and spiritual

---

13. This is one of the psalms without a title. That it needs to be read as the continuation of Ps. 70 – which is explicitly Davidic – is clear from the quasi-refrain that features at 70:2, 71:13 and 71:24b. The two psalms are tied in many Hebrew manuscripts.

depression tied to God's absence – twin problems confronting an individual (Pss 42 – 43) and the nation of Israel as a whole (Ps. 44). Joseph, Simeon and Anna, surrounded by Romans, can identify with this dual problem. These psalms contain the seeds of the solution, which lies with the *ḥesed*, or covenant loyalty, of Yahweh (42:8; 44:26). The promises of 2 Samuel 7, which form part of the backdrop to Psalm 2, had foreshadowed this *ḥesed* and had made it clear that this covenant loyalty must find concrete expression in the shape of ever-lasting Davidic, messianic rule. In line with this expectation, the rest of Book 2 is framed by two psalms (45 and 72) clearly reminiscent of Psalm 2, and, in both cases, the king in question is *Solomon*. Such, at least, is the traditional, and least problematic, understanding of the identity of the bridegroom in the historical context of Psalm 45.[14] As for Psalm 72, we need, for a variety of reasons,[15] to understand the title as meaning '*for* Solomon' (so AV, Darby): David is the author, Solomon the subject matter of the psalm – it is David's twilight prayer for his 'royal son' (v. 1). What ambitious hopes these two psalms express in relation to Solomon – with regard to supremacy, righteousness and status on a par with Yahweh! Here,

---

14. And even if it is not absolutely secure, a 'Solomonic atmosphere' in this psalm is scarcely in doubt. The splendour and luxury of the king's court, the marriage to a foreign princess (1 Kgs 3:1) and dealings with the King of Tyre (1 Kgs 5:15; cf. Ps. 45:12) may be cited in favour of Solomon as bridegroom. See Alexander F. Kirkpatrick, *The Book of Psalms: Books II and III*, CBSC (Cambridge: Cambridge University Press, 1895), p. 244.

15. The reasons are as follows: (1) LXX, which disambiguates the Hebrew preposition; (2) the juxtaposition with Ps. 71, which presents David in the twilight of his life and makes it plausible to suggest that Ps. 72 constitutes his closing prayer (cf. Jean-Marie Auwers, 'Les Psaumes 70–72, Essai de lecture canonique', *RB* 101 [1994], pp. 242–257; *La Composition*, p. 136 [although the historical authenticity of the titles should be affirmed]); (3) the links between Ps. 72:6–7 and David's 'last words' in 2 Sam. 23:3b–4 (Derek Kidner, *Psalms 1–72*, TOTC [Downers Grove: Inter-Varsity Press, 1973], p. 255); (4) the numerous links between Ps. 72 and the portrait of Solomon provided by 1 Kings (e.g. Auwers, 'Les Psaumes 70–72', p. 248); (5) the juxtaposition with 72:20 (Jean Calvin, *Commentaires sur le livre des Pseaumes*, vol. 2 [Paris: Ch. Meyrueis, 1859], p. 25); cf. Brevard S. Childs, *Introduction to the Old Testament as Scripture* (Philadelphia: Fortress, 1979), p. 516.

indeed, are hopes worthy of a 'Psalm 2 king'! With regard to military achievements, it is envisaged, or at least desired,[16] that 'the nations fall beneath [him]' (Ps. 45:5), that he 'rule from sea to sea, / and from the River to the ends of the earth', that 'his enemies lick the dust', that 'all kings bow down to him, / and all nations serve him' (Ps. 72:8–11). The righteous character of this king takes up three verses of Psalm 45 (vv. 4, 6–7) and eight of Psalm 72 (vv. 1–4, 7, 12–14). With regard to his status, Psalm 72 opens with the request that the king be able to exercise divine justice; his throne is to endure 'for ever and ever' (Ps. 45:6); he is to be feared 'as long as the sun' (Ps. 72:5 mg.), and 'his name' is, likewise, to 'endure for ever' (Ps. 72:17).

There is a third noteworthy distinction between the first two books that strikes the macro reader of the psalter. The doxology that closes Book 2 clearly echoes that of Book 1, but it incorporates a yearning that 'the whole earth be filled with his glory' (72:19). The appeal to the nations to praise God is an important theme in this book (notably Pss 65 – 68). Indeed, the end of the closing psalm picks up on the language of the Abrahamic covenant in speaking of blessing flowing to all nations; but this blessing can come about only through the righteous king of kings (Ps. 72:17b).

Joseph, Simeon and Anna understand that messianic expectations are now concentrated on great David's prospectively greater son. Much is riding on this figure of Solomon – hope for Israel (the Davidic covenant), hope even for the nations (the Abrahamic covenant).

Book 3 (Pss 73 – 89): 'Exile means crisis!'

Enter Book 3, and hope is in short supply. The book is bounded by near despair, the truth of Psalm 1 being called into question at the start (first half of Ps. 73) and the truth of Psalm 2 being called into question at the end (second half of Ps. 89). At the beginning of the book, in Psalm 73, the near despair is expressed by only one individual. Yet at the end of the book, in Psalm 89, the perspective is

---

16. The hesitation here stems from the fact that Hebrew imperfective and jussive are often not morphologically distinguished.

that of the nation as a whole. To be sure, in Psalm 73 there is a healthy 180-degree turnaround in the second half of the psalm. Yet in Psalm 89 the turnaround moves in the opposite direction, from positive to negative, and it is on a note of crisis that the book concludes. Even the book's closing doxology (Ps. 89:52) is stripped to its barest bones relative to those of the first two books. Moving inwards to consider the psalms adjacent to those of the extremities of the book, Psalms 74 and 88 reinforce the anguish and gloom, respectively from a national and an individual perspective. In terms of what has given rise to the crisis, the Babylonian exile is centre stage (Pss 74:3–7; 89:39–45). As Psalm 74 makes clear, the temple has been razed to the ground: Zion is no longer even Yahweh's holy hill. As Psalm 89 makes clear, there is no longer a Davidic king to speak of – let alone one that fits the bill of Psalm 2. This set of circumstances squares with what Joseph, Simeon and Anna are experiencing: several centuries have gone by since Jehoiachin, and, if there has been a return from exile, there has not been a return to Davidic kingship – not even with Zerubbabel. The oath that God had sworn to David, celebrated in the first three-quarters of Psalm 89, now appears to be weightless (Ps. 89:38–39, 49). Where is Yahweh's *ḥesed* when the Davidic crown has been 'defiled . . . in the dust' (Ps. 89:39), the Davidic throne 'cast . . . to the ground' (Ps. 89:44)?

Anxious questioning ('Why . . . ?'; 'How long . . . ?') characterizes much of the middle of the book as well (Pss 77:7–9; 79:5; 80:4; 85:6). But more than this is going on between the book's boundaries, and two features are particularly noteworthy. First, we find some clues as to why the crisis is occurring. In particular, it is clear that the people have not been obedient to the Law of Moses (Pss 78:5–10; 81:8–16): under the Sinaitic covenant, blessings would be contingent on obedience, and curses would result from disobedience. Secondly, once the long group of Asaph psalms comes to an end, we come across four optimistic psalms that precede the gloomy closing boundary. These psalms provide shafts of light in relation to precisely those Israelite institutions that are lacking in exile: temple, land, king, city (Pss 84, 85, 86, 87 respectively). It is true that Psalm 86 does not speak directly of a king, but the speaker is a 'servant' (v. 2) who expresses confidence in God's *ḥesed* (v. 5) – and, according to the superscription, that speaker is David! Given that we have been told that David's prayers are ended (Ps. 72:20), we are forced to wrestle with this, and the macro psalter context points not to the (immediate) son of Jesse, but to a *coming* Davidic figure.[17] Similarly, Psalm 87 presents a vision of Yahweh's holy hill, Zion, which requires transposition – it can be said of *this* Zion that *Gentiles* were *born* there.

If the fulfilment of the Abrahamic and Davidic covenants remains on the agenda, the question that Joseph, Simeon and Anna are asking at this stage is 'On what grounds?' What solid reasons could there be for believing in the prospect of a supreme king established on Yahweh's holy hill?

Book 4 (Pss 90 – 106): 'Meditate on the Law of Moses!' (or, 'Get your biblical theology sorted out!')

The answer is found in Book 4 and turns on the Pentateuch. It is as if the compiler-editor is saying at this stage, 'If you're looking for a solution to the crisis of the exile, your starting point is to get some basic matters of biblical theology straight in your mind. Before you start imagining that God's covenant loyalty doesn't amount to much, that the prospect of the coming of the Psalm 2 king is wishful thinking, go back and study the Law of Moses.' The book is bounded by the psalter's only psalm 'of Moses' (Ps. 90) and, at the other end, three long psalms that work their way through Yahweh's post-flood commitment to creation (Ps. 104), the era of Abraham (Ps. 105) and the era of Moses (Ps. 106).

---

17. See Christopher R. Seitz, 'Royal Promises in the Canonical Books of Isaiah and the Psalms', in *Word Without End: The Old Testament as Abiding Theological Witness* (Grand Rapids: Eerdmans, 1998), p. 159: 'Not David the man, but David the paradigmatic ruler, will now be the focus of interest.' David, son of Jesse, may have been the original author of this psalm (prior to its being placed in its Book 3 context), but that is not the point at issue; and, in line with our associating this psalm with a 'new David', it is interesting to note, with Childs (*Introduction*, p. 514), that 'almost every line [of Ps. 86] has picked up a phrase from another portion of Scripture and fashioned it into a poem' (see also Allan M. Harman, *Commentary on the Psalms* [Fearn: Christian Focus, 1998], p. 293). It is fitting that the new David serve a 'recapitulative' function.

We learn from these psalms that the crisis of the exile needs to be understood through particular lenses. Intertextual dialogue between Psalms 89 and 90,[18] between Psalm 90 and Exodus 32[19] and between Psalm 90 and Genesis 3[20] requires us to tie the problem of the exile to the problem of the golden calf episode and to the disobedience of Adam. They are all part of one massive human-sin-leading-to-divine-wrath package. But what Psalm 90 draws our attention to is the role played by Moses in interceding for the people. Given the background in the Pentateuch, we know that the *ḥesed* or covenant loyalty for which he pleads (v. 14) is that of the Abrahamic covenant (Exod. 32:11–14; Deut. 9:27).

The same pattern is found at the other end of the book: following the golden calf episode, Moses the mediator intercedes on behalf of the rebellious people to assuage God's wrath (Ps. 106:19–23) – and does so on the basis of the Abrahamic covenant (Pss 105:5–11; 106:40–46). There are, though, several other incidents in Psalm 106 that also presuppose or indicate this scenario of major rebellion followed by mediation on the part of Moses (or Phinehas) on the basis of the Abrahamic covenant. The message is clear: despite the seriousness of the people's sin in the past, the promises to Abraham were never abandoned, and why should it be any different now, in the exile? Had not the books of Moses always specified that the exile would not spell the end of God's covenant loyalty – that the promises to Abraham would remain on track (Lev. 26:42–45; Deut. 4:25–31; 30:1–10)? Significantly, at the end of Book 4 we observe that the *exiles* seem to have understood this and pray for their restoration to the land (Ps. 106:47).

Joseph, Simeon and Anna are already conscious of the close connection between the Abrahamic covenant and the Davidic covenant, and so they can now grasp that, in principle, it is realistic to expect a supreme king to be established on Yahweh's holy hill.

18. Cf. Ps. 89:46–48 with Ps. 90; also Ps. 90:13 with Ps. 89:46, 49–51.

19. Cf. Ps. 90:13 with Exod. 32:12–13.

20. Cf. Ps. 90:2 with Gen. 2:4, Ps. 90:3 with Gen. 3:19, Ps. 90:8 with Gen. 3:9–10, 17, Ps. 90:8–9 with Gen. 3:19, 22, 24–25, and Ps. 90:10b with Gen. 3:16–19. The flouting of the commandment of Gen. 2:17, and its consequences, may be considered to be in the background to Ps. 90.

Yet, with half a millennium having elapsed since the exile, they could nonetheless be wondering whether other factors are not at work to derail this scenario. This question, in particular, may come to mind: Is God really powerful enough? Psalms 93 – 100 answer the question affirmatively: as the refrain of this section has it, 'it is *Yahweh* who is king' (my tr.). These psalms correlate closely with Isaiah 40 – 55,[21] and they serve a similar purpose – that of assuring the exilic community that *its* God is the world's Creator-Ruler-Judge, superior to the nations' gods, and powerful to orchestrate a new exodus. In other words, meditating on the Law of Moses in the context of Book 4 also means looking for a recapitulation of Yahweh's powerful intervention in Moses' day[22] – though on a superior plane.

Indeed, meditating on the Law of Moses entails recognizing the need for a solution that lies beyond the Mosaic regime.[23] For all that Moses' and Phinehas' mediation was essential for keeping the Abrahamic promises alive, Psalm 106 highlights three ways in which it fell short: (1) it was only partially effective in keeping God's wrath at bay, for many Israelites were put to death; (2) it was only temporarily effective, for it needed to be repeated following each act of rebellion; and (3) the intercessors were themselves affected by the sin problem they were purporting to deal with (vv. 32–33; cf. Num. 20:7–12). Thus the Psalm 106 cycle contains an implicit call for a mediator who is greater than Moses.

It is possible that Book 4 provides us with a glimpse of the solution. Psalm 101, a 'Psalm of David', presents us with a king who is – or, at least aspires to be – beyond reproach. This is immediately followed by a psalm that portrays an 'afflicted' one who represents the exiled people in his intercessory ministry, and who suffers God's

---

21. See e.g. André Feuillet, 'Les psaumes eschatologiques du règne de Yahvé', *Etudes d'exégèse et de théologie biblique: Ancien Testament* (Paris: Gabalda, 1975), pp. 364–365; Jerome F. D. Creach, 'The Shape of Book Four of the Psalter and the Shape of Second Isaiah', *JSOT* 80 (1998), p. 68.

22. E.g. Ps. 98:1–3, or the exodus imagery of shepherd and the powerful 'hand' of God (Pss 95:7; 100:3; cf. Exod. 14:31; Ps. 78:42).

23. Henri Blocher speaks of 'the pedagogy of failure': *La Doctrine du péché et de la rédemption* (Vaux-sur-Seine: Edifac, 2000), p. 126.

wrath, in connection with the rebuilding of Zion – even for the benefit of all nations. I am not alone in seeing here the 'suffering servant' figure of Isaiah 42 onwards.[24]

Whatever one makes of those two psalms, the bottom line of this key book for the macro psalter reader is assurance at precisely the point where it was lacking in Book 3. In the three psalms in this book that have yet to be commented on, confidence in Yahweh's *ḥesed* is in view (Pss 91:4; 92:2; 103). In particular, Psalm 103, a second Davidic psalm in the book, may be viewed as an answer to Moses' prayer in Psalm 90, its vocabulary and themes echoing this earlier psalm in several places.[25]

Book 5 (Pss 107 – 144/145): 'His covenant loyalty endures for ever!'

The key that unlocks the final book is its refrain. In its full form the refrain reads as follows: 'Give thanks to the LORD, for he is good; / his *ḥesed* endures for ever'; but, in most of its occurrences, it is only the last part ('his *ḥesed* endures for ever') that is quoted. In figure 1.4 below, 'P1' ('praise type 1') and the thick vertical lines indicate the junctures at which the refrain appears. The larger the 'P1' print, the more the refrain is repeated. Note the crescendo building up to the climax in Psalm 136 where the refrain appears in every verse. The other type of summons to praise, 'P2' ('praise type 2'), is *halĕlû yâ*

---

24. So (briefly) Erich Zenger, 'Das Weltenkönigtum des Gottes Israels (Ps. 90–106)', in N. Lohfink and E. Zenger (eds.), *Der Gott Israels und die Völker: Untersuchungen zum Jesajabuch und zu den Psalmen*, SBS 154 (Stuttgart: Verlag Katholisches Bibelwerk, 1994), p. 171.

25. Note, in particular, Moses the mediator in relation to the golden calf episode (vv. 7–8); the notions of *ḥesed* and satisfaction (vv. 4–5; cf. Ps. 90:14); the descriptions of human beings (vv. 14–16; cf. Ps. 90:3, 5, 10); the depiction of Yahweh as reigning over creation (vv. 19–22; cf. Ps. 90:2); God or his *ḥesed* as being 'from everlasting to everlasting' (v. 17; cf. Ps. 90:2 – the importance of this phrase may be appreciated by its featuring both at the beginning of the book and [with slight variants] at the end). There is, however, a significant contrast to note: whereas God's reaction to sin in Ps. 90 is one of wrath, in Ps. 103 it is one of grace and forgiveness – for here, indeed, is the answer needed to Moses' prayer.

107	108–110	111–118	119	120–136[26]	138–144[27]	145	146–150
P1	DAVID	P2 → P1		ASCENTS → P1	DAVID		P2

Figure 1.4 Structure of Book 5.

– 'Praise the LORD!' Psalms 111 – 117 and 146 – 150 begin and/or end this way.[28]

This book is shot through with calls to praise that are tied to a recognition of Yahweh's covenant loyalty. According to the opening psalm, this *ḥesed* has been manifested in Yahweh's orchestrating a return from exile: 'the redeemed of the LORD' have been 'gathered' (107:2–3) – an answer to the exiles' prayer from the end of the previous book and psalm (106:47). To portray this salvation, the psalm deploys a range of motifs subsequently redeployed in the book – a new exodus (vv. 4–9; cf. Pss 114; 135; 136), a journey to a city (v. 7; cf. Pss 118; Songs of Ascents, esp. 120 – 122), the liberation of captives (vv. 10–16; cf. Pss 130; 146:7), deliverance from death (vv. 10, 14, 17–20; cf. Pss 116; 118; 124), healing (v. 20; cf. Ps. 147:3), salvation of sinners by the word (vv. 17–20; cf. Pss 119; 130), a reversal of fortunes for the poor (vv. 40–41; cf. Pss 113; 146).

But what about the king of Psalm 2? Does he not have a role to play in this salvation? Some scholars argue that he is strikingly absent from Book 5,[29] and it is true that this book is not teeming with royal

---

26. To see why Pss 135 – 136 have been tacked on to the Songs of Ascents, cf. 134:1 with 135:1–2, and 135:8–12 with 136:10–22.

27. Ps. 137 is transitional: it is not a psalm of David, but it serves as a fitting introduction to this David sequence. Ps. 145 is also a psalm of David, concluding the preceding group and introducing the flourish of praise with which the psalter closes.

28. With the exception of Ps. 114. 'Praise the LORD!' is found at the beginning of this psalm in the Greek version of the OT.

29. M. A. Vincent, 'The Shape of the Psalter: An Eschatological Dimension?', in Peter J. Harland and C. T. Robert Hayward (eds.), *New Heaven and New Earth: Prophecy and the Millennium, Essays in Honour of Anthony Gelston* (Leiden: Brill, 1999), p. 78; Gerald H. Wilson, *passim*, e.g. 'Psalms and Psalter: Paradigm for Biblical Theology', in Scott J. Hafemann (ed.), *Biblical Theology: Retrospect and Prospect* (Leicester: Apollos, 2002), pp. 106–109.

psalms. We might be tempted to think that this simply reflects the character of the sixth- and fifth-century returns from exile under Zerubbabel, Ezra and Nehemiah: there was no king. Yet, as they meditate on this final book of the psalter, Joseph, Simeon and Anna are all too conscious that the return from exile that Book 5 portrays is far more glorious than anything experienced by their Israelite ancestors. Indeed, they are, so to speak, still praying the prayer of the end of Psalm 106, and their experience on the ground is that of a journey still in progress and that is tough because there are scoffers, enemies and persecutors along the way. Their experience thus reflects that of the major Psalm 119 and the Songs of Ascents. Psalm 119 reminds them that the word of God is sufficient to sustain them as they persevere: their job is to keep meditating on divine *tôrâ*. As they do so, they recognize that Psalm 107 is reminiscent of Isaiah 40 – 55,[30] and this helps them to understand that the new exodus of which this book speaks is the one that will be led by a Servant-King (Isa. 11; 49). But where is this Servant-King in Book 5?

In fact, he is centre stage. It comes as no surprise that there is a close connection between the covenant loyalty of Yahweh and the presence of the Messiah who features, in essence, at the end of each major section of the book. First, in a clear match of Psalm 2, the king of Psalm 110 rules on Zion and is absolutely victorious over his enemies. As has become clear by this stage, this king must be superior to David, son of Jesse, and must even be on a par with Yahweh. Here, in Psalm 110, we learn that he is David's 'lord' and that his status indeed correlates with that of Yahweh. As has also become clear by this stage, a figure greater than Moses is required to break the cycle of sin and wrath followed by intercession that is only partially and temporarily effective. Here, in Psalm 110, we discover that the king also fulfils a priestly function. Indeed, while this would have been unthinkable under the old covenant, it turns out that the Messiah is 'a priest for ever' in connection with a new

---

30. As noted by many authors. See the table in John W. Roffey, 'Beyond Reality: Poetic Discourse and Psalm 107', in Eugene E. Carpenter (ed.), *A Biblical Itinerary: In Search of Method, Form and Content, Essays in Honor of George W. Coats*, JSOTSup 240 (Sheffield: Sheffield Academic Press, 1997), pp. 72–73.

regime – 'in the order of Melchizedek' (v. 4). This mediation is fully effective (cf. Ps. 130:7)[31] and permanent.

At the end of the next section, Psalm 118 sets forth a figure who has been delivered from death, having been in the grip of the nations. This rejected stone has become the key foundation stone, in other words, one who comes in Yahweh's name has secured salvation – of which the people are beneficiaries (vv. 2–4, 22–27). This victory is attributed to Yahweh's covenant loyalty, and the little psalm that precedes Psalm 118 reminds us that *all nations* benefit from this *ḥesed*.

The next key psalm stands out within the Songs of Ascents by virtue of its length. Psalm 132 speaks of the definitive establishing of Zion as Yahweh's dwelling place in connection with the definitive establishing of David's throne. If we had trouble squaring the Sinaitic conditionality (of, say, Ps. 78) with the unconditional promises made to David (Ps. 89), this psalm enables us to harmonize these perspectives: the Messiah must observe the Law of Moses. No other psalm responds more directly to Psalm 89,[32] and Psalm 132 closes on a note of assurance that the Davidic crown, having been 'defiled . . . in the dust' at the time of the exile (Ps. 89:39) will shine once again (v. 18).

The final climax of the book is Psalm 144, which replays much of Psalm 18. It depicts David as a servant whose victory wins blessings for the people. Significantly, as specified in the penultimate verse, another exile is precluded ('no breach, no going out' [my tr.])[33] – which means that the problem of sin is definitively dealt with. It may be that the macro psalter reader is meant to take the double

---

31. The link between new exodus and total pardon is clear in Ps. 130, and, as already noted, the king is the leader of the new exodus.

32. Timo Veijola, *Verheissung in der Krise: Studien zur Literatur und Theologie der Exilszeit anhand des 89. Psalms*, AASF B 220 (Helsinki: Suomalainen Tiedeakatemia, 1982), pp. 49, 72–75, has listed twenty-eight points of contact between these two psalms, conveyed by sixteen words and phrases.

33. The threat of exile in Amos 4:3 employs the same Hebrew roots, and the first features in Ps. 89:40 in relation to the exile. See e.g. John Goldingay, *Psalms*, vol. 3: *Psalms 90–150* (Grand Rapids: Baker Academic, 2008), p. 690.

'happy' (my tr.) of the final verse as an echo of the double 'happy' of the psalter's introduction (Pss 1 – 2).

If Joseph, Simeon and Anna are struck by these four key psalms, and led to praise God for his covenant faithfulness, they are also intrigued by the sheer number of Davidic psalms in this book. As they meditate on the first one, Psalm 108, they recall having seen these words before – in Book 2. This psalm, in common with a number of others in this book,[34] is a composite, combining (in this case) passages from Psalms 57 and 60. But the verses of Psalm 57 that speak of distress are not found in Psalm 108, whose picture is of confidence and victory. At the same time, Psalm 57 is also reflected in the title of Psalm 142, whose picture is the very opposite – one of considerable distress. Such is the character of the David to come – one who recapitulates, on a higher plane, both the victories and the sufferings of David, son of Jesse. The ministerial scope of this greater King-Priest-Servant David is an impressive dimension of this final book.

Conclusion (Pss 145 / 146 – 150): 'Hallelujah!'

The psalter closes with an extended doxology. These closing psalms seem to express praise to Yahweh from a perspective that envisages the people gathered in the rebuilt city of Zion (Pss 146:10; 147:2–3, 12–13; 149:1–2; 150:1). The summons to praise grows louder until it reaches its climax in Psalm 150 with the call for 'resounding cymbals' and the exhortation that 'everything that has breath' should praise Yahweh. The reasons for the praise are highlighted at the end of Psalm 148, which may lie at the centre of a concentric structure across the last five psalms:[35] 'his name alone is exalted' and 'he has raised up for his people a horn' (vv. 13–14). The language here echoes that of Psalms 89 and 132

---

34. Cf. Pss 144 (mentioned above) and 140, which recalls five Davidic psalms from Book 2 (v. 3: cf. Pss 52:2; 57:4; 58:4; 64:3; v. 4: cf. Ps. 71:4; v. 5: cf. Pss 57:6; 64:5). Perhaps Pss 118 and 135 could be added to this list, although they contain fewer allusions to other psalms.

35. Cf. Erich Zenger, '"Daß alles Fleisch den Namen seiner Heiligung segne" (Ps. 145,21): Die Komposition Ps. 145 – 150 als Anstoß zu einer christlich-jüdischen Psalmenhermeneutik', *BZ* 41 (1997), p. 18.

and throws the realization of Psalm 2 messianic expectations into sharp relief.

One day, as Joseph ponders the prospect of the Psalm 2 king being established on Zion, he is interrupted by some news. His fiancée Mary has been feeling unwell for some time, and it turns out she is pregnant by the Holy Spirit. A few months later, she gives birth to the Psalm 2 king. Joseph comes to see him with his own eyes (cf. Matt. 1:18–25). A few weeks later, Simeon, having awaited the 'consolation of Israel', takes this child, Jesus, into his arms and praises God, for, with his very eyes, he sees 'salvation' for Jew and Gentile alike (Luke 2:25–32). And the time has come for Anna to speak to those awaiting the 'redemption of Jerusalem' (Luke 2:38).

As far as we are concerned, we may not have seen the Psalm 2 king in the flesh, but we do have a clearer grasp of the person and work of the Messiah than did Joseph, Simeon and Anna thanks to the illumination of New Testament revelation. It turns out that the establishment of the anointed as king on Yahweh's holy hill takes place at two related moments: his resurrection from the dead – moment one – demonstrates that he is 'the Son of God in power' (Rom. 1:4; Acts 13:33) and portends a day – moment two – when he will be Yahweh's instrument for judging 'the world with justice' (Acts 17:31). The fact that we live in between these two moments means that our circumstances are remarkably similar to those of our forebears of the post-exilic period. To be sure, the first coming of Christ was welcomed as the end of the exile (Luke 2 – 4), and his death is to be understood as a new 'exodus' (Luke 9:31 [my tr.]); he has secured, for his people, the forgiveness of sins, deliverance from death, and the destruction of all enemies. But the consummation of his work lies in the future for us: we await the day when his enemies will 'be made his footstool' (Heb. 10:13; cf. Ps. 110:1). In one sense we have arrived at the end of the journey of which Book 5 speaks: in Christ we 'have come to Mount Zion . . . the heavenly Jerusalem' (Heb. 12:22). At the same time, we are 'foreigners and strangers on earth' (Heb. 11:13; cf. 1 Pet. 1 – 2): 'For here we do not have an enduring city, but we are looking for the city that is to come' (Heb. 13:14). May God grant that we meditate day and night on the *tôrâ* concerning his Son, that we hold on to gospel promises, that 'through the encouragement [the Scriptures] provide we might have hope' (Rom. 15:4). For the Psalm 2 king has come, and he will return. 'Happy are all who take refuge in him' (Ps. 2:12 [my tr.])!

Consideration of babies and bathwater

If such a reading is suggested by the final form of the book of Psalms, where does all this leave us in terms of our traditional teaching of individual psalms, without reference to psalter context? And where does it leave us in terms of the traditional use of psalms whereby one takes the words of individual psalms on to one's lips in a subjective manner – as if one were David or another psalmist – in one's personal and community prayer life?

It seems to me that we enjoy the freedom and flexibility to benefit from both the macro and the micro approaches and from both objective and subjective use of psalms (as both God's word to us and our word to God). I can understand why we might want to suggest otherwise: in our excitement regarding the macro (gospel) shape of the psalter, we might be liable to reject any hermeneutic that fails to take account of this big picture. But this would be reductionist. Defending the study of individual psalms – and demonstrating that psalter context is not equivalent to context within, say, a Pauline letter – is straightforward. In brief, (1) New Testament authors show very little interest in psalter context; (2) individual psalm numbering – unlike that of other chapter (and verse) divisions in Scripture – is inspired by the Holy Spirit (Acts 13:33), implying that units of psalm text are demarcated for us; (3) Gerald Wilson's appeal to the analogy of a symphony[36] is apposite (in the film *The King's Speech*, it is no scandal that the second movement of Beethoven's Seventh is 'lifted from its symphony context'). Thus it would be legitimate to study and teach Psalm 73 without taking account of the psalms that

---

36. Gerald H. Wilson, 'Shaping the Psalter: A Consideration of Editorial Linkage in the Book of Psalms', in J. Clinton McCann (ed.), *The Shape and Shaping of the Psalter*, JSOTSup 159 (Sheffield: Sheffield Academic Press, 1993), p. 82.

precede and follow it (even if additional benefits would accrue if one were to consider the psalter context).

Defending the subjective use of psalms – our stepping into the shoes of David and appropriating his words as we speak to God – is somewhat harder, but the case is robust. (1) There are at least three places where it is practised in the New Testament (Rom. 8:35–37; 2 Tim. 4:17; Heb. 13:6).[37] (2) David sometimes serves as an (exemplary) ordinary Israelite more than as a king, for example in Psalm 19 (note the echo of Ps. 1 in v. 14) or in Psalm 32 (cf. Rom. 4:4–8). (3) Given the importance of prayer and praise for the believer as prescribed in Scripture in general, and the principle of *lex orandi, lex credendi*,[38] it would be surprising if the psalter contained no dimension of exemplarity. (4) An important metaphor, 'pouring out one's heart/soul to God' (1 Sam. 1:15; Pss 42:4; 62:8; Lam. 2:19), conveys what prayer is and is often precisely what we see psalmists doing. (5) We Christians are united to Christ in his sufferings (Rom. 8:17; Phil. 3:10; Col. 1:24), and these sufferings are typologically anticipated by those of David (e.g. John 15:25 draws on Pss 35:19; 69:4).[39] (6) The non-specificity of the historical context of so many of the psalms lends itself to their being applied *generally* to comparable circumstances to those the twenty-first-century believer may be experiencing.[40]

There are, of course, pitfalls to avoid. First, there must be a danger of developing an unhealthy subjectivism or egocentrism: the New Testament use of the psalms should lead us to focus primarily on God's attributes and Christology. Secondly, we should be on our guard against allegorization (that we read of David's being 'in the Desert of Judah' in Ps. 63 is not a direct invitation for us to appropriate this psalm when we are in a metaphorical desert). Thirdly, we should strive to take account of the change of salvation-historical era (e.g. in relation to Ps. 51:11, a Christian does not need to fear

---

37. Two of these are mentioned by Harman, *Commentary on the Psalms*, pp. 62–63; I owe the third reference to David Gibbs.

38. The principle that prayers are indices of beliefs (2 Cor. 4:13 expresses the principle that Christians' words should reflect their beliefs).

39. I owe this insight to Dominique Angers.

40. I owe this insight to Jamie Grant.

that the Holy Spirit will be taken from her; in relation to Ps. 100:4, the equivalent for us of entering God's courts is not entering a church building; dashing Babylon's children against the rock [Ps. 137:9] does not carry over in any direct way to our era of redemptive history).

For what it is worth, my practice in the pulpit is generally not to mention psalter context, but I do sometimes cover the big picture of the psalter by giving a number of successive talks during single weekends. I have come to be persuaded that we have a moral responsibility to avoid so majoring on the macro/objective perspective that we run the risk of leaving fellow-believers daunted by the idea of studying the Psalms or fearful of looking to benefit from them from a micro/subjective perspective.

Conclusion

Micro psalm exegesis needs to remain firmly on the agenda, as does subjective use of the psalms in personal and corporate piety, and these approaches are explored elsewhere in this volume. At the same time, sensitivity to the macro psalter shape yields a particular appreciation of its clear gospel message. When the risen Lord Jesus Christ explained the Psalms' fulfilment in his sufferings and resurrection (Luke 24:27, 44–47), he may or may not have adopted an approach similar to the one I have sketched above, but it is the testimony of many that a grasp of the unfolding flow of the psalter leads to hearts that 'burn' for joy (cf. Luke 24:32). We should not be surprised if our reading of the psalter leads us to proclaim God's *ḥesed* in Christ and exclaim, 'Hallelujah!'

2. READING THE PSALMS AS CHRISTIAN SCRIPTURE

John Woodhouse

To claim that the book of Psalms is Christian Scripture is to see a particular relationship between the psalter and Christian faith. This relationship is undoubtedly multifaceted. The present chapter will not do justice to the complexity, but will attempt to explore the heart of it.

The chapter has two parts. In the first I will discuss what it means to call the book of Psalms 'Christian Scripture'. In the second we will begin to explore the heart of what the Christian believer receives from the Psalms.

Christian Scripture and the Psalms

What is 'Christian Scripture'?
To regard the book of Psalms as Christian Scripture is to understand these writings to have the characteristics of Christian Scripture. For our purposes, let us focus on three qualities of Christian Scripture, each of which is highlighted in the apostle Paul's famous words about Scripture in 2 Timothy 3:15–16.

First, to say that the book of Psalms is Christian Scripture is to say that it is 'God-breathed' (Gk. *theopneustos*, 2 Tim. 3:16a).[1] The person who reads the Psalms as Christian Scripture hears them as God's words, breathed to us by God himself.

Secondly, if the Psalms are Christian Scripture, then they are 'profitable' (Gk. *ōphelimos*) for shaping the Christian life. The person who hears the Psalms as Christian Scripture expects from them *teaching* of Christian truth, *reproof* for unchristian behaviour, *correction* of departures from the Christian way and *training* in the righteousness expected of Christian believers (2 Tim. 3:16b).

Thirdly, that the Psalms are Christian Scripture means they 'are able' (Gk. *dynamai*) to make one 'wise for salvation through faith in Christ Jesus' (2 Tim. 3:15b). The person who knows the Psalms to be Christian Scripture is one who has found them to be a source of this saving wisdom: faith in our Lord Jesus Christ.

While much more might be said, if the Psalms are Christian Scripture at least these three things must be true of them. It is the question of what it means for these things to be true of the Psalms that I will explore.

Three puzzles

Three puzzles emerge as soon as we speak in these terms of the Psalms as Christian Scripture.

Whose words?

The first is that (in the main) the Psalms are explicitly, obviously and importantly *human* words, often addressed to God, rather than *divine* words addressed to humans. In much of Scripture it is relatively

---

1. There is an ambiguity in the Greek of 2 Tim. 3:16a, understood here as 'all Scripture is God-breathed' (so NIV; similarly ESV and most English versions). Other possible translations include, 'Every scripture inspired by God is also profitable' (RSV margin); 'All inspired scripture has its use for teaching' (REB). The ambiguities are made much of by James Barr, 'Basic Thoughts about Biblical Inspiration and Authority', in *Escaping from Fundamentalism* (London: SCM, 1984), pp. 1–7. A careful consideration of the issues is provided by George W. Knight III, *Commentary on the Pastoral Epistles*, NIGTC (Grand Rapids: Eerdmans, 1992), pp. 444–450.

straightforward to understand the words of a narrator, teacher, lawgiver or prophet to be God's message to the human hearer or reader. 'Thus says the Lord' makes sense as an introduction to such texts, whether or not it actually appears. The human speaker or writer is understood to have spoken '*from God* as they were carried along by the Holy Spirit' (2 Pet. 1:21). While the Psalms contain explicitly divine words (such as the decree of the Lord in Ps. 2:7–9), and words of instruction that can be received as 'from God' (as e.g. Ps. 37), much of the language of the psalter is in the first person and the words cannot straightforwardly be regarded as 'from God'. What does it mean, for example, to regard words such as the following as '*God*-breathed'?

> Listen to my words, LORD,
>   consider my lament.
> Hear my cry for help,
>   my King and my God,
>   for to you I pray.
> (Ps. 5:1–2)

What does it mean to hear these words as words 'from God', when they are in fact addressed from David *to* God?

There is one quite simple approach to this issue. The Psalms are often regarded as a divinely inspired hymn (or prayer) book. The Psalms are 'from God' in a different sense from, say, prophetic oracles. In the Psalms we have God-given words for us to take on *our* lips. To treat the Psalms as Christian Scripture, in this view, is no more nor less than regarding the Psalms as given to Christians for their Christian prayers and praises. Within this approach there are certainly problems (and I will comment on some of those shortly). However, in principle it is straightforward. The continuity of the faith of Old Testament believers and the faith of Christians allows the words that give expression to the first to become an expression of the second.[2]

---

2. T. Worden, *The Psalms Are Christian Prayer* (London: Geoffrey Chapman, 1964), is one of many examples of this approach.

This approach is encouraged by three references to psalms in the New Testament, which indicate that psalms are to be spoken or sung by believers to one another when they meet together (1 Cor. 14:26; Eph. 5:19; Col. 3:16).[3]

Those who take this approach find that much in the book of Psalms can readily (and wonderfully) be turned into the words of a Christian believer:

> The LORD is my shepherd;
>   I lack nothing.
> (Ps. 23:1)

> The LORD is my light and my salvation –
>   whom shall I fear?
> The LORD is the stronghold of my life –
>   of whom shall I be afraid?'
> (Ps. 27:1)

However, anyone who has read the Psalms in this way (making the words of the psalms my own in the sense that the 'I' and 'me' in the psalms become *me*) has found problems:

> Vindicate me, LORD,
>   for I have led a blameless life;
> I have trusted in the LORD
>   and have not faltered.
> (Ps. 26:1)

Can the following words ever be an expression of Christian faith?

> May the table set before them [my enemies] become a snare;
>   may it become retribution and a trap.
> May their eyes be darkened so they cannot see,
>   and their backs be bent for ever.

---

3. While it is not certain, I regard it as most likely that *psalmos* in the three texts cited is a reference to the psalms of the Old Testament Scriptures.

> Pour out your wrath on them;
>> let your fierce anger overtake them.
> May their place be deserted;
>> let there be no one to dwell in their tents.
> For they persecute him whom [NIV those] you wound,
>> and talk about the pain of those you hurt.
> Charge them with crime upon crime;
>> do not let them share in your salvation.
> May they be blotted out of the book of life
>> and not be listed with the righteous.
> (Ps. 69:22–28)

The emphatic and unqualified assertion of complete personal integrity and the cry for vengeance on his enemies are just two points at which the Christian believer is right to feel uncomfortable in making the words of the Psalms his or her own words.

A dimension of this problem that is less often noted is what I will cautiously call the self-centredness of the Psalms. The speaker in the Psalms speaks more of his own difficulties than of anyone else's; he prays for the alleviation of his own troubles more than those of others. Nothing in the world seems to matter more than the troubles of the speaker. This is a generalization and exceptions may be noted, but part of the appeal to many of the psalms as Christian prayer is that they can be so personal in giving voice to *my* distress, *my* joys, *my* fears, *my* faith. However, Christian prayer in the New Testament is marked by intercession for others (see 1 Tim. 2:1). Is there a problem here with thinking of the Psalms as Christian prayer?

These problems suggest that regarding the Psalms as God-given prayers and praises for Christian believers to make their own may not be an adequate explanation of how these human words are to be received by Christians as God's words.

The Psalms and Christian living

The second puzzle arises from regarding the Psalms as 'profitable' for shaping the Christian life. Again there are some parts of the Psalms where this seems straightforward. Consider, for example, the wisdom of Psalm 37 with respect to trusting the Lord in the face of wickedness:

Do not fret because of those who are evil
    or be envious of those who do wrong;
for like the grass they will soon wither,
    like green plants they will soon die away.
Trust in the LORD, and do good;
    dwell in the land and enjoy safe pasture.
Take delight in the LORD,
    and he will give you the desires of your heart.
(Ps. 37:1–4)

Here are words that are indeed 'profitable . . . for training in right-eousness'. However, many readers of the Psalms wonder what they are to make of the particular circumstances and experiences that seem to be reflected in many of the psalms. How does the prayer for the destruction of enemies in Psalm 69 relate to the life of the follower of Jesus who said, 'Love your enemies' (Matt. 5:44; Luke 6:27, 35)?

The Psalms and faith in Jesus

The third puzzle is common to all of the Old Testament Scriptures, but is answered differently in different places. It is the question of how these texts 'are able to make you wise for salvation through faith in Christ Jesus'. It is one thing to think that the Psalms may display elements of a spirituality shared by Christian believers and Israelites of old. It is another to regard these texts as formative particularly for *Christian* faith. But no less than this is entailed in considering the Psalms to be Christian Scripture.

The thesis of this chapter is that the threefold key to understanding the Psalms as Christian Scripture is (1) recognizing the importance of King David, the Lord's anointed, with respect to the book of Psalms; (2) believing the gospel announcement that 'Jesus is the Christ (the anointed one)'; and (3) reading the Psalms as one who belongs to the Christ and knows the benefits of belonging to him.

We will consider these points in turn.

The psalms of David

The book of Psalms is particularly associated with David. Just as the book of Proverbs is known as 'The Proverbs of Solomon' and

the Pentateuch is known as 'The Torah of Moses', the book of
Psalms is appropriately called 'The Psalms of David'. As in the case
of Proverbs and the Pentateuch this is more than an assertion about
authorship. Parts of Proverbs and the Pentateuch were clearly not
written by Solomon or Moses.[4] Nonetheless, the former is associated in the canon of Scripture with the wisdom of Solomon's
kingdom, and the latter has at its heart the instruction given by God
through Moses at Mount Sinai. In each case the association with
the figure of Old Testament history is highly significant. Proverbs
is more than a collection of good ideas for coping with life. Here is
the wisdom of God's king: it is about life in his kingdom. The Torah
has an analogous focal point in Moses.

Just so, the Psalms are the psalms 'of King David'. They are
associated (in a way fully comparable with Proverbs and the
Pentateuch) with the kingship of David. The superscription of many
psalms (Hebr. *lĕdawîd*, 'of David') may not always indicate authorship. Both the preposition and the name have a range of possibilities.
The psalm in question may be 'to', 'for', 'concerning' or 'belonging
to' David. 'David' may be David himself or a king in David's line.
The ambiguity is less important than the fact that the designation
associates the psalm with the remarkable kingship of David. If the
speaker is David or the psalm is in some other way associated with
David, it is not simply David the pious Israelite composing prayers
for all the faithful to make their own. It is David the king, God's
king, the Lord's anointed. Furthermore it is reasonable to assume
that any particular psalm is 'Davidic' in this sense, unless there is
reason to think otherwise.[5]

---

4. See e.g. Prov. 30:1; 31:1; Deut. 34:1–12.

5. This is contrary to the approach of many scholars who require evidence
   that any particular psalm should be regarded as a 'royal psalm'. I am
   suggesting that the onus is the other way around. I acknowledge here that
   my thinking about this matter has been stimulated and helped by rereading
   a decades old monograph by John H. Eaton, *Kingship in the Psalms*, SBT, 2nd
   Series, 32 (London: SCM, 1976). I do not by any means follow his theory
   entirely, but am persuaded that he is essentially right to see very many of
   the psalms as the words of or about the Davidic king, and I have found his
   drawing together of the psalms' portrayal of 'the ideal of the king's office'

I am confident that many of the psalms were in fact composed
by David, 'the sweet psalmist of Israel' (2 Sam. 23:1),[6] and indeed
a number of the superscriptions imply as much (despite alternative
interpretations that have been proposed).[7] However, my point here
is that the psalter as a whole is associated with David, the Lord's
anointed one, and his kingdom. The association is multifaceted and
interesting, and we turn now to examine the book of Psalms from
this perspective.

'The man' [NIV 'one'] of Psalm 1 who is 'blessed' may well be an
allusion to this king. I will not argue for this here, but there are
certainly interesting connections between the descriptions of the
Psalm 1 'man' and things that are said elsewhere about Israel's king
or Israel's leader.[8]

Be that as it may, the focus of Psalm 2 is unambiguously 'the
LORD and his anointed' (Ps. 2:2c). Psalm 2 introduces a major reality
that casts its bright light on the whole psalter. The Lord's anointed
(or Messiah) bears the Lord's promise that he will receive the nations
as his inheritance and the ends of the earth as his possession (Ps.
2:8). The hostile rulers of the earth who set themselves against the
Lord and his anointed are on the way to their destruction (Ps. 2:12).
As a later psalm puts it, he will make his enemies a footstool for his

---

(as Eaton puts it) very helpful. But with that acknowledgment, I need
to add that I am confident that what I am going to say would not win
agreement from John Eaton.

6. Note that the TNIV renders this phrase suggestively, 'the hero of Israel's
songs'.

7. For an argument that the superscriptions have a purpose that has nothing
to do with the circumstances of the composition of the psalm in question,
see Brevard S. Childs, 'Psalm Titles and Midrashic Exegesis', *JSS* 16 (1971),
pp. 137–150; cf. John Goldingay, *Psalms Volume 1: Psalms 1–41*, BCOT
(Grand Rapids: Baker Academic, 2006), pp. 28–30.

8. Compare Ps. 1:2–3 with the requirement laid on the king in Deut. 17:18–19,
the expectation and promise given to Israel's leader Joshua in Josh. 1:8, and
David's word to his son Solomon in 1 Kgs 2:3. If 'the one' of Ps. 1:1 is
indeed a reference to the king, who will be explicitly introduced in Ps. 2,
this adds significance to the frequently noted *inclusio* of Pss 1:1a and 2:12d:
'Blessed is the one . . . Blessed are all who take refuge in him.'

feet (Ps. 110:1). Psalm 2 proclaims and celebrates the promise of God given to King David: 'O how blessed are all who take refuge in *him*!'

Psalm 3 introduces what I will describe as the theological problem of the book of Psalms. It is already there in Psalm 2, where the kings of the earth and the rulers take counsel together against the Lord and his anointed. In Psalm 3, however, we encounter the perplexing situation that the Lord's anointed suffered at the hands of many foes (Ps. 3:1). This psalm takes us to the days when David 'fled from his son Absalom'. Psalm 3 is the first of many psalms of lament.

Any reader of the psalter after its compilation in exilic or post-exilic times knows well that the David who fled from Absalom has died, and did not rule the world (at least not in the extravagant terms anticipated in Ps. 2). The theological problem of the psalter is the tension between the promises made to David (and David's son), set out in Psalm 2 and presupposed throughout, and the reality of historical experience (encountered first in Ps. 3). Psalm 89 (closing Book 3) gives full expression to this tension.

> Lord, where is your former great love,
>   which in your faithfulness you swore to David?
> Remember, Lord, how your servant has been mocked,
>   how I bear in my heart the taunts of all the nations,
> the taunts with which your enemies, LORD, have mocked,
>   with which they have mocked every step of your anointed one.
> (Ps. 89:49–51)

The reader of the Psalms is not allowed to forget Psalm 2. The Lord and his anointed will reign. His kingdom will come. That is the promise of the one who sits in the heavens and has set his king on Zion, his holy mountain (Ps. 2:4, 6). However, the historic experience of David and of those around him, and of subsequent generations who sang the Psalms, finds expression in the cry 'How long, LORD?' (Ps. 89:46).

I am suggesting that the Lord's promises to David, trumpeted in Psalm 2, reverberate through the psalter. Of course there are psalms far removed from David himself. Perhaps the most obvious is the exilic or post-exilic Psalm 137, 'by the rivers of Babylon'. But Psalm

137 *is* about the promises to David. What else does 'we remembered Zion' (Ps. 137:1) mean? Psalm 137 is about the city of David, and the promises of God associated with it. 'If I forget you, Jerusalem, may my right hand forget its skill' (Ps. 137:5).

Jesus is the Christ

The second of my keys to understanding the Psalms as Christian Scripture is the gospel that announces, '*Jesus* is the Christ.'[9] This simple statement identifies a historical person (Jesus) with an office designated by the title 'the Christ', 'the anointed one'.

The background that gives the gospel announcement its weighty meaning and significance is, on the one hand, the Old Testament history of David's kingdom (David was the Lord's anointed one) and, on the other hand, the promises of the Old Testament prophets concerning a new David. While it is true that anointing was applied in the Old Testament to various persons (particularly, we might note, to priests and prophets), 'the anointed one' or 'Yahweh's anointed' became specifically a designation for the king.

The books of Samuel introduce the idea of a royal figure who is the Lord's 'anointed one'. Hannah concluded her majestic prayer:

the LORD will judge the ends of the earth.
He will give strength to his king
    and exalt the horn of his anointed.
(1 Sam. 2:10b; cf. 2:35)

This expectation was fulfilled in the kingdom of David, anointed as the Lord's king, and his son Solomon.[10]

After the collapse of the Davidic kingdom, when Old Testament prophetic eschatology took shape, a prominent theme was a coming

---

9. See Matt. 16:16; Mark 8:29; Luke 9:20; 24:26, 46; John 4:29; 11:27; 20:31; Acts 5:42; 9:22; 17:3; 18:5, 28; 1 John 2:22; 5:1.

10. See 1 Sam. 16:1, 6, 13; 2 Sam. 2:4, 7; 3:39; 5:3, 17; 12:7; 19:21; 22:51; 23:1; 1 Kgs 1:39, 45; 5:1. Before David, Saul had been anointed at the Lord's word, and therefore became 'the LORD's anointed' (1 Sam. 10:1; 12:3, 5; 15:17; 24:6, 10; 26:9, 11, 16, 23; 2 Sam. 1:14, 16). Saul, however, failed and was rejected. It was David who unambiguously became 'the LORD's anointed'.

king, a new David, an anointed one.[11] The announcement that 'Jesus is the Christ' identifies Jesus as the promised new David.

The book of Psalms plays an important role in the Old Testament presentation of this theme. We may appropriately speak of the Christology of the Psalms. Fundamental to the Psalms being Christian Scripture is the recognition that their multifaceted association with David finds fulfilment in Jesus, the son of David, who is the Christ, to whom all authority in heaven and on earth has been given (Matt. 28:18). He is the one who 'must reign until he has put all his enemies under his feet' (1 Cor. 15:25). He is the one in whom the decree of the Lord in Psalm 2 will be fulfilled (see Rev. 2:27; 12:5; 19:15).

To understand the Psalms as Christian Scripture is to believe that Jesus, the Christ of whom the Psalms speak, has come. This is the perspective from which the Psalms make true sense to the one who has come to believe the gospel of Jesus.

How to read the Psalms 'as Christian Scripture'
This means that regarding the Psalms as Christian Scripture is far more important than seeing them as God-given words to express my faith, my emotions, my longings and my pain. As a Christian believer, reading the Psalms is about me, but not *all* about me.

I find it helpful to think of four related levels of meaning in the Psalms. Sometimes I will read a psalm four times over, deliberately hearing each of these levels.

First, we may read the psalm, recognizing words that directly express our own experience of difficulties in life and our faith in God. But we will often notice that there are at least parts of a psalm that we cannot directly make our own. They do not really 'fit' us.

Secondly, we can read historically. Often this will mean understanding a psalm as David's words, or words about David, or words related in some way to David's kingdom. But we will notice again that there are ways in which the psalm does not really 'fit' even David. He never ruled the world.

---

11. See Isa. 9:7; 16:5; 22:22; 61:1; Jer. 23:5; 30:9; 33:15, 17; Ezek. 34:23–24; 37:24–25; Hos. 3:5; Amos 9:11; Zech. 12:7–8, 10; 13:1.

Thirdly, as we listen to the psalm we may consider how the psalm 'fits' Jesus. How does the psalm illuminate the news that *'Jesus* is the Christ'? In what ways does Jesus fulfil the psalm? In what ways does this fulfilment surpass the David we hear in the Psalms?

Then, on a fourth reading I consider the wonder that I belong to the Christ. By faith I am united to him. This will mean that I identify, not first of all with the 'I' of the Psalms, but with the people who benefit from the deliverance of the Christ. I am among those who are blessed because they take refuge in him.

In a secondary and derivative sense we may then find that we join in the words of the Christ. Just as we know that the one who raised Christ Jesus from the dead will give life to our mortal bodies (Rom. 8:11), so we find that we join in his words of trust in God, his words of longing for deliverance, his prayers for the overthrow of the enemies of the Lord and of his Christ, his joy in God's salvation. For his deliverance is our deliverance.

Christian people love the Psalms because they are the Psalms of the Christ. That is why, as we sing them to one another, the word *of Christ* dwells richly among us (Col. 3:16).

The Christology of the Psalms

In the second part of this chapter I propose to outline what I have called 'the Christology of the Psalms'. In what ways do the Psalms make us wise for salvation through faith in the Christ?

The fundamental 'Christology' of the Psalms is found in Psalm 2, which has an important introductory function to the whole psalter. In many of the points I am going to make we will begin with the Lord's anointed one in Psalm 2, and follow the point as it is developed in other psalms.

The kingdom of God and of his Christ
Let us begin by observing the close relationship between the reign of the anointed one and God's own kingship.

This is clearly set out in Psalm 2. In verse 2 the enemies are plotting 'against the LORD and against his Messiah [NIV, 'anointed']'.

The Lord is then described in verse 4 in terms of his heavenly kingship. He is 'the one *enthroned* in heaven'. And the Messiah, in verse 6, is *his* king, installed by the Lord on *his* holy mountain, Zion. The closeness (indeed 'identification' is not too strong a word) of the Messiah's rule with God's own reign is expressed in verse 7 in terms of sonship (echoing 2 Sam. 7:14): 'You are my son; today I have become your father.'

The Christ of the Psalms is seen in the context of God's sovereignty and is most closely related to it. There is one kingdom, and it is God's. The Lord God says to his king:

Sit at my right hand
    until I make your enemies
    a footstool for your feet.
(Ps. 110:1)

The Christ is king by virtue of the word of God. This 'decree of the Lord' is at the centre of Psalm 2, and in various ways appears in Psalms 89, 110 and 132.

I will not violate my covenant
    or alter what my lips have uttered.
Once for all, I have sworn by my holiness –
    and I will not lie to David –
that his line will continue for ever
    and his throne endure before me like the sun;
it will be established for ever like the moon,
    the faithful witness in the sky.
(Ps. 89:34–37; cf. v. 49)

Interestingly, a certain conditionality is introduced to this word of God in Book 5:

The LORD swore an oath to David,
    a sure oath that he will not revoke:
'One of your own descendants
    I will place on your throne.
If your sons keep my covenant

and the statutes I teach them,
then their sons will sit
on your throne for ever and ever.'
(Ps. 132:11–12)

God's own kingship is never lost sight of in the Psalms. The following is a selection of statements from the early part of the psalter (where David features prominently):

The LORD reigns for ever;
he has established his throne for judgment.
(Ps. 9:7)

The LORD is King for ever and ever;
the nations will perish from his land.
(Ps. 10:16)

The LORD is in his holy temple;
the LORD is on his heavenly throne.
He observes everyone on earth;
his eyes examine them.
(Ps. 11:4)

Indeed David himself, the king, addresses God as *his* King:

Listen to my cry for help,
my King and my God,
for to you I pray.
(Ps. 5:2)

Likewise, David speaks of God's kingship in the well-known royal image of a shepherd in the most famous of the psalms:

The LORD is my shepherd,
I lack nothing.
(Ps. 23:1)

Therefore we see the closest identification of the Christ's reign with

God's own kingdom, at the same time as it is subordinate to and derived from it.

In Books 4 and 5 of the psalter the kingship of God becomes a climactic theme: 'The LORD reigns' we hear again and again (Pss 93:1; 96:10; 97:1; 99:1; 146:10).

When we hear the New Testament proclamation 'God has made this Jesus, whom you crucified, both Lord and Messiah' (Acts 2:36), or 'the kingdom of the world has become the kingdom of our Lord and of his Messiah, and he will reign for ever and ever' (Rev. 11:15), we should have no difficulty hearing the fulfilment of the Christology of the Psalms. Jesus is the Christ.

The enemies of God and of his Christ

Our second observation is that the enemies of the Messiah are the enemies of God and the enemies of God are the enemies of the Messiah.

Again this is clear in Psalm 2, where the nations and their rulers are the enemies of 'the LORD and his Messiah [NIV: 'anointed']' (Ps. 2:1–2). The enemies appear in the Psalms in many forms and under many descriptions, but are very commonly described by reference to the king: 'the king's enemies' (Ps. 45:5), 'my enemies' (Ps. 3:7), 'those who hate me' (Ps. 35:19), they 'rise up against me' (Ps. 3:1), they are 'false witnesses against me' (Ps. 27:12), 'those who fight against me' (Ps. 35:1), and so on.

It does appear that the king in the Psalms understands himself to be the particular target of the enemies of God. In this he is a lonely figure (Pss 31:11; 38:11; 69:8). However, in a number of ways we hear the converse, namely that the king's enemies are God's enemies too:

> Banish them for their many sins,
>   for they have rebelled against you.
> (Ps. 5:10)

> Arrogant foes are attacking me;
>   ruthless people are trying to kill me –
>   people without regard for God.
> (Ps. 54:3)

the insults of those who insult you fall on me.
(Ps. 69:9)

The enemies are portrayed in a number of extreme ways. They are wild
beasts (Pss 22:16; 59:6). They are the forces of death (Pss 18:4–5; 23:4).
The enemies of the king (who are the enemies of God) have this
purpose: to destroy the Lord's anointed at a moment when God may
have forsaken him. They watch for the moment when they can say:

God has forsaken him;
> pursue him and seize him,
> for no one will rescue him.
(Ps. 71:11)

The Psalms recognize that among the enemies (and it may be fair
to say that this is the ultimate enemy) is death:

LORD, see how my enemies persecute me!
> Have mercy and lift me up from the gates of death.
(Ps. 9:13)

The cords of death entangled me;
> the torrents of destruction overwhelmed me.
The cords of the grave coiled around me;
> the snares of death confronted me.
(Ps. 18:4)

My heart is in anguish within me;
> the terrors of death have fallen on me.
(Ps. 55:4)

Even though I walk
> through the valley of the shadow of death,
I will fear no evil,
> for you are with me;
your rod and your staff,
> they comfort me.
(Ps. 23:4)

It is important to recognize that this is part of the complex background to Jesus' words 'the Christ must suffer'. In the Psalms the Christ finds himself the object of the hostility of the enemies of God. Jesus is the Christ.

I am not sure that we can clearly see a doctrine of substitutionary atonement in the Psalms, but we certainly find essential elements of such a doctrine that give depth to its unambiguous expression in Isaiah 53:

- The Christ of the Psalms suffers, and this suffering does not appear to be accounted for only in terms of his own sins.
- The Christ in the Psalms is righteous (Ps. 17:1) (whatever that precisely means).
- The Christ in the Psalms endures God's wrath (Pss 38:3; 88:7, 16; 89:46; 102:10).
- The obedience of the Christ of the Psalms surpasses (supersedes?) sacrifices, offerings, burnt offerings and sin offerings (Pss 40:6–8; 51:16).

I have no doubt that this (and probably much more) was involved in Jesus' assertion 'the Christ must suffer . . . and rise again'.

What will be the outcome of the suffering of the Christ in the Psalms? Here we come to our third observation.

The Christ trusts in God
God's promise to his anointed one is that he will rule the hostile ones 'with a rod of iron, [and] dash them to pieces like pottery' (Ps. 2:9). Such a promise of victory for the king over the enemies recurs often:

> Your hand will lay hold on all your enemies;
> > your right hand will seize your foes.
> When you appear for battle,
> > you will burn them up as in a blazing furnace.
> The LORD will swallow them up in his wrath,
> > and his fire will consume them.
> You will destroy their descendants from the earth,
> > their posterity from mankind.

> Though they plot evil against you
>> and devise wicked schemes, they cannot succeed.
> You will make them turn their backs
>> when you aim at them with drawn bow.
> (Ps. 21:8–12)

More particularly it is God himself who will overthrow the king's enemies:

> The enemy will not get the better of [David my servant];
>> the wicked will oppress him.
> I [God] will crush his foes before him
>> and strike down his adversaries.
> (Ps. 89:22–23)

This promise includes deliverance from death:

> Our God is a God who saves;
>> from the Sovereign LORD comes escape from death.
> (Ps. 68:20)

Put positively, the Lord promises life to his king:

> The king rejoices in your strength, LORD.
>> How great is his joy in the victories you give!
> . . .
> He asked you for life, and you gave it to him –
>> length of days, for ever and ever.
> Through the victories you gave, his glory is great;
>> you have bestowed on him splendour and majesty.
> Surely you have granted him unending blessings
>> and made him glad with the joy of your presence.
> (Ps. 21:1, 4–6)

There is a 'for ever' theme. God has blessed his king for ever (Ps. 45:2), given him a throne for ever and ever (Ps. 45:6), made him a priest for ever (Ps. 110:4), he is enthroned in God's presence for ever (Ps. 61:7), and so on.

It is characteristic of the king that, in the face of his enemies, he trusts in the Lord who has made such promises concerning him:

> For the king trusts in the LORD;
>> through the unfailing love of the Most High
>> he will not be shaken.
> (Ps. 21:7)

> It is better to take refuge in the LORD
>> than to trust in humans.
> It is better to take refuge in the LORD
>> than to trust in princes.
> (Ps. 118:8–9)

This confidence extends to death itself:

> Therefore my heart is glad and my tongue rejoices;
>> my body also will rest secure,
> because you will not abandon me to the realm of the dead,
>> nor will you let your holy one see decay.
> (Ps. 16:9–10)

And so he prays:

> LORD, see how my enemies persecute me!
> Have mercy and lift me up from the gates of death.
> (Ps. 9:13)

Particularly we should remember that the anointed king has a specific word of promise from the Lord, and so his affirmations of confidence in God's word should not be taken as vague and general, but directed to the specific promises made to him:

> As for God, his way is perfect;
> the LORD's word is flawless.
> (Ps. 18:30)

We should think here, not of God's word as a general concept, but of his promise to his king. Likewise:

In God, whose word I praise,
in the LORD, whose word I praise –
in God I trust, I will not be afraid.
What can man do to me?
(Ps. 56:10–11)

The king's people learn this lesson too:

Now this I know:
the LORD gives victory to his anointed.
He answers him from his heavenly sanctuary
with the victorious power of his right hand.
(Ps. 20:6)

While there are descriptions of the king's being active in overthrowing his enemies by God's power, often he is passive: it is God who gives him the victory:

Sit at my right hand
until I make your enemies
a footstool for your feet.
(Ps. 110:1)

Here [in Zion] I will make a horn grow for David
and set up a lamp for my anointed one.
I will clothe his enemies with shame,
but his head will be adorned with a radiant crown.
(Ps. 132:17–18)

The king's chief weapon of both defence and offence, therefore, is prayer. Again and again we hear him:

For your name's sake, LORD, preserve my life;
in your righteousness, bring me out of trouble.
In your unfailing love, silence my enemies;
destroy all my foes,
for I am your servant.
(Ps. 143:11–12)

Likewise, every one of the laments of the king.

We note that the king's trust in God is intimate. He speaks again and again of his love for God (Ps. 18:1), his joy in God's salvation (Ps. 21:1), and so on. There is no greater good for him than to be near God (Ps. 27:4). The enemies, however, mock the king's trust in God:

> 'He trusts in the LORD,' they say,
>> 'let the LORD rescue him.
> Let him deliver him,
>> since he delights in him.'
> (Ps. 22:8)

Here, of course, we are touching on the very terms in which the faithfulness of Jesus before his enemies and in death is understood in the New Testament (see the mockery he received in Matt. 27:43). Jesus is the Christ who trusts in God.

The Christ is himself obedient to God and applies his ways to his people

The fourth observation I will make is that the Christ of the Psalms is obedient to God and applies his ways to his people. He can say:

> For I have kept the ways of the LORD;
>> I am not guilty of turning from my God.
> All his laws are before me;
>> I have not turned away from his decrees.
> (Ps. 18:21–22)

David's prayer for Solomon, at the end of his life (if that is what Ps. 72 is) begins like this:

> Endow the king with your justice, O God,
>> the royal son with your righteousness.
> He will judge your people in righteousness,
>> your afflicted ones with justice.
> (Ps. 72:1–2; cf. Ps. 101, *passim*)

This could be illustrated much more widely, but it is certainly one of those points where the reader is conscious that the Christ of the Psalms is represented only in pale shadow in the David of history. Jesus is fully this Christ.

The Christ and God's majesty

The anointed king in the Psalms is at times a very human figure. His suffering and vulnerability, his dependence on God, the precariousness of his life, are all evident.

However, he is also seated at the right hand of God (Ps. 110:1) and his kingship (and even his person) are, in remarkable ways, caught up in the glory and majesty of God, in ways that cannot be understood until their fulfilment in the Lord Jesus Christ. The fifth group of observations is of the virtually divine majesty of the Christ of the Psalms.

In Psalm 61:7 the king is pictured as enthroned in God's presence for ever, protected by faithfulness (*ḥesed*) and truth (*'ĕmet*). The king's closeness to God is captured a number of times by this image of the shelter of God's wings:

> I long to dwell in your tent for ever
> > and take refuge in the shelter of your wings.
> (Ps. 61:4)

> Because you are my help,
> > I sing in the shadow of your wings.
> I cling to you;
> > your right hand upholds me.
> (Ps. 63:7–8)

Similarly, 'Because of my integrity you uphold me, / and set me in your presence for ever' (Ps. 41:12); 'Surely you have . . . made him glad with the joy of your presence' (Ps. 21:6). This closeness means that the king is surrounded and caught up in God's own holiness and glory: 'with my sacred oil I have anointed him' (Ps. 89:20b); 'you have bestowed on him splendour and majesty' (Ps. 21:5b); 'I ask . . . to gaze upon the beauty of the LORD' (Ps. 27:4).

The king's glory is not his own, but a reflection or extension of God's own majesty: 'you, LORD, are . . . my glory, the one who lifts

my head high' (Ps. 3:3); 'my salvation and honour depend on God'
(Ps. 62:7a). Well known, and controversial, is Psalm 45:6, addressed
to the king, boldly (but correctly) translated in the NIV as 'your
throne, O God, will last for ever and ever' (Ps. 45:6). Hebrews 1:8
understands this to indicate that the Son (clearly a Christological
term) is greater than any angel. Jesus is the Christ.

The Christ is God's Son

In the next two observations we will notice two ways in which the
close relationship between the Christ and God are presented in
the Psalms. The first of these (and my sixth observation) is as
God's son.

Sonship has a background in the history of Israel's relationship
with God. Israel as a people is called by God 'my firstborn son'
(Exod. 4:22; cf. Hos. 11:1). The promise to David concerning his
own son who would succeed him was 'I will be his father, and he
will be my son' (2 Sam. 7:14). In both of these instances the context
of thought does not suggest that the 'son' is in any direct sense
divine. The son is not by *nature* God's son, but by grace is taken to
be (or adopted as) God's son. In each case, of course, the son turned
out to be disobedient and rebellious.

> I reared sons [NIV 'children'] and brought them up,
>   but they have rebelled against me.
> (Isa. 1:2)

As we enter the psalter we are introduced to the anointed one
emphatically as the son. We hear his own testimony:

> [The LORD] said to me, 'You are my son;
> today I have become your Father.'
> (Ps. 2:7)

At the end of Book 3, where the situation anticipated in Psalm 2
has apparently been lost, the promise of Psalm 2 is remembered:

> He will call out to me, 'You are my Father,
>   my God, the Rock my Saviour.'

I will also appoint him to be my firstborn,
>   the most exalted of the kings of the earth.
(Ps. 89:26–27)

The Psalms, in quite remarkable ways, develop this idea of the
Messiah king as God's son, and God as the anointed one's Father.
At the same time the Psalms (perhaps most strikingly in Ps. 89)
testify to the failure of David and his successors in Israel's historical
experience to be what one might expect of such a privileged one.
The following are examples of the sonship idea as it is expressed in
the Psalms.

Psalm 89 makes clear the two-sided implications of sonship
(already stated in 2 Sam. 7), namely that sonship means the father's
unfailing commitment to the son, but also chastisement for the son
who does wrong:

I will maintain my love to him for ever,
>   and my covenant with him will never fail.
I will establish his line for ever,
>   his throne as long as the heavens endure.
If his sons forsake my law
>   and do not follow my statutes,
if they violate my decrees
>   and fail to keep my commands,
I will punish their sin with the rod,
>   their iniquity with flogging;
but I will not take my love from him,
>   nor will I ever betray my faithfulness.
(Ps. 89:28–33)

In fact we often see the king of the Psalms chastised as indicated:

The LORD has chastened me severely,
>   but he has not given me over to death.
(Ps. 118:18)

The king, however, in whatever suffering comes his way (and it is
not always chastisement of course), trusts in God in sonlike terms:

> Yet you brought me out of the womb;
>> you made me trust in you
>> even at my mother's breast.
> From birth I was cast upon you;
>> from my mother's womb you have been my God.
> (Ps. 22:9–10; cf. 71:5–6)

It seems to me that the well-loved Psalm 139:13–16 belongs to this developed concept of sonship. David can say:

> For you created my inmost being;
>> you knit me together in my mother's womb.
> I praise you because I am fearfully and wonderfully made;
>> your works are wonderful,
>> I know that full well.
> (Ps. 139:13–14)

His divine Father can be depended on more surely than his natural parents:

> Though my father and mother forsake me,
>> the LORD will receive me.
> (Ps. 27:10)

If this is an expression of sonship, it is interesting to hear David continue with a prayer that his Father will teach him his ways. A father teaches his son. This aspect of God's fatherhood finds expression in several places (e.g. Pss 18:34; 71:17; 132:12; 143:10; 144:1).

At the baptism of Jesus by John, the voice from heaven echoed the words of Psalm 2, 'This is my Son, whom I love; with him I am well pleased' (Matt. 3:17). Any reflection on the significance of that statement must listen to the Psalms' portrayal of the sonship of the Messiah. Any reflection on the sonship of the Messiah in the Psalms must take notice of the words at Jesus' baptism, for there we meet the one who is truly the Son of whom the Psalms have spoken. Jesus is the Christ.

The Christ is God's servant

A second very important way of presenting the relationship between the Messiah and the Lord in the Psalms is that the anointed one is the servant of the Lord. Here I will simply note some illustrative texts, worth examining individually: Psalms 18 (superscription); 35:27; 69:17; 78:70; 89:3, 20, 39, 50; 132:10; 143:12.

The Christ is the Lord's chosen servant, a designation conveying both humility and high status. This, too, has an important place in the recognition that Jesus is the Christ, and in understanding the meaning of that claim.

The Christ and his people

My eighth observation is that the Messiah of the Psalms lives and reigns for the benefit of his people. His people are God's people. When God delivers his king, his people are blessed. We see this clearly expressed in David's prayer in Psalm 144:

> From the deadly sword deliver me;
>   rescue me from the hands of foreigners
> whose mouths are full of lies,
>   whose right hands are deceitful.
> Then our sons in their youth
>   will be like well-nurtured plants,
> and our daughters will be like pillars
>   carved to adorn a palace.
> . . .
> Blessed are the people of whom this is true;
>   blessed are the people whose God is the LORD.
> (Ps. 144:11–12, 15)

In Psalm 22 the deliverance of the king has positive consequences for the whole world:

> All the ends of the earth
>   will remember and turn to the LORD,
> and all the families of the nations
>   will bow down before him.
> (Ps. 22:27)

More than this, Psalm 69 sees the king's deliverance as a reason for the *creation*, and in particular the people of Zion, to rejoice:

> Let heaven and earth praise him,
>> the seas and all that move in them,
> for God will save Zion
>> and rebuild the cities of Judah.
> (Ps. 69:34–35)

The Psalms testify to the fact that God will bring blessing to his people (indeed to his creation) by redeeming his king from his enemies and giving him life. Jesus is the Christ.

The Christ and the nations

The king in Psalm 2 calls on the rulers of the earth to cease their rebellion, to serve the Lord and kiss the son (Ps. 2:10–11). In Psalm 4 we hear the king preaching this gospel:

> How long will you people turn my glory into shame?
>> How long will you love delusions and seek false gods?
> Know that the LORD has set apart his faithful servant for himself;
>> the LORD hears when I call to him.
> (Ps. 4:2–3)

This king, on the basis of the authority given to him, brings the nations under his sway:

> You have delivered me from the attacks of the people;
>> you have made me the head of nations.
> People I did not know now serve me,
>> foreigners cower before me;
>> as soon as they hear of me, they obey me.
> (Ps. 18:43–44)

The king will preach the gospel among the nations:

> Therefore I will praise you, LORD, among the nations;
>> I will sing the praises of your name.

He gives his king great victories;
>   he shows unfailing love to his anointed,
>   to David and to his descendants for ever.
(Ps. 18:49–50)[12]

This study is far from exhaustive. The Psalms have much more to teach us about 'the Christ' of whom they speak. My hope is that sufficient has been said to demonstrate that reading, hearing or singing 'the Psalms as Christian Scripture' is more important than finding the psalms to be relevant to the joys and sorrows of human life. When Jesus said, 'These are the very Scriptures that testify about me' (John 5:39), he was speaking about the Psalms (and the other Old Testament scriptures). We read them to learn of him. We sing them to one another that the word of Christ may dwell richly among us (Col. 3:16). Knowing that Jesus is the Christ, the Psalms are able to make us wise for salvation through faith in Christ Jesus (2 Tim. 3:15).

---

12. This theme should be studied in more detail. Relevant passages include Pss 22:27–28; 45:17; 47:1, 4; 57:9; 65:7; 67:2, 4; 72:11, 17; 86:9; 96:3, 7, 10; 98:2; 99:1–2; 102:15; 105:1; 108:3; 117:1; 126:2.

3. CHRISTOLOGICAL USE OF THE PSALMS IN LUKE-ACTS AND HEBREWS

David G. Peterson

The Gospels indicate that Jesus used biblical psalms to express his unique relationship with God the Father and to explain the nature of his calling and its consequences. His way of using two particular psalms appears to have given rise to an important strand of Christological interpretation evidenced in Acts and many other New Testament documents. The focus in this study will be on the pattern that can be discerned in Luke-Acts and Hebrews.

Jesus as suffering and exalted Messiah: the evidence of Luke

Understanding events in the light of Scripture
On two occasions in Luke 24 the resurrected Jesus interprets the Scriptures for his disciples. First, he encounters two men on the road to Emmaus, and says:

> 'How foolish you are, and how slow to believe all that the prophets have spoken! Did not the Messiah have to suffer these things and then

enter his glory?' And beginning with Moses and all the Prophets, he explained to them what was said in all the Scriptures concerning himself. (Luke 24:25–27)

Then he appears to the Eleven and those gathered together with them (24:33). He instructs them about the necessity for his death and resurrection in terms of scriptural fulfilment (24:44–49), pointing also to the need for repentance and forgiveness of sins to be 'preached in his name to all nations, beginning at Jerusalem', indicating that they are 'witnesses of these things', and promising the empowerment of the Spirit for the task of proclamation.

In both these narratives Jesus highlights the importance of a Christocentric interpretation of the Scriptures, but he does not actually illustrate what he means. He says to those he encounters, 'This is what I told you while I was still with you: Everything must be fulfilled that is written about me in the Law of Moses, the Prophets and the Psalms' (Luke 24:44).

Jesus claims a post-resurrection continuation and development of the teaching he had previously given them, encouraging a comprehensive approach to the Hebrew Canon as a basis for interpreting the significance of his life and ministry.[1] We must look earlier in Luke's Gospel to see how he 'interpreted to them in all the Scriptures the things concerning himself'. Acts and the epistles will show how Jesus' creative handling of the Scriptures became for his disciples 'both the source of their own understanding and the paradigm for their exegesis of the Old Testament'.[2]

---

1. Jesus could be singling out 'the Psalms' for special attention (24:44), but it is more likely that the third part of the Hebrew Canon is indicated by mentioning its first and principal component. See I. H. Marshall, *The Gospel of Luke: A Commentary on the Greek Text* (Exeter: Paternoster, 1978), p. 905, who compares the way Philo (*Contemplative Life*, p. 25) describes the third part of the Hebrew canon.

2. R. N. Longenecker, *Biblical Exegesis in the Apostolic Period* (Grand Rapids: Eerdmans, 1975), p. 51. Longenecker goes on to outline some of the key issues involved in discovering and evaluating Jesus' use of the Old Testament.

Biblical citations in the teaching of Jesus

Predictions by Jesus of his death and resurrection are found in Luke
9:22, 44; 17:25; 18:31–33. As in the other Synoptic Gospels, these
sayings progressively reveal the full extent of his approaching
betrayal and suffering, without referring to any particular Old
Testament text. But Luke 22:37 uniquely records a climactic revelation to the disciples at the Last Supper, using a citation from
Isaiah 53:12 ('And he was numbered with the transgressors'). A
portion of a verse is used to refer to the passage as a whole. The
importance of this saying is highlighted by the introductory
claim that 'this [Scripture] must be fulfilled in me' and by the
emphatic conclusion that 'what is written about me is reaching its
fulfilment'.

Luke also uniquely has Jesus begin his public ministry with the
reading of Isaiah 61:1–2 in the synagogue at Nazareth, adding words
from Isaiah 58:6 as an interpretative gloss ('to set the oppressed
free'). This is followed by the claim that 'Today this Scripture
is fulfilled in your hearing' (Luke 4:16–21). Jesus implies that he is
the promised individual who has been anointed by the Spirit for the
prophetic task of announcing the eschatological redemption of
Israel and bringing it into effect.

Jesus quotes only two other Scriptures when teaching about
himself in Luke's Gospel. Psalm 118:22 (LXX 117:22) is cited after
Jesus alludes to his rejection by the leaders of Israel in the parable
of the wicked talents (Luke 20:17). Psalm 110:1 (LXX 109:1) is then
quoted when Jesus challenges his opponents about how David can
call his son Lord (Luke 20:42–43).[3] There is a further allusion to
this text in Jesus' answer to the question about his identity at his trial
(Luke 22:66–71).

So, of the four major scriptural citations in Luke's presentation
of Jesus' teaching about himself, two are from Isaiah and two from

---

3. On the cross Jesus adapts the prayer of Ps. 31:5 (LXX 30:6), addressing
   God as Father and saying, 'into your hands I commit my spirit' (Luke
   23:46). We do not hear Jesus cry the words of Ps. 22:1 in Luke's narrative
   (cf. Matt. 27:46; Mark 15:34), though there are allusions to some of the
   sufferings described in that psalm. Cf. W. J. Larkin, Jr., 'Luke's Use of
   the Old Testament', *JETS* 20.4 (1977), pp. 326–336.

the Psalms. In different ways, each is significant for understanding the saving plan of God and the role of Jesus in fulfilling that plan.

Space does not permit an exploration of the many possible quotations and allusions in the other Gospels.[4] However, it is noteworthy that Psalm 82:6 is used by Jesus when challenged about claiming to be the Son of God (John 10:33–36). Psalm 41:9 is used to predict his betrayal by Judas (John 13:18–19; cf. Matt. 26:23–25; Mark 14:20–21; Luke 22:21–23). Psalm 69:4 is cited by Jesus in John 15:25 and is said to have been fulfilled in the hatred of his enemies 'without a cause'.[5]

Two key citations from the Psalms

In each of the Synoptic Gospels Jesus' use of Psalms 118:22 and 110:1 is significant because of the narrative context and because of the implied claims he makes about his identity and role in fulfilling God's saving purpose (cf. Matt. 21:42–44; 22:41–45; Mark 12:10–11; 12:35–37). This threefold Synoptic witness points to the authenticity of the tradition and explains how Jesus' interpretation of these texts was critical for the development of a Christological reading of certain psalms by his disciples.

The rejected but vindicated son/king

After his triumphal entrance into Jerusalem, Jesus cleanses the temple and engages in 'teaching the people in the temple and proclaiming the good news' (Luke 20:1). The parable of the wicked talents is told in response to challenges from the religious authorities about his authority to act and speak in this way. The parable climaxes with the killing of the 'beloved son' of the owner of the vineyard and the claim by Jesus that the owner will 'come and kill those tenants and give the vineyard to others' (Luke 20:15–16).

---

4. See Longenecker, *Biblical Exegesis*, pp. 133–157; D. A. Brueggemann, 'The Evangelists and the Psalms', in P. S. Johnstone and D. G. Firth (eds.), *Interpreting the Psalms: Issues and Approaches* (Downers Grove: InterVarsity Press Academic, 2005), pp. 263–278.
5. In John 2:17, Ps. 69:9 is remembered by the disciples after Jesus' death with reference to his zeal in cleansing the temple. In John 19:28 Jesus says 'I thirst' to 'fulfil the Scripture', apparently alluding to Ps. 69:21.

In Luke's record those who hear the parable say, 'God forbid!', and Jesus responds by looking directly at them and saying, 'Then what is the meaning of that which is written?' (20:17). A citation from Psalm 118:22 (LXX 117:22) follows:

> the stone that the builders rejected
> has become the cornerstone.

Matthew and Mark also include the next verse from the psalm:

> the Lord has done this,
> and it is marvellous in our eyes.

In Luke 20:18 Jesus gives a midrashic interpretation of this text: 'everyone who falls on that stone will be broken to pieces; anyone on whom it falls will be crushed'. This incorporates the language of Isaiah 8:14–15 and Daniel 2:34, 44–45 (cf. Rom. 9:32–33; 1 Pet. 2:6–8). Mark has no parallel, and Matthew 21:43 interposes the words 'Therefore, I tell you that the kingdom of God will be taken away from you and given to a people who will produce its fruit,' before concluding in the same way.

Although some scholars have suggested that the link between the citation, the interpretation and the parable is not very direct and must be secondary, N. T. Wright argues that there is a logical flow of thought, which most likely goes back to Jesus himself:

> The prophetic story of the rejected servants climaxes in the rejected
> son; he, however, is the messianic stone which, rejected by the builders,
> takes the chief place in the building. Those who oppose him will find
> their regime (and their Temple) destroyed, while his kingdom will be
> established.[6]

Psalm 118 begins and ends with a call for God's people to acknowledge that the Lord is good and that 'his love endures for ever' (vv. 1–4, 29). The bulk of the psalm contains the thanksgiving of

---

6. N. T. Wright, *Jesus and the Victory of God* (London: SPCK, 1996), p. 501.

an individual, 'probably the king or some other representative of the community'.[7] He bears witness to the Lord's help in time of crisis: he has been delivered from death and given victory over his enemies (vv. 5–18). A festal procession to the Jerusalem temple provides the opportunity to give thanks and pray to God to save his people again (vv. 19–28).

The crowd going up with Jesus to celebrate the Passover in Luke 19:38 echo the words of the pilgrims in Psalm 118:26 (LXX 117:26), 'Blessed is the king who comes in the name of the Lord!'[8] Jesus implicitly claims to be the promised messianic ruler by riding into the city as he does, weeping over Jerusalem and predicting its destruction, then driving out those who sold in the temple precincts (Luke 19:28–46).

In the flow of Psalm 118 the miniature parable in verse 22 points to the king as one who has been in great distress, in danger of being rejected, but vindicated by God as 'the cornerstone' of the building he is constructing.[9] In the context of Jesus' public ministry this becomes a prophecy of his impending betrayal and death, but inevitable exaltation by God through resurrection and ascension. It is this kind of teaching that Jesus apparently resumes and develops when he encounters his disciples again in Luke 24.

The Messiah / Son who rules at God's right hand

As the confrontation between Jesus and the religious authorities in Jerusalem progresses, he deals with the question of paying taxes to Caesar and then the question about the resurrection of the dead (Luke 20:19–40). Finally, he turns to them and says:

---

7. R. Davidson, *The Vitality of Worship: A Commentary on the Book of Psalms* (Grand Rapids: Eerdmans; Edinburgh: Handsel, 1998), p. 383. Cf. L. C. Allen, *Psalms 101–150* (Waco: Word 1983), pp. 122–125.

8. In Mark 11:9 and Matt. 21:9 the crowd also cry out, 'Hosanna (to the Son of David)!', abbreviating the cry of Ps. 118:25 (LXX 117:25), 'LORD, save us!'

9. There has been debate over the meaning of the expression *kephalēn gōnias* (lit. '[the] head of [the] corner'). But whether 'keystone' or 'capstone' is meant, the reference is to a stone that is crucial to the whole structure. See J. A. Fitzmyer, *The Gospel According to Luke X–XXIV* (Garden City: Doubleday, 1985), p. 1282.

Why is it said that the Messiah is the son of David? David himself declares in the Book of Psalms:

> The Lord said to my Lord:
> 　'Sit at my right hand,
> until I make your enemies
> 　a footstool for your feet.'

David calls him 'Lord'. How then can he be his son? (Luke 20:41–44).

Jesus' use of Psalm 110:1 (LXX 109:1) suggests that a messianic interpretation was known to the teachers of the law in his day.[10] But he challenges accepted views and questions the sense in which David could address his son as 'my Lord'. David's son is treated as his superior in this text and the messianic kingdom is portrayed as more than a renewal of David's earthly dominion.

Once again, Wright points to the nexus between Messiah and temple in Jesus' actions and words: 'by posing this question, Jesus implies that he has gained his authority over the Temple not merely as David's son but, more particularly, as David's lord'.[11] But how does Jesus indicate that his rule will be inaugurated and expressed?

When he is on trial in Luke 22:69 and is asked about whether he is the Christ, he combines words from Psalm 110:1 with an allusion to Daniel 7:13, predicting that 'from now on the Son of Man shall be seated at the right hand of the mighty God'. Wright resists the idea that Jesus with this claim portrays himself as a 'transcendent' figure.[12] However, if Jesus sees the supernatural events of his resurrection and ascension inaugurating his heavenly rule, this raises questions about his identity and relationship with 'the Lord'. As we shall see, Psalm 110:1 is understood in Acts and in the argument of

---

10. D. M. Hay, *Glory at the Right Hand: Psalm 110 in Early Christianity* (Nashville: Abingdon, 1973), pp. 22–33, examines interpretations of this text in Jewish tradition. However, Wright, *Jesus and the Victory*, p. 508, n. 116, contends that there is no clear pre-Christian evidence of this text being used in a messianic sense.

11. Wright, *Jesus and the Victory*, p. 509.

12. Ibid., pp. 526–528.

Hebrews to point to his divinity, as well as to the dominion established through his resurrection and ascension.

Conclusions about Luke's Gospel

Jesus' use of Psalms 118:22 and 110:1 appears to have been critical for the Christological application of the Psalms by the earliest Christians. These significant texts were used in a pattern of self-disclosure following his entrance into Jerusalem and his cleansing of the temple (Luke 20:17–18, 41–44). An allusion to Psalm 110:1 appears again in his answer to the question about his identity posed at his trial (Luke 22:66–71).

In the context of his teaching as a whole, these texts point to Jesus as the promised saviour-king of Israel, who experiences rejection and death at the hands of Israel's leaders, but who is exalted by God to reign from heaven. The interpretative principle being used here is patterning or typology. As part of the unfolding revelation of God's plan for Israel and the nations, what happens to David, or is predicted concerning his 'house', is taken as a blueprint for understanding the person and work of the Messiah.[13]

Jesus' approach to the Psalms involves viewing them in the context of prophetic teaching about Davidic kingship and the future of Israel (e.g. Luke 1:32–33, 68–75). Specifically in Luke's Gospel, Jesus' use of psalms is set within the context of his application of the prophecies of Isaiah 53 and 61 to himself.

Jesus as Messiah and Lord: the evidence of Acts

Jesus as Son of David

The first two citations from the Psalms in Acts form part of Peter's speech explaining the defection of Judas and the need for another to take his place as an apostle and witness of the resurrection of Jesus (1:16–22). The Davidic authorship of both texts is the basis

---

13. Cf. G. Goldsworthy, *Preaching the Whole Bible as Christian Scripture* (Grand Rapids: Eerdmans; Leicester: Inter-Varsity Press, 2000), pp. 46–52, 76–78.

of Peter's understanding of the fulfilment of Psalms 69:25 (MT 69:26; LXX 68:26) and 109:8 (LXX 108:8).[14]

The apostle claims that David spoke the words cited, but it was the Holy Spirit who spoke through him, and so the psalms attributed to him are regarded as being inspired by God (Acts 1:16; cf. 2:25, 30; 4:25). Following the lead of Jesus, his disciples looked for the way the inspired Scriptures pointed to the Christ event.

As Luke's description of the death of Judas in Acts 1:18–19 suggests, Psalm 69:25 had been 'fulfilled' when Judas, who betrayed the Messiah to his enemies, died as one cursed by God. His 'place' was 'deserted' and there was 'no one to dwell in it'. Peter personalizes this text by turning the plural of the original into the singular.

When it is said that David spoke 'concerning Judas', the meaning is that David's words have their ultimate application or fulfilment in the betrayal of Jesus as the Son of David. There is an underlying, and frequently surfacing, Davidic Christology in Acts that makes it possible for passages related to David and his experiences to be applied to Jesus and his experiences. Following Jesus' own use of this psalm, the enemies of David or of the righteous sufferer could be seen as foreshadowing his opponents, without implying that the primary or only reference of Psalm 69:25 was to Judas himself.[15]

---

14. D. J. Moo, 'The Problem of Sensus Plenior', in D. A. Carson and J. D. Woodbridge (eds.), *Hermeneutics, Authority and Canon* (Grand Rapids: Zondervan, 1986), pp. 179–211, discusses the 'appropriation techniques' of the New Testament writers as they interpreted and applied Old Testament texts. Cf. K. D. Litwak, 'The Use of the Old Testament in Luke–Acts: Luke's Scriptural Story of the "Things Accomplished among Us"', in S. A. Adams and M. Pahl (eds.), *Issues in Luke–Acts: Selected Essays* (Piscataway: Gorgias, 2012), pp. 147–169.

15. Longenecker, *Biblical Exegesis*, p. 97, argues that the Jewish exegetical rule *qal waḥomer* (light to heavy) is being applied here, 'allowing Peter to assert that what has been said of false companions and wicked men generally applies, *a minore ad majorem*, specifically to Judas, the one who proved himself uniquely false and evil'. But these texts are particularly applicable to Judas because he betrays the eschatological Son of David and because Jesus himself cites Ps. 69 in John 15:25 to explain the hatred of his enemies 'without a cause'.

Such an understanding of this text may well have led to the application of Psalm 109:8 to the situation. This psalm also calls for God's judgment upon David's enemies. Part of verse 8 is used with slight modification as a justification for replacing Judas as an apostle of Christ. The expression 'may another take his place of leadership [ESV, 'office']' (LXX *tēn episkopēn autou*) is used in a non-technical sense here for his 'oversight' or 'leadership'. The narrative concerning the appointment of Matthias goes on to show how this happened.

The pattern of relating an explicitly Davidic psalm to Jesus continues in Peter's Pentecost sermon.[16] Jesus' resurrection is proclaimed as his ultimate accreditation and vindication by God (2:22–24). In making this point, Peter claims that God loosed Jesus from the pangs of death, 'because it was impossible for death to keep its hold on him'. The expression 'agony [*ōdines*, 'birthpangs'] of death' is found in Psalms 18:4 (LXX 17:5) and 116:3 (LXX 114:3). This mixed metaphor regards death as being 'in labour' and unable to hold back its child. God 'brought the pangs to an end' so that 'the "birth" which is to bring Christ to light, may attain its goal'.[17] It was *impossible* for the Son of David to be prevented by death from exercising his eternal, kingly rule, because of who he is.

The implication is that Jesus was resurrected because he already was the Messiah, not that he 'became' Messiah through resurrection. Psalm 16:8–11 (LXX 15:8–11) is not quoted to 'prove' the resurrection as a historical event – the apostles present themselves as witnesses in that particular respect (Acts 2:32) – but to show how the resurrection testifies to Jesus' messiahship.

Old Testament scholars continue to debate whether there is any hint of bodily resurrection or life after death in the Psalms, but Peter manifests no such doubts. The connective 'for' (*gar*) at the beginning of Acts 2:25 makes it clear that it was impossible for death to keep its hold on Jesus because of what David says 'concerning him'.

---

16. The treatment of Acts 2:22–36 that follows is a condensation of the argument in D. G. Peterson, *The Acts of the Apostles* (Grand Rapids: Eerdmans; Nottingham: Apollos, 2009), pp. 144–153.

17. BDAG (λύω). Cf. G. Bertram, 'ὠδίν, ὠδίνω', *TDNT*, vol. 9, p. 673.

Psalm 16 celebrates the benefits of a life lived under the rule of God. These include the protection mentioned in verse 8 (Acts 2:25), 'because he is at my right hand, I will not be shaken'.[18] But David's joy reaches beyond his present circumstances to include the hope that he will always be with God (Ps. 16:9–10; Acts 2:26–27). Death no longer terrifies him and he affirms:

> you will not abandon me to the realm of the dead,
> you will not let your holy one see decay.

The impotence of death to destroy his relationship with God is David's confidence. Since God has already made known to him 'the paths of life', David anticipates that God will continue to fill him with joy in his 'presence' (Ps. 16:11; Acts 2:28).

The fact that the patriarch David 'died and was buried, and his tomb is here to this day' is sufficient proof for Peter that Psalm 16 speaks about something beyond David's personal experience. Bodily resurrection is the key issue. If David's own body had been raised, his grave would have been disturbed or would no longer be present. Peter again claims that David was a prophet (cf. 1:16; 4:25).[19] Jesus himself suggested the prophetic status of David when he gave a messianic interpretation of Psalm 110:1. Since that passage is paired with Psalm 16:8–11 in Acts 2:24–36, it is possible that Jesus' interpretation of Psalm 110 was the basis for this messianic reading of Psalm 16.

There is also an allusion in Acts 2:30–33 to another important Davidic psalm. David knew that 'God had promised him on oath

---

18. The text quoted in Acts 2:25–28 follows the LXX where it differs from the Hebrew in minor details. The first verb, 'I saw', is substituted for the Hebrew 'I have set'; 'my tongue' for the Hebrew 'my glory'; the expression 'in hope' for the Hebrew 'securely'; and 'decay' for the Hebrew 'the Pit'. None of these changes is decisive for a new understanding of the text. See D. L. Bock, *Proclamation from Prophecy and Pattern: Lucan Old Testament Christology* (Sheffield: JSOT Press, 1987), pp. 174–177.

19. J. A. Fitzmyer, 'David, Being Therefore a Prophet . . . (Acts 2:30)', *CBQ* 34 (1972), pp. 332–339, shows that this was a common theme in Palestinian Judaism.

that he would place one of his descendants on his throne'. The wording of Psalm 132:11 is recalled, reflecting the divine promise in 2 Samuel 7:12–16, establishing the throne of David's offspring for ever (cf. Ps. 89:3–4, 35–37). The implication is that the resurrection and ascension of a suffering and rejected Son of David is essential for the fulfilment of God's covenant purpose.

Peter in this Acts passage claims that in writing Psalm 16 and 'seeing what was to come, [David] spoke about the resurrection of the Messiah, that he was not abandoned to the realm of the dead, nor did his body see decay'. Only through resurrection from the dead could a son of David rule for ever over God's people. David's confidence about this was an oracular statement through the prophet Nathan, inspired by the Spirit of God and reflected in Psalm 132:11. This enabled him to indicate many centuries beforehand how God's covenant with him would ultimately be fulfilled.

When Psalm 16:10 is cited again in Acts 2:31, two significant changes are made. The past tense is employed to emphasize fulfilment ('he was not abandoned to the realm of the dead') and 'his body' is substituted for 'your Holy One'. This last change 'guarantees that the point of the passage is not merely spiritual translation, bodily preservation, or terminal illness, but bodily resurrection'.[20] God's Holy One is saved from death in his body.

Most likely, the title 'your Holy One' (*ton hosion sou*; Hebr. *ḥĕsîdĕkā*) was taken to be another way of referring to the messianic Son of David and is a key for understanding Peter's use of this text. In Psalm 16:10 David is God's 'holy one', meaning that he is one of the faithful in Israel 'whose life is lived in accordance with the principles of *ḥesed*', that is, 'faithfulness, steadfast love, or more generally kindness'.[21]

---

20. Bock, *Proclamation*, p. 178. This change reflects the explanatory parallelism of the psalm as recorded in Acts 2:26b, 27, where 'the last two elements of the line define how *the flesh* shall dwell in security with hope'.

21. D. A. Baer and R. P. Gordon, '*ḥsd* II', *NIDOTTE*, vol. 2, p. 213. A messianic interpretation of Ps. 16:9 is found in the much later *Midrash Tehillim* ('my glory rejoices over the Lord Messiah, who will rise from me'; i.e. from David). As the Messiah, Jesus was God's Holy One par excellence (cf. Acts 3:14; 4:27, 30, where the adjective *hagios* [holy] is used).

Peter specifically links the hope of the psalmist with Jesus and his resurrection when he says, 'God has raised this Jesus to life, and we are all witnesses of it' (2:32). The resurrection demonstrates that Jesus is the Messiah, who fulfils a complex of Jewish hopes (cf. 3:15, 26; 4:10–12; 5:30–32; 10:40–43; 13:30–39). He is the saviour-king of David's line, who reigns for ever over God's people, bringing the blessings of forgiveness and peace with God. As the one appointed to be the judge of the living and the dead he offers salvation and a share in his resurrection life to all nations (cf. 13:46–48; 16:30–31; 17:30–31). The psalms cited in Acts help to define the *nature* or character of his messiahship.

Jesus and God

The climax of Peter's Pentecost sermon in Acts 2:33–36 is a threefold claim. First, Peter asserts that Jesus was exalted to the right hand of God and that 'he has received from the Father the promised Holy Spirit, and has poured out what you now see and hear'. Secondly, he asserts that Jesus' exaltation is a fulfilment of Psalm 110:1 (LXX 109:1). Thirdly, the challenge is given to acknowledge Jesus' true identity: 'let all Israel be assured of this: God has made this Jesus, whom you crucified, both Lord and Messiah'.

Returning to the events that provoked this address in the first place, Peter insists that what the crowd could see and hear were signs of Jesus' exaltation to the situation of absolute glory, power and authority in the universe. As the dispenser of the Spirit he was now acting with 'the Father', sharing fully in his heavenly rule. Given the relationship between God and his Spirit in the Old Testament, an implicit trinitarianism is being expressed here.[22]

Max Turner has suggested a fusion of Davidic and Mosaic

---

22. M. M. B. Turner, *Power from on High: The Spirit in Israel's Restoration and Witness in Luke–Acts* (Sheffield: Sheffield Academic, 1996), p. 277, argues that the fulfilment of the promise envisaged in Acts 2:17–18, 33 'takes the reader beyond anything Judaism conceived of the messiah, for it relates the Spirit to Jesus in the same way as to God, the Father, himself'.

Christologies here, as part of a new exodus soteriology in Luke-Acts.[23] David did not ascend to God to receive a gift for God's people, but Moses did (see Exod. 19; 24; 34). Moreover, Moses was involved (at least passively) in the distribution of the Spirit to other Israelites, and it was his wish that the Spirit might be given to all Israel (Num. 11:26–30), which the promise of Joel 2:28–32 (MT and LXX 3:1–5) 'fulfils'.

David's authorship of a psalm citation is once again critical for Peter's messianic application (2:34). The fact that David himself did not ascend to heaven compels us to look for the interpretation of this oracle beyond his own experience. Psalm 110 speaks about the enthronement of a son of David as king of Israel. God's invitation to 'sit at my right hand / until I make your enemies / a footstool for your feet' suggests that David's son will be the Lord's representative, through whom he will rule his people and put down all his enemies (a theme developed in Ps. 110:5–6). Peter proclaims that Jesus' resurrection and ascension are the events by which his heavenly rule as the saviour-king of his people was inaugurated.

The conclusion to Peter's argument in 2:36 challenges his immediate audience, but also subsequent readers of Acts to 'be assured of'[24] who Jesus is and how God has vindicated him: 'God has made this Jesus, whom you crucified, both Lord and Messiah.' The two titles given to Jesus here relate back to the psalm citations in 2:25–34 and the prior claim of Joel 2:32 that whoever calls on the name of 'the Lord' will be saved (2:21). Jesus is 'the Lord' on whom to call, since he is 'the Messiah [Christ]', resurrected by God in fulfilment of Psalm 16:8–11 and now exalted to his right hand in fulfilment of Psalm 110:1.

The first occurrence of *kyrios* (Lord) in Psalm 110:1 represents the sacred name of God in Hebrew, whereas the second is qualified by 'my' and represents the ordinary Hebrew expression 'my lord'.

---

23. Ibid., pp. 279–289. Cf. L. W. Hurtado, 'Christology in Acts: Jesus in Early Christian Belief and Practice', in S. A. Adams and M. Pahl (eds.), *Issues in Luke–Acts: Selected Essays* (Piscataway: Gorgias, 2012), pp. 217–237.

24. 'Be certain' (*asphalōs ginōsketō*) in 2:36 recalls Luke's promise at the beginning of his work to provide 'certainty' (*asphaleian*) to Theophilus and other readers of the things they have learned (Luke 1:4).

The one whom David addresses as 'my lord' is distinguished from
God ('the LORD'). However, since Jesus has been uniquely exalted
to the Father's side through heavenly ascension and has poured out
the promised Spirit, he can be called 'LORD' in the full sense that
God is. God now calls people to himself though Jesus and offers
them forgiveness and the Holy Spirit 'in the name of Jesus Christ'
(2:38–39).[25]

When Peter says God 'made' (*epoiēsen*) him Lord and Messiah,
this does not mean that Jesus was somehow adopted as God's
heavenly co-regent at this point in time. Peter is proclaiming 'not
an adoptionist Christology but a functional one with ontological
overtones'.[26]

In Luke's Gospel Jesus is proclaimed as Saviour, Messiah and
Lord from his birth (2:11; cf. 1:31–35, 43; 3:22). Peter's sermon
highlights the way in which this became known, as Jesus was pro-
gressively attested by God through 'miracles, wonders and signs'
(Acts 2:22), and then climactically through the resurrection (2:24).
Since he *was* the Christ, he was raised from death and exalted to
God's right hand. In the final analysis Luke shows that 'the Messiah
Jesus is not merely the Son of David or the messianic Son of God.
He is Son in a fuller sense that entails complete authority and direct
access to God.'[27]

However, just as there are several important stages in the life of
a king, from birth as heir to the throne, to anointing, to actual
assumption of his throne, so it is with Jesus in Luke-Acts.

---

25. L. W. Hurtado, *One God, One Lord: Early Christian Devotion and Ancient Jewish
    Monotheism* (Minneapolis: Fortress; London: SCM, 1988), pp. 94–95, 100,
    argues that we have here a mutation of Jewish 'divine agency' thinking,
    involving 'an unprecedented reshaping of monotheistic piety to include
    a second object of devotion alongside God'.

26. R. N. Longenecker, 'The Acts of the Apostles', in F. E. Gaebelein (ed.), *The
    Expositor's Bible Commentary*, vol. 9: *John–Acts* (Grand Rapids: Zondervan,
    1982), p. 281. Contrast C. K. Barrett, *A Critical and Exegetical Commentary on
    the Acts of the Apostles*, vol. 1 (Edinburgh: T. & T. Clark, 1994), pp. 140–141,
    151–152.

27. Bock, *Proclamation*, p. 143.

Although Jesus was called Lord and Messiah previously, the full authority of these titles is granted only through death, resurrection and exaltation. Peter's proclamation in 2:36 makes it clear that something new and important has happened through these events. Jesus has been enthroned as Lord and Messiah for Israel, to fulfill all the divine promises. This newly enthroned ruler will also offer salvation to the world, having been granted universal power to rule and judge.[28]

Jesus and his opponents

Psalm 118 in an apologetic and evangelistic context

When Peter and John were called to account for 'proclaiming in Jesus the resurrection of the dead' (Acts 4:2), the presenting issue was also the 'power' or 'name' by which they healed a man lame from birth (4:7; cf. 3:1–10).[29] Standing before the rulers, elders, scribes and high-priestly authorities, Peter was quick to claim that 'by the name of Jesus Christ of Nazareth, whom you crucified but whom God raised from the dead, that this man stands before you healed' (4:10; cf. 3:16). Peter alludes to Psalm 118:22 (LXX 117:22) as he continues, 'Jesus is "the stone you builders rejected, which has become the cornerstone". Salvation is found in no one else, for there is no other name given under heaven by which we must be saved' (4:11–12). The citation used by Jesus in his challenge to the religious authorities is modified here to highlight even more directly the tragic error of his opponents. The verb 'rejected' in the Greek version of the psalm (*apedokimasan*) is replaced with another, which more literally means 'scorned' (*exouthenētheis*), and the word 'you' (literally 'by you', *hyph' hymōn*) is inserted before 'the builders' to make the application to Peter's audience abundantly clear.[30]

---

28. R. C. Tannehill, *The Narrative Unity of Luke–Acts: A Literary Interpretation*, vol. 2: *The Acts of the Apostles* (Minneapolis: Fortress, 1990), p. 39.

29. My discussion of Acts 4:11–12, 23–28 here largely follows the argument in Peterson, *Acts*, pp. 191–193, 197–201.

30. Barrett, *Acts*, p. 230, observes that the modifications in the quotation imply 'a preaching context', and does not think that Luke himself reworded the psalm. The change of verb suggests 'the identification of the *stone* with a person' (emphasis original).

The claims of Acts 4:10 parallel the two phases of the quotation. Jesus is the despised 'stone', scorned by the leaders of Israel, but exalted by God to the place of highest honour and significance. He is now 'the cornerstone' because he plays an essential part in the building God is constructing.[31] In other words, he is the key figure in God's plan for the restoration of Israel and the whole created order: 'God's purpose for Israel finds its fulfilment in the single-handed work of the Christ.'[32]

Members of the Sanhedrin would have agreed that the God of Israel is humanity's only true saviour (cf. Exod. 15:1–11; Isa. 43:11–12; 45:22; Ps. 96:1–5), but Peter insists that the name of Jesus is the exclusive means by which God's saving power can now be invoked and experienced (4:12). God's ultimate act of salvation in the death and exaltation of Jesus makes him the one upon whom to call for deliverance in the coming 'day of the Lord' (2:20–21, 33–36). The leaders of Israel needed to acknowledge their utter dependence on him.

Psalm 2 used to explain opposition to Jesus and his followers
When the apostles were released from captivity, they returned to their friends and reported what the chief priests and elders had said to them. Then they prayed together, acknowledging God's rule over nature and history, especially his good providence in revealing beforehand the pattern of opposition that would be experienced by the Messiah and those associated with him (4:25–28).

God is addressed in this prayer as 'Sovereign Lord' or 'Master' (*despota*), who 'made the heavens and the earth and the sea, and everything in them'. The last words are almost a direct quote from Psalm 146:6 (LXX 145:6), where they are the basis for confidence in God's ability to help his people when they are oppressed (cf. Isa. 37:16–20).

God is also addressed as the one who 'spoke by the Holy Spirit through the mouth of your servant, our father David'. David was

---

31. Cf. Longenecker, 'Acts', pp. 304–305, and n. 9 above.
32. F. F. Bruce, *The Book of the Acts*, rev. ed. (Grand Rapids: Eerdmans, 1988), p. 93.

the human author of Psalm 2:1–2, which is then quoted in its LXX form. What David uttered is once more declared to be the word of God, because God's Spirit was speaking through him. David was God's 'servant' in this prophetic role, and Jesus is actually the anointed one mentioned in the psalm: he truly is God's 'holy servant', whom he anointed (Acts 4:27).

Once Jesus was acknowledged as the anointed ruler of Psalm 2, it was easy enough to relate his opponents to the other characters in the psalm and for his disciples to see themselves sharing in the suffering of the Messiah. But only here in Acts 4 are the opening verses of the psalm quoted. In this way the disciples expressed their confidence that the problems they faced were an extension of the opposition to Jesus as Messiah and, as such, 'part of the will of God'.[33]

Psalm 2:1–2 is applied to their situation by matching up its predictions with the events of recent history. The emphatic expression 'for truly' (*gar ep' alētheias*) introduces the application. Herod and Pontius Pilate are identified as 'the kings of the earth' and 'the rulers' who met together 'with the Gentiles and the peoples of Israel in this city' to conspire against Jesus. The surprising fulfilment of the psalm is that Israelites aligned themselves with foreigners and their rulers in opposing the Lord and his anointed one.

Acknowledging that the opponents of Jesus were doing what Scripture predicted, the apostles and those gathered to pray with them were able to confess, that they did 'whatever your power and will had decided beforehand should happen' (4:28). With this understanding of God's sovereignty and purpose, they were able to pray for the continuing ability to proclaim the gospel in the face of such opposition (4:29–30).[34]

---

33. Bock, *Proclamation*, p. 206. A Jewish messianic application of Ps. 2 is found in the first-century BC document *Pss Sol.* 17.26, where the Lord's Anointed will 'dash the sinner's pride in pieces like a potter's vessels, break all their substance with a rod of iron'. For a similar use of Ps. 2:9, see Rev. 2:27; 12:5; 19:15.

34. Tannehill, *Narrative Unity*, p. 71, observes that 'the opponents of Jesus and the opponents of the church are viewed as one continuous group, a simplification facilitated by the Sanhedrin's leading role in both situations'.

Jesus and the promises of God

The final two psalm citations in Acts occur in the sermon preached by Paul in the synagogue at Antioch in Pisidia (13:16–41).

Psalm 2:7

The argument begins with shared premises about God's election of Israel to be his people and David to be their king (13:17–23). As Paul goes on to describe the rejection of Jesus by 'the people of Jerusalem and their rulers' he claims that 'they did not recognize him nor understand the utterances of the prophets, which are read every Sabbath' (13:27 ESV). Nevertheless, they fulfilled those Scriptures by condemning him! The rest of the sermon shows how Jesus is the fulfiller of God's promises to David and is therefore the key to Israel's future (13:28–37), before Paul appeals to the congregation not to miss out on the salvation being offered through Jesus (13:38–41).[35]

The 'good news' that Paul brings is first described in terms of God's fulfilling what he promised 'to our ancestors' by raising Jesus (13:32–33). The promises Paul has in mind could include those made from the time of Abraham onwards, but he cites what is written in Psalm 2:7, 'You are my son; today I have become your father' [or, 'begotten you']. 'Begetting' is related to enthronement in this psalm. As in 2:33–36 Jesus' resurrection and exaltation to the right hand of God are viewed as linked events. Jesus' use of Psalm 110:1 appears to have inspired the application of Psalm 2:7 to his heavenly enthronement.[36]

'My son' is to be understood in a royal and messianic sense. When the Davidic king is installed on Zion, God's holy mountain (v. 6), the Lord in heaven recognizes him as his own son (v. 7), promising to put down his enemies and make the nations his

---

35. This sermon is discussed in more detail in Peterson, *Acts*, pp. 384–396.

36. F. F. Bruce, *The Acts of the Apostles: The Greek Text with Introduction and Commentary*, 3rd rev. ed. (Grand Rapids: Eerdmans 1990), p. 310, relates this 'begetting' to the baptism of Jesus, when he was anointed 'with the Holy Spirit and power' (10:38). But the parallels with Ps. 110 are strong and the enthronement in that psalm is applied to Jesus' resurrection and ascension in Acts 2:33–36.

inheritance (vv. 8–9). Applied to Jesus and his resurrection, the psalm suggests that his resurrection and ascension bring him to the full experience of his messianic destiny in a heavenly enthronement and rule (cf. Rom. 1:3–4; Heb. 1:3–5).[37]

In this context Paul says nothing about the pre-existence of the Son of God, though his letters indicate that such teaching needs to be taken into account when seeking to give a full account of what it means to call Jesus the Son of God (e.g. Rom. 8:3; Gal. 4:4–5; Col. 1:15–20; cf. Luke 1:31–33, 35; John 1:1–18; Acts 9:20).

Psalm 16:10

The messianic significance of Jesus' resurrection is further explained by means of two scriptural quotations. The paragraph begins and ends with a reference to 'decay' (13:34–35, *diaphthoran*), picking up a key word from the citation of Psalm 16:10 (LXX 15:10), which lies at the centre of the argument here. As we have seen, a more extensive quotation and application of this psalm are found in 2:25–31. God raised Jesus from the dead so that he might 'never be subject to decay'. This is another way of explaining the fulfilment of Psalm 2:7. To reign for ever at the Father's side, the Son had to be delivered from death and decay (cf. Luke 1:32–33).

Before citing a portion of Psalm 16:10 and saying something more about it, Paul quotes from Isaiah 55:3 ('I will give you the holy and sure blessings promised to David'). This compares with the use of Psalm 132:1 in 2:30, establishing the covenantal basis for the predictions about the Son of David. The plural 'you' makes it clear that the promise of God in this context is for Israel and so for Paul's listeners.

But the key text is a promise for the Messiah himself ('you will not let your holy one see decay'). As in 2:27–31, 'your holy one' is understood as a Christological title. The messianic significance of this promise is argued by noting that, when David had served God's

---

37. Longenecker, 'Acts', p. 428, misreads the flow of the argument when he suggests that *anastēsas* in 13:33 refers to Jesus' being 'brought forth' for his people Israel.

purpose in his own generation, he 'fell asleep; he was buried with his ancestors and his body decayed'. The words spoken by David in Psalm 16 find their true fulfilment in the bodily resurrection of Jesus Christ ('but the one whom God raised from the dead did not see decay').

Linking together the promises from Psalm 16:10 and Isaiah 55:3, we see that the Messiah's deliverance from death and decay is one of 'the holy and sure blessings promised to David' and that this means salvation for Israel too.[38] Israel's future is intimately connected with what happens to her Messiah, though there is no explicit mention of the return of Christ or eternal life here.

Conclusions about Acts

Jesus taught his disciples that psalms attributed to David could be read prophetically in connection with the Messiah and those associated with him. David's enemies included those who were close to him and betrayed him. Jesus' use of Psalm 69 encouraged his followers to see a prediction of his betrayal by Judas there and to view Psalm 109:8 as a call to replace Judas as one of the twelve apostles.

Psalm 2 is close to Psalm 110 in emphasis and theme. Psalm 2:7 is specifically related to the resurrection of Jesus in Acts 13:33, though resurrection also implies heavenly exaltation here, as in 2:33–36. The deeper implications of Jesus' divine sonship are not explored in Paul's sermon. But Peter's argument about Jesus being the Lord who sits at God's right hand, who provides salvation from the coming judgment of God, and who relates to the Spirit as the Father does, provides the elements for a trinitarian theology. The early Christians also saw the combined opposition of Jewish and Gentile authorities predicted in Psalm 2:1–2 as applying to themselves, as well as to Jesus, the Son of David.

Reflection on the meaning of Psalm 118:22 in relation to Jesus and his rejection by the leaders of Israel led to the conclusion that

---

38. Tannehill, *Narrative Unity*, p. 171, notes verbal correspondence between the two citations, understanding them as 'the positive and negative expression of the same promise'.

'there is salvation in no one else, for there is no other name under heaven given to mankind by which we must be saved' (Acts 4:12). While continuing to offer this salvation to Jews who would repent and believe, the earliest preachers were clearly also being prepared to apply their message about Jesus being 'the cornerstone' of God's saving plan to the nations more generally. At the same time, they were able to explain how the rejection of the Messiah by Israel's leaders furthered God's plan for the establishment of his New Covenant people.

Psalm 16 expresses David's confidence that God will not abandon him to the realm of the dead nor let his holy one see corruption. It is used by both Peter and Paul to argue that it was impossible for the Son of David to be prevented by death from exercising his eternal, kingly rule. Psalm 16 is paired with Psalm 132:11 to recall the divine promise in 2 Samuel 7:12–16, thus establishing that rule. Psalm 110:1 is quoted to make the climactic point that 'God has made this Jesus . . . both Lord and Messiah' (Acts 2:36).

So the use of these psalm texts is not arbitrary, but is guided by a hermeneutic based on the biblical portrait of David and his role in the plan of God for Israel and the nations. The wider context for this understanding of the Psalms is the prophetic literature of the Old Testament, and God's covenant with David is the specific basis for the Christological interpretation of psalms.

Jesus as Son of God and high priest: the evidence of Hebrews

Hebrews begins with an impressive statement about the Son, who is the supreme revealer of the glory and power of God and who has been appointed 'heir of all things, through whom also he made the universe' (1:1–2). When he had accomplished the high-priestly work of making 'purification for sins', 'he sat down at the right hand of the Majesty in heaven', having become 'as much superior to the angels as the name he has inherited is superior to theirs' (1:3–4).

This passage is rich with biblical allusions, many of which

anticipate the catena of biblical quotations that follows.[39] Seven Christological affirmations in 1:1–4 are undergirded by seven citations with introductory and concluding comments in 1:5–14.[40] There is a notable dependence on psalms in this section, with five of the seven citations coming from that biblical source.

The Son who is greater than the angels

Psalm 2:7 is first paired with 2 Samuel 7:14 to explain the Son's superiority to the angels in terms of his unique relationship with God the Father (Heb. 1:5). The psalm citation continues the enthronement theme from Hebrews 1:3, where there is an allusion to Psalm 110:1 ('he sat down at the right hand of the Majesty in heaven').[41] So the expression 'today I have become your Father' most likely refers to Jesus' entrance into 'the full exercise of all the prerogatives of his Sonship when, after his sufferings had proved the completeness of his obedience, he was raised to the Father's right hand'.[42]

As in Acts, the promise to David and his offspring in 2 Samuel 7:11–14 is the basis for interpreting Psalm 2 with reference to Jesus. The ultimate expression of God's kingship over his people through a Davidic ruler is exercised by one who is intimately related to God the Father and operates from his throne in heaven.

---

39. I have written more generally about the use of the Old Testament in Hebrews in D. G. Peterson, 'God and Scripture in Hebrews', in P. Helm and C. Trueman (eds.), *The Trustworthiness of God: Perspectives on the Nature of Scripture* (Grand Rapids: Eerdmans; Leicester: Apollos, 2002), pp. 118–138.

40. P. T. O'Brien, *The Letter to the Hebrews* (Grand Rapids: Eerdmans; Nottingham: Apollos, 2010), pp. 64–66, outlines the general correspondence between the themes and movement of thought in these passages. R. T. France, 'The Writer of Hebrews as a Biblical Expositor', *TynB* 47 (1996), pp. 245–276, discusses the expository method of Hebrews more generally.

41. There is also an allusion to Ps. 2:8 in Heb. 1:2 ('whom he appointed heir of all things'). Ps. 2, with 2 Sam. 7:11–14, is linked with a messianic interpretation at Qumran (4QFlor).

42. F. F. Bruce, *The Epistle to the Hebrews*, rev. ed. (Grand Rapids: Eerdmans, 1990), p. 54.

The next two citations affirm the necessity for the Son to be worshipped by angels, specifically supporting the claim that he has become 'as much superior to angels as the name he has inherited is superior to theirs' (1:4). Psalm 97:7 in the Greek version (LXX 96:7) reads, 'worship him, all [you] his angels'. However, Deuteronomy 32:43 may be the actual text quoted, because the LXX reads, 'and let all the sons of God worship him'. Hebrews 1:6 takes 'sons of God' to mean 'angels', perhaps using this psalm text as a gloss on the words from Deuteronomy.[43] The enthroned Son is worthy of the angelic adoration due to the Lord God of Israel.

Psalm 104:4 in the Hebrew text speaks about God's use of wind and fire as 'messengers' and 'ministers' to serve his purpose in creation. But the LXX version (103:4) 'reverses the objects so that the text now speaks of the transitory nature of the angels, who receive their rank and task from God'.[44]

Then, by way of contrast, two lengthy citations in Hebrews 1:8–12 return to the theme of the Son's supremacy. First, Psalm 45:6–7 (LXX 44:7–8), which celebrates a royal wedding, is quoted. When the psalmist says, 'your throne O God will last for ever and ever', the implication is that the king rules as God's representative. Moreover, he is praised for ruling over Israel 'in a manner that is supposed to resemble God's ruling authority over the universe'.[45]

The psalmist's attribution of divinity to the Davidic king is figurative, but in the argument of Hebrews the text is understood literally with reference to Christ. Like the God of Israel he rules for ever with uprightness. His love of justice and hatred of evil have

---

43. Cf. O'Brien, *Hebrews*, pp. 70–71. This text is preceded by the words 'and again, when God brings his firstborn into the world, he says . . . '. O'Brien rightly takes this to be another reference to the ascension and enthronement of Christ.

44. Ibid., p. 71. However, P. Ellingworth, *The Epistle to the Hebrews: A Commentary on the Greek Text* (Grand Rapids: Eerdmans; Carlisle: Paternoster, 1993), pp. 120–121, argues that the LXX means the same as the Hebrew text.

45. H. W. Bateman, 'Psalm 45:6–7 and Its Christological Contribution to Hebrews', *TrinJ* 22 (2001), p. 10. Cf. Exod. 7:1, 'I have made you like God to Pharaoh'. O'Brien, *Hebrews*, pp. 72–73, discusses different ways in which Ps. 45:6 has been understood and translated.

led God to 'anoint' him with gladness beyond his partners or companions (cf. 12:2). Based on the writer's view of divine inspiration, the seven quotations in Hebrews 1 are presented as 'a succession of words spoken by God to the Son, which the Church on earth is permitted to overhear'.[46]

With the simple connective 'and' God continues to address his Son through the words of Psalm 102:25–27 (LXX 101:26–28). The Lord is acknowledged as the one who laid the foundation of the earth 'in the beginning' and formed the heavens by the work of his hands. Everything created will wear out and perish, but he remains the same and his years will have no end. Hebrews 1:2 has already affirmed that God created 'the whole universe of time and space'[47] through the agency of the Son. So the words of the psalm are applicable to him (cf. Heb. 13:8).

Hebrews simply takes the words about God from Psalm 102:25–27 and applies them to the Son, without focusing on the expressions of human suffering that precede them. Together with Psalm 45:6–7 this prepares for the argument concerning the eternity of Christ's priesthood (Heb. 5:6; 6:20; 7:3, 17, 21, 24–25, 28) and 'the heavenly "abiding" reality of the Christian heritage, which stands over against what does not "remain" in the structures of this world (10:34; 12:25–27; 13:14)'.[48]

Psalm 110:1 is the seventh and final citation in Hebrews 1. Like the first quote from Psalm 2:7, it is preceded by the rhetorical question 'to which of the angels did God ever say' (1:13). The heavenly enthronement of Christ is proclaimed in 1:3 with an allusion to Psalm 110:1 and is further asserted by the citation from Psalm 2:7. When Psalm 110:1 is quoted in full, Christ's enthronement is linked to the promise about making his enemies a footstool for his feet (cf. 10:12–13; 1 Cor. 15:25–27).[49] Further allusions to Psalm 110:1 can be found in Hebrews 8:1; 12:2.

46. W. L. Lane, *Hebrews 1–8* (Dallas: Word, 1991), p. 32.

47. Bruce, *Hebrews*, p. 47, translating and explaining *tous aiōnas*.

48. O'Brien, *Hebrews*, p. 77.

49. Ibid., n. 210, observes from the Greek grammar that 'the focus is less on the single event of Christ's exaltation than on the period inaugurated by his sitting at the right hand of God (*kathou . . . heōs an thō*)'.

The Son who fulfils human destiny

In Hebrews 2:5–12 two psalm citations are critical for the development of the argument about the Son and his work of salvation: Psalms 8:4–6 (LXX 8:5–7) and 22:22 (LXX 21:13).

The first citation is introduced with the words 'there is a place where someone has testified' (Heb. 2:5). Since every scripture is regarded by Hebrews as the word of God, the identity of the human author in this case is relatively unimportant. The oracle reflects on God's purpose for humanity in creation, but in the flow of the argument in Hebrews it is applied to the Son who enables us to fulfil our destiny through his suffering and heavenly exaltation (2:5–10).

The Christological significance of the original text is indicated by highlighting two clauses.[50] 'You made him for a little while lower than the angels' (ESV) is taken to refer to the incarnation of the Son and 'you have crowned him with glory and honour' (ESV) is taken to refer to the heavenly enthronement of Christ.[51] Then it is claimed that the exaltation of Christ was 'because of the suffering of death, so that by the grace of God he might taste death for everyone'.[52]

The theme of Christ's representative and redemptive work for humanity continues in Hebrews 2:10–18. He brings 'many sons and

---

50. Cf. E. Otto, 'Hermeneutics of Biblical Theology, History of Religion and the Theological Substance of Two Testaments: The Reception of Psalms in Hebrews', in D. J. Human and G. J. Steyn (eds.), *Psalms and Hebrews: Studies in Reception* (New York: T. & T. Clark, 2010), p. 17.

51. NIV (2011) unfortunately translates Ps. 8:4–6 in Heb. 2:6–8 by using 'mankind' for *anthrōpos* and the plural 'them' for *auton*. This presumes that the text is not applied to Christ until 2:9 and makes it clear that humanity comprises both male and female. However, ESV rightly translates as if the text speaks of Christ from the beginning. See D. G. Peterson, *Hebrews and Perfection: An Examination of the Concept of Perfection in the 'Epistle to the Hebrews'* (Cambridge: Cambridge University Press, 1982), pp. 51–54.

52. O'Brien, *Hebrews*, p. 98, observes that 'in different contexts, the Hebrew expression rendered "a little" can refer to either time or degree'. But Hebrews understands the LXX translation (*brachy ti*) to be temporal in sense ('for a little while'). Significant also for the writer's purpose is the LXX rendering 'lower than the angels', for the Hebrew 'lower than God/the heavenly beings' (*mē'ĕlōhîm*).

daughters to glory' by his own perfecting through sufferings and sanctifies those whom he is not ashamed to call his 'brothers and sisters'. At this point Psalm 22:22 (LXX 21:13) is introduced into the argument: 'I will declare your name to my brothers and sisters; in the assembly I will sing your praises.' Although Jewish interpreters do not appear to have understood this psalm messianically, Jesus' use of its opening words on the cross (Matt. 27:46; Mark 15:34) doubtless encouraged the application of the whole psalm to his suffering and exaltation.

Following the LXX, Hebrews 2:12 uses the word *ekklēsia* (congregation, church) in parallel with 'my brothers and sisters'. In 12:23 the writer, using the same term, speaks about the ultimate, eschatological assembly of all those gathered around Christ in heaven. It is likely, therefore, that Christ is viewed as proclaiming his victory in that heavenly context. However, the writer may also mean that the exalted Lord is present to declare and celebrate the character of the one who delivered him from death when believers on earth gather to 'offer to God a sacrifice of praise' through him (13:15).[53]

The Son who is a priest for ever

Another two citations are critical for developing the Christology of Hebrews. Psalm 110:4 (LXX 109:4) is extensively quoted and expounded in Hebrews 5 – 10, and Psalm 40:6–8 (LXX 39:7–9) is used to explain the priestly and sacrificial role of Jesus in Hebrews 10:5–10.

The idea that Jesus is 'a merciful and faithful high priest in service to God' first becomes explicit in 2:17, as a development of the representative and redemptive Christology earlier in that chapter. He is identified as the one 'we acknowledge as our . . . high priest' (3:1) and as 'a great high priest who has ascended into heaven' (4:14), before the writer begins an extended contrast between the Aaronic high priests and Jesus (5:1–10).

The text of Psalm 110:4 is first introduced into the argument in Hebrews 5:6 in conjunction with a further citation of Psalm 2:7. The one who said to him, 'You are my son, today I have become your Father,' also says, 'you are a priest for ever, in the order of

---

53. See ibid., pp. 111–112.

Melchizedek'. The reappearance of Psalm 2:7 recalls the teaching of Hebrews 1:5–13 about the absolute supremacy of the messianic Son and the salvation he came to bring. Indeed, the presentation of Jesus as Son of God predominates from Hebrews 1:1 to 4:14.

The theme of Jesus as heavenly high priest becomes the central concern in Hebrews 4:14 – 10:18. So the linking of these two key psalm texts in 5:5–6 demonstrates the vital connection between Jesus as Son and high priest in the writer's Christology: 'he who is the perfect Son of God from the beginning becomes the perfect high priest for his people'.[54]

Psalm 110 is structured around two divine declarations to the Davidic king (vv. 1, 4), followed by a commentary on each one. The first declaration in Psalm 110:1 is the most frequently cited text in the New Testament. The second is introduced by a solemn oath from the Lord that is elsewhere associated with 'the Lord's covenant and promises to David (cf. 89:35)'.[55] This oracle concerns the king's priestly functions, which are related to Melchizedek in Genesis 14:18–19, who was the pre-Israelite priest-king of Salem (probably Jerusalem).[56]

Psalm 110:4 is alluded to again in Hebrews 5:10, 6:20, before the writer begins his extensive explanation in 7:1–28 of how the promise is fulfilled by Jesus. The eternity of his priesthood is based on 'the power of an indestructible life' (7:16), which refers to his resurrection and ascension. His self-offering in death and his heavenly exaltation perfect him as high priest of the New Covenant (7:26–28) and make it possible for him to hold his priesthood permanently, 'because Jesus lives for ever' (7:24). 'Therefore he is able to save completely those who come to God through him, because he always lives to intercede for them' (7:25).[57]

---

54. Ibid., p. 197.
55. Davidson, *Vitality of Worship*, pp. 366–367.
56. Allen, *Psalms 101–150*, pp. 86–87, speaks of the Davidic king as 'a divinely appointed successor to the dynastic line of Jebusite priest-kings, but his rule was destined not to be superseded as theirs had been'.
57. I have expounded Heb. 7 in Peterson, *Hebrews and Perfection*, pp. 104–125, and there explain why I think that 7:16 refers to the resurrection and ascension of Jesus.

The divine oath in Psalm 110:4 is said to make Jesus 'the guarantor of a better covenant' (7:22). He replaces the Levitical priesthood that was foundational to the Mosaic Covenant (7:11–12) and inaugurates the New Covenant promised in Jeremiah 31:31–34 by the shedding of his blood (8:6–13; 9:11–22). This argument leads the writer of Hebrews to cite Psalm 40:6–8 (LXX 39:7–9) in 10:5–10 to support his claim that the better priesthood of Jesus has introduced a once-for-all sacrifice that cleanses and sanctifies his people definitively.

Psalm 40 is called 'a psalm of David' and a typological relationship between David and Christ is suggested by its use in Hebrews. Christ is said to have spoken these words when he 'came into the world' (10:5). This implies that the incarnate Son saw the words of the psalmist as a perfect expression of his mission, which was to fulfil and replace the sacrificial system by his perfect obedience: 'Here I am – it is written of me in the scroll – I have come to do your will, my God' (10:7).[58]

David lists the various types of sacrifice ordained by God for Israel ('sacrifices and offerings', 'burnt offerings and sin offerings') and indicates that their purpose was to facilitate the obedience of his people. God's preference for obedience over animal sacrifice is expressed in the strongest possible terms in Psalm 40:6–8, though there are parallels in other psalms and prophetic texts (e.g. Ps. 50:7–23; Amos 5:21–24; Mic. 6:6–8).

The Hebrew literally reads 'but ears you have dug for me', which is rendered by the NIV 'but my ears you have opened' (REB 'you have given me receptive ears'). The LXX renders this strange expression, 'but a body have you prepared for me', which is probably 'an interpretive paraphrase' of the Hebrew.[59] 'The body which was "fashioned" for the speaker by God is given back to God as a "living sacrifice", to be employed in obedient service to him.'[60]

58. M. Karrer, 'LXX Psalm 39:7–10 in Hebrews 10:5–7', in Human and Steyn, *Psalms and Hebrews*, pp. 126–146, argues that it is the pre-existent Jesus who speaks through this psalm in Hebrews. But compare Peterson, *Hebrews and Perfection*, pp. 147–148.

59. O'Brien, *Hebrews*, p. 350. Cf. Karrer, 'LXX Psalm 39:7–10', pp. 137–145.

60. Bruce, *Hebrews*, p. 46.

David expresses his commitment to do the will of God revealed in 'the scroll' (Heb. 10:7), which seems to refer to the Mosaic law (cf. 9:19–20). The Son of David echoes these words in speaking to his heavenly Father about his willingness to fulfil what is written about him. The significance of the Son's perfect obedience for redemptive history is then outlined in the interpretation of the psalm that follows: 'he sets aside the first' (the pattern of sacrifice in the law) 'to establish the second' (the way of perfect obedience that inaugurates the New Covenant). The benefit for the Messiah's people is then revealed in the concluding claim that, by the will of God revealed in Scripture, 'we have been made holy through the sacrifice of the body of Jesus Christ once for all' (10:10).

As a climax to the argument in Hebrews 9:1 – 10:4, the writer uses Psalm 40:6–8 to reinforce the claim that the pattern for cleansing, sanctifying and perfecting the people of God is revealed in the law. It is fulfilled and replaced by the obedience of Christ, culminating in the shedding of his blood and his entrance into heaven, 'now to appear for us in God's presence' (9:24).

Conclusions about Hebrews

Hebrews foundationally uses the Pentateuch to reflect on redemptive history and its significance for Christians. The writer also sees in the Pentateuch the pattern for Christ's priestly ministry and sacrificial offering. By means of his death and heavenly exaltation Jesus has fulfilled the prophetic hope of a new covenant and made its benefits available for believers. Psalms are mainly used to expound two interrelated Christological themes: Jesus is the Son of God who fulfils the promises made to David in the prophetic literature, and he is the priest 'after the order of Melchizedek', who lives for ever to intercede for and save his people.

The writer quotes portions of psalms to establish and confirm the Christological claims made at critical points in his argument. These citations are sometimes presented as words from the Father to the Son (1:5, 8–13) and sometimes as words from the Son to the Father (2:12; 10:5–9). An underlying Davidic typology can often be discerned from understanding the citations in their original context and then observing the way they are employed in Hebrews.

But Psalm 8:4–6 is used to set the work of Christ within the broader context of biblical theology. The Son becomes incarnate for the sake of fallen humanity and experiences the suffering of death, so that he might be 'crowned with glory and honour' and bring many to share in the dominion originally promised by God to humankind. Psalms therefore play a critical role in what might be termed the 'canonical' approach to Scripture exhibited in Hebrews. They are treated as prophetic in the sense that they indicate how God's creation purpose and redemptive plan are fulfilled in Christ. But they are also vehicles of praise, by which God's people can acknowledge the greatness of his work in the person of his Son and offer to God through Jesus 'the fruit of lips that openly profess his name' (13:15).[61]

---

61. I have not said anything about the use of Ps. 95:7–11 in Heb. 3 – 4, because it is part of an exhortation to the readers to persevere in faith and obedience. However, the Christological implication of the argument in these chapters is significant. It is now the 'word' of the Son that is critical for the salvation of God's people, because it promises that eternal rest is possible through his faithfulness to the Father's will.

4. THE PSALMS AND CHRISTIAN DOCTRINE

Mark D. Thompson

Christian engagement with the Psalms as a source of the knowledge of God and his purposes, purposes that find their focus and fulfilment in the person and work of Jesus Christ, stretch right back to the pages of the New Testament itself. With 79 direct quotations and more than 330 allusions to the Psalms in the New Testament (according to the apparatus of the Nestle-Aland text) it is undisputed that Jesus and his apostles regarded the Psalms as a source of the truth about God and how he is engaged with the world he has made, and, in particular, how he is involved with the Messiah and his people. If for these purposes we discount the parallels in the four Gospels, we discover that Jesus quoted from the Psalms at least ten times, with another seven quotations made by others. What is more, in a well-known statement from the end of Luke's Gospel Jesus spoke of the fulfilment of everything written about him 'in the Law of Moses, the Prophets and the Psalms' (Luke 24:44).[1] So there

---

1. For reasons that will become obvious later in this chapter, the slightly
   different reference a little earlier (Luke 24:27) to 'Moses and all the
   prophets' need not exclude the psalms.

would seem to be abundant licence from the pages of the New Testament for the practice of 'doing theology' from the Psalms.

Two thousand years of theological reflection testifies to the importance of this part of the Bible in establishing and explaining Christian doctrine. Leaving aside the plethora of commentaries and monographs produced in the last one hundred years or so, classic expositions were produced by Chrysostom, Augustine, Aquinas, Luther, Bucer and Calvin, in each case moving with ease between exegetical observation and theological assertion. In almost every case these collected expositions (some, originally sermons, and others, lectures) included serious reflection upon the appropriate principles for expounding the Psalms. Contemporary concerns about drawing theology from the Psalms are not entirely without precedent in the various theological traditions, but there is ample testimony to its being done and being done confidently.

So how might we go about the task of theologizing on the basis of what is recorded for us in the book of Psalms? Further, how might the exercise of drawing theological conclusions from the Psalms inform the discipline more broadly? Let us begin with a case study.

A case study in doing theology from the Psalms: Psalm 22

Perhaps the most evocative of all the psalm quotations in the New Testament are the words from Psalm 22 uttered by Jesus from the cross, 'My God, my God, why have you forsaken me?' (Matt. 27:46; Mark 15:34). This 'cry of dereliction' was once described by Jürgen Moltmann as 'either the end of all theology or the beginning of a specific Christian theology'.[2] Moltmann himself made a great deal of these words as a hermeneutical key to what was going on at the cross, concluding that here was God's own act of loving solidarity with suffering, a taking of the problem of suffering into his own history. Whatever we might say about Moltmann's conclusion – and

---

2. J. Moltmann, *History and the Triune God*, tr. J. Bowden (London: SCM, 1991), p. 172.

it seems to me there is more than a grain of truth in it, while at the same time it is woefully inadequate as a summary statement about the meaning of the cross – Psalm 22 promises to be an important case study for a 'theology from the Psalms'.[3] In the current context the briefest of outlines will have to suffice.

The proper theological use made of Psalm 22 (Ps. 21 in the LXX) becomes clear when close attention is given to its location, identification, structure and form, content, and the echoes of its words and ideas in the wider canon. In terms of *location*, the psalm is placed in Book 1 of the Psalms (Pss 1 – 41), bookended as it is with descriptions of blessing in the midst of opposition:

> Blessed is the one
>> who does not walk in step with the wicked,
> or stand in the way that sinners take,
>> or sit in the company of mockers . . .
> For the LORD watches over the way of the righteous.
> (Ps. 1:1, 6a)

> I know that you are pleased with me,
>> my enemy does not triumph over me.
> Because of my integrity you uphold me
>> and set me in your presence for ever .
> (Ps. 41:11–12)

The righteous person of Psalm 1 is confronted by the reality of sin, mockery and wickedness and yet lives in the light of another reality: the promise of God, his faithfulness to his promise, and his determination to vindicate his own and judge those who stand against him.

More specifically, though, Psalm 22 is located in the midst of a group of psalms that extol God's salvation of the king (Pss 20 – 21,

---

3. In what follows I am heavily indebted to the excellent article by Kelly M. Kapic of Covenant College: 'Psalm 22: Forsakenness and the God Who Sings', in R. M. Allen (ed.), *Theological Commentary: Evangelical Perspectives* (London: T. & T. Clark, 2011), pp. 41–56.

on one side, and 23 – 24, on the other). Psalm 20 ends with the prayer 'LORD, give victory to the king' (v. 9); Psalm 21 tells of how the king greatly exults 'in the victories you give' (v. 1);[4] Psalm 23 delights in the one whose presence is a comfort even in 'the valley of the shadow of death' (v. 4); and Psalm 24 speaks of the one who receives 'blessing from the LORD / and vindication from the God their Saviour' (v. 5). In such an immediate context the genuine agony of Psalm 22:1, 'My God, my God, why have you forsaken me?', is matched with the praise of God that will be given 'in the assembly' (vv. 22, 25). The one anointed by the Lord inhabits a world where opposition to God and his purposes is real, as is the accompanying suffering, but it is also the arena in which God's salvation and its attendant blessings are genuinely experienced as well. Critically, Psalm 22 ends with the proclamation to a generation yet unborn that 'he has done it'.

In terms of *identification*, Psalm 22 is marked as a psalm of David. However precisely that phrase is to be understood, it is clear that the intention is to associate this psalm, like those immediately surrounding it, with the person and perhaps the career of David, son of Jesse and King of all Israel. David was pre-eminently the man of God's choice, the one anointed at God's direction to deliver Israel and to rule. It was not his own decision. God took him 'from the pasture, from tending the flock' and made him prince over Israel (2 Sam. 7:8). Nor was it an uncomplicated matter. David's journey to the throne was fraught with difficulties and his tenure as king was not one of unalloyed joy. Nevertheless, he was the Old Testament Messiah, the deliverer, king and executor of God's purposes. In the first instance, then, this psalm gives voice to the Messiah and speaks of the nature of his presence in the world.

When we turn to *structure and form*, it becomes apparent that the psalm oscillates between expressions of grief at what is happening to the one speaking and recollections of God's deliverance in the past. Lament is interlaced with praise, and despair is tempered by

---

4. The Hebrew verb *yš'* and cognate noun *yĕšû'â*, usually translated 'save, salvation' (so ESV, AV), are more narrowly translated 'give victory, victory' in this context by RSV, HCSB and NIV.

confidence that the one who delivered in the past will be able to deliver yet again. So, following the chilling cry of dereliction in verses 1–2, the psalm goes on to speak of how our fathers' trust in God was vindicated:

> My God, my God, why have you forsaken me?
>> Why are you so far from saving me,
>> so far from my cries of anguish?
> My God, I cry by day, but you do not answer,
>> by night, but I find no rest.
> Yet you are enthroned as the Holy One,
>> you are the one Israel praises.
> In you our ancestors put their trust;
>> they trusted and you delivered them.
> To you they cried out and were saved;
>> in you they trusted and were not put to shame.
> (Ps. 22:1–5)

This oscillation resolves into a prayer for deliverance in verses 19–21 and the prospect of praise in the congregation and the proclamation of God's righteousness in the world.

Attention to the detailed *content* of the psalm emphasizes the reality and depth of the anguish the psalmist experiences. It is not lightly dismissed with a simple assurance that God's purpose will prevail as it always has. It keeps pressing in on the one who literally feels God's silence in contrast to the all-too-audible mockery of those who surround him. What is more, the intensity of what is expressed here reveals something that has been lost. As Kelly Kapic has observed:

> to feel forsaken there had to be a time when you felt you belonged, you were secure. How can someone really consider himself forsaken without presupposing a real relationship or commitment. This cry of abandonment is so painful to hear partly because the psalmist and reader know that the crying heart aches for what is lost.[5]

---

5. Kapic, 'Psalm 22', p. 42.

Nevertheless, for all this intensity – and of course for the Christian reader this is heightened by its ultimate reference to the crucifixion – the anguish and sense of God-forsakenness does not prevail. There is a certainty that cannot be overturned by the sense of loss and abandonment the psalmist expresses in the first few verses. Reminded of how God rescued 'our ancestors' when they cried out to him, moved to recall how trust in God has been a feature of his life from the very beginning, how 'from my mother's womb you have been my God' (v. 10b), after one final round of recognizing the terrifying reality of his predicament, the Messiah once more casts himself upon God:

> But you LORD, do not be far from me.
> You are my strength; come quickly to help me.
> (v. 19)

Instead of giving expression to his sense of abandonment, this one calls on God to end it. This journey had begun a little earlier in the psalm: 'Be not far from me, for trouble is near, and there is none to help' (v. 11). The deliverance he expects will become a cause of praise in the great assembly and of proclamation in the world. And once again we notice the final words of the psalm: he has done it. It is done. It is finished.

At which point we come quite naturally to the *echoes* of this psalm in the New Testament. In Matthew and Mark the cry of dereliction is found on the lips of Jesus as he bears the full consequence of human sin on the cross. In John, Psalm 22:18 with its reference to the division of garments and the casting of lots for clothing is recalled as the Roman soldiers do precisely that with the Lord's tunic and other garments. In Hebrews 2, after drawing attention to the way Jesus was 'crowned with glory and honour because he suffered death' (v. 9) and how he, the founder of our salvation, was made 'perfect through what he suffered' (v. 10), the writer quotes Psalm 22:22:

> I will declare your name to my brothers and sisters;
>   in the assembly I will sing your praises.
> (Heb. 2:12)

So each of the three New Testament quotations of this psalm draws a connection to the death of Jesus. There, at that singular point, the paradox of abandonment and salvation was at its most intense. For was he not the one who had always done his father's will? Was not he the one the voice from heaven had declared was 'my beloved Son in whom I am well pleased'? How could these words be his words?

Questions like these take us to that task of drawing conceptual connections that lies close to the heart of the discipline of systematic theology. Historically, three more specific questions have shaped much of the theological discussion of this psalm: (1) How does Jesus' use of these words relate to David's use of these words? (2) In what sense are these words a reflection of what was actually happening at the cross? (3) How can, or perhaps should, Christians take these words upon their own lips as part of their own response to God's mercy in Christ? Let us look briefly at each of these questions in turn, with a sideways glance at how those before us have come to an answer.

How does Jesus' use of Psalm 22:1 relate to David's use of Psalm 22:1?

Another way of putting this might be to ask whether these words are first and foremost David's words or Jesus' words? In their original setting are they descriptive or prophetic (in the sense of pointing to an event in the future)?

There have been three basic approaches to this complex of questions. There is a long-standing Christian custom of reading these words as always and only referring to Jesus. Partly this is because it has proven difficult to identify a point at which this specific kind of suffering is reflected in David's experience (so, for instance, Lactantius, Justin Martyr and Tertullian),[6] but also partly because, as Charles Spurgeon famously put it in the nineteenth century, once the link with Jesus has been made, believers 'will

---

6. Lactantius, 'The Divine Institutes', *ANF* 7, p. 121; Justin Martyr, 'Dialogue with Trypho', *ANF* 1, pp. 247–248; Tertullian, 'Answer to the Jews', *ANF* 3, pp. 166, 169. These and others are identified by Kapic, 'Psalm 22', p. 45.

probably neither see nor care to see David'.[7] Martin Luther followed
this line of interpretation:

> There are two parts to this Psalm. The first part describes the passion of
> Christ, the second part describes his glorification and its benefits, which
> clearly lay hold of us on account of the passion of Christ.[8]

Others, such as Theodore of Mopsuestia and his late-sixteenth-
century namesake Theodore Beza, insisted that the psalm referred
chiefly to David and warned against jumping too hastily to a
Christological reference.[9] They did not deny that there was a connection to Jesus, but this was because Jesus took David's words and
applied them to himself, thereby explaining his death in terms of
the Old Testament pattern of the suffering righteous one. A third
group saw other intentional connections between David and Christ,
connections that allowed neither reference to be minimized in the
interests of the other. Often this involved an appeal to the prophetic
character of David and the psalter or to biblical typology. Not all
attempts remain convincing to modern ears. Pope Leo I (Leo the
Great) wrote:

> What human ears did not yet know as about to be done, the Holy Spirit
> was announcing as accomplished. King David, whose offspring Christ is
> according to human lineage, preceded the day of the Lord's crucifixion
> by more than eleven hundred years. He had suffered none of those
> tortures which he mentions as having been inflicted upon himself.
> Because the Lord – who was going to take the suffering flesh from
> David's stock – spoke through his mouth, the history of the crucifixion
> has rightly been prefigured in the person of David. David bore in

---

7. C. H. Spurgeon, *The Treasury of David: An Expository and Devotional
   Commentary on the Psalms*, repr. (Grand Rapids: Baker, 1978), p. 365.
8. M. Luther, *Kleinere Arbeiten über Psalmen* (1530–32), *WA* 31, p. 522 (my tr.).
9. Theodore of Mopsuestia, *Commentary on Psalms 1–81*, tr. and ed. Robert C.
   Hill (Atlanta: Society of Biblical Literature, 2006), pp. 241–243; Théodore
   de Bèze, *In historiam passionis et Sepulturae domini nostri J. Christi Homiliae*
   (Geneva: Ioannes le Preux, 1592), p. 816. Once again, see Kapic, 'Psalm 22',
   pp. 45–47.

himself the bodily origin of the Saviour. Truly David suffered in Christ, because Jesus was truly crucified in the flesh of David.[10]

So wrote the famous author of the *Tome* which so influenced orthodox Christology. Calvin's way of explaining the connection is representative of the mainstream and more convincing:

> In short, there is no doubt that Christ, in uttering this exclamation upon the cross, manifestly showed, that although David here bewails his own distresses, this psalm was composed under the influence of the Spirit of prophecy concerning David's King and Lord.[11]

Calvin was not suggesting that David was aware of the reference to Jesus and what it would involve. However, in keeping with an understanding that there is a prophetic dimension to the Psalms, Calvin was not afraid to draw the connection in this way.

More could, perhaps, be made of the messianic connection between David and Jesus as a key to understanding why Jesus would take David's words upon his own lips at such a significant moment in his earthly ministry. Coming from David's pen, these are the words of Israel's Messiah. Though Jesus was careful to avoid the distorted messianic expectations of his contemporaries, he nonetheless saw that it was fitting that he, the fulfilment of all that David anticipated as the anointed deliverer and ruler of Israel, should both express the genuine agony of his death as the sinless yet sin-bearing human being and explain its significance by using David's words. Which leads us to the second question.

In what sense are these words a reflection of what was actually happening at the cross?

I mentioned earlier that Jürgen Moltmann saw in these words an explanation of the cross as Jesus entering into solidarity with those

---

10. Leo the Great, 'Sermon 67', §2 in *St Leo the Great: Sermons*, tr. J. P. Freeland and A. J. Conway (Washington, D.C.: Catholic University of America Press, 1996), p. 291.

11. J. Calvin, *Commentary on the Book of Psalms*, tr. J. Anderson, 2 vols., repr. (Grand Rapids: Eerdmans, 1963), vol. 1, p. 362.

who suffer. Yet this still leaves unresolved the deeper question of whether the beloved Son was actually abandoned at the cross, and, if so, in what sense? Popular hymnody has sometimes spoken of the Father departing from Jesus at this point, or turning his face away. But how would this cohere with the statements elsewhere in the Bible about the unbroken unity of the Father and the Son, a unity that goes deeper than any we could possibly imagine. The Father is in the Son and the Son is in the Father, so how could he be abandoned? He took upon himself an undeserved judgment in order to free those who deserved it and yet the resurrection itself is evidence that he never ceased to be the beloved Son in whom the Father is well pleased.

Nevertheless, the solution cannot lie in minimizing the agony of what was endured on the cross for us. The cross was in no sense a charade. Jesus really suffered and died. Bearing the sin of men and women meant that more was going on than the physical torture and the humiliation of the injustice and the mockery. Exhausting the penalty for sin in the place of all who would be united to him by faith and in the Spirit meant dying this particular death without relief. This really is a cry of dereliction. Kelly Kapic has drawn attention to the way the word for 'forsaken' can bear the sense of 'to withhold one's hand from' and in that sense is the opposite of 'to deliver'. He explains:

> God withheld his hand from rescuing Jesus from the cross, 'leaving' him there but without departing from him. Jesus *is* the action and Word of God in this event. God neither abandons his Son nor does the Trinity dissolve, but God enters into the affliction of his people through his Son. This awful silence and inaction constitutes the forsakenness – this is the only way to penetrate the gates of hell . . . According to the biblical story of redemption, all of humanity, including God's representative Israel, has forsaken and aban-doned God. God deals with the dereliction, not by ignoring it, but by entering into it and exhausting it through the Messiah. Jesus does not cease to be God in this moment. Instead, the eternal, holy, righteous God who cannot be manipulated or beaten, answers the damning cry of humanity in their sin . . . In other words, the cross does not represent a rupture in the Trinity, but the greatest expression of the Triune God's holy love and purpose.[12]

---

12. Kapic, 'Psalm 22', pp. 52–53 (emphasis original).

And always we must remember that just as Psalm 22 does not end at verse 1 or even verse 2, his real suffering was not the end either. As the resurrected one he stands amid the congregation – 'who walks among the seven golden lampstands' as Revelation 1 and 2 puts it – holding the keys of death and Hades. The death and agony and all who stand behind them cannot win. Jesus wins.

How can Christians take these words upon their own lips as part of their own response to God's mercy in Christ?

Since these are the words of the Messiah, prefigured in David's experience but fully realized only in the incarnate Son born of David's line, it might seem that it would be inappropriate for Christians to take these words as their own. Yet through the centuries a different answer has been given to this question. Philip Melanchthon spoke of how in the Psalms 'often the voice of David is at the same time the voice of Christ, and conversely the voice is David's or our own'.[13] The profound union of the believer with Christ, so that his death is our death and his rising ours (Eph. 1 – 2), gives these words a powerful resonance in our own lives. More than that, his acknowledgment of genuine grief and agony, while at the same time maintaining his trust in the God who has proven faithful and will do so again, finds other echoes in the experience of those who live in the same broken world awaiting its final redemption. Both these lines of response converge in a little pamphlet published by Dietrich Bonhoeffer in 1940, entitled *The Psalms: Prayer Book of the Bible*:

> How is it possible that at the same time a man and Jesus Christ should both pray in the Psalter? It is the Son of God made man, who has borne all our human weakness in his own flesh, who here pours out the heart of all mankind before God, who stands in our place and prays for us. He has known pain and anguish, guilt and death more deeply than we have. Thus it is the prayer of that humanity he has assumed that comes before God in the Psalms. It is indeed our prayer, but since he knows us better than we know ourselves, since for our sake he became true man,

---

13. P. Melanchthon, *Commentarii in Psalmos* (1555), *CR* 13, p. 1022.

it is also truly his prayer, and it can only become our prayer because it was his.[14]

This brief case study could easily have been extended in a number of directions. However, even the bare outline I have drawn should be sufficient to demonstrate that a theological approach to the Psalms need not do violence either to their poetic form or their immediate and canonical context.

The distinctive contribution of the Psalms to the practice of theology

The discipline of systematic theology is at its best when it is in the closest possible relation to biblical exegesis. Whenever that relation is strained, for whatever reason, systematic theology runs the risk of becoming abstract, removed from the concrete historical realities of God's revelation, and suffering distortion as a result. Alternatively, it begins to privilege other conversations, too often accommodating itself to the world view currently prevailing in the academy. Examples of both tendencies in contemporary systematic theology could be multiplied, even among essentially conservative practitioners. Perhaps a little counter-intuitively given the imaginative play usually associated with poetry, the Psalms raise a challenge to such abstract systems, not least by forging an essential link between the content of our belief and its embodiment in a world where opposition and challenge are undeniable. In short, the Psalms demonstrate again and again that the knowledge of God is not merely an intellectual phenomenon but it necessarily engages the will and the emotions as well. It is in the Psalms that the discipline appropriately takes on a distinctively Calvinistic flavour, as an attempt to expound the sum of Christian piety. In the preface to his Psalms commentary, Calvin writes:

> not only will we here find general commendations of the goodness of God, which may teach men to repose themselves in him alone, and to

---

14. Tr. Isabel Mary (Oxford: SLG, 1982), p. 6.

seek all their happiness solely in him; and which are intended to teach true believers with their whole hearts confidently to look to him for help in all their necessities; but we will also find that the free remission of sins, which alone reconciles God towards us, and procures for us settled peace with him, is so set forth and magnified, as that here there is nothing wanting which relates to the knowledge of eternal salvation.[15]

Too often, even while railing against the distorting influence of pagan Western philosophy, systematic theology has been trapped in its basic quest for universals by using the tools of logic, rationality and sequential thinking.[16] The assumption is sometimes made that the more abstract the formulation the more profound the truth it is conveying. This can even happen in ethical discourse, which should properly be considered a branch of the systematic theological enterprise. But the Psalms, with their imaginative but powerfully concrete imagery, cut through all that intellectual self-indulgence, grounding theology more securely in the delight and frustration of life in a world compromised by human sin and yet the arena of God's deliverance through his Messiah. Nevertheless, we should be wary of overstatement even here, as for instance when Brueggemann claims that 'the spirituality of the Psalms is shaped, defined and characterized in specific historical, experiential categories and shuns universals'.[17] Rather, the truth about God, which is constant throughout human history, is manifested in the experience of the psalmist.

---

15. Calvin, *Commentary*, p. xxxix.

16. B. Tanner, 'Rethinking the Enterprise: What Must Be Considered in Formulating a Theology of the Psalms', in R. A. Jacobson (ed.), *Soundings in the Theology of Psalms: Perspectives and Methods in Contemporary Scholarship* (Minneapolis: Fortress, 2011), pp. 139–140. Tanner's solution, which discards singularity as a relic of the past, embraces an interpretative community of voices in conversation and insists that the biblical-theological enterprise has now become contextual and thus canonical, transitory and pluralistic (p. 142), strangely follows the same trajectory away from the biblical text rather than being disciplined by it.

17. W. Brueggemann, *The Message of the Psalms: A Theological Commentary* (Minneapolis: Augsburg, 1984), p. 175.

The Psalms also provide a challenge to what Kevin Vanhoozer calls 'the epic ambition' of propositionalist theology. Propositional revelation and what George Lindbeck called a 'cognitive-propositional approach to theology' have had a bad press in recent years, often but not always caricatured by those who have not taken the time to consider carefully their grounding in Scripture. Vanhoozer is not among that number. In his book *The Drama of Doctrine* he explicitly aims 'to rehabilitate the cognitive-propositional approach to theology by expanding what we mean by "cognitive" and by dramatizing what we mean by "proposition"'.[18] Nevertheless, he is alert to the danger that attends a preoccupation with theological propositions. Appropriating Ricœur's description of Hegel's philosophy – 'the greatest attempt and the greatest temptation' – to describe works such as Charles Hodge's monumental three-volume *Systematic Theology*, Vanhoozer spells out the danger:

> What is *tempting* in propositionalist theology is the idea that one can 'master' divinity by learning the system of truths communicated through the language and literature of the Bible. What is tempting is the thought that one can package the Bible in a conceptual scheme that is tidier than the original. What is tempting is the suggestion that it is enough to *know* the information thus packaged. It is precisely this sense of distantness, even more than the grandeur of the systematizing vision, that makes propositionalist theology look epic. It is ultimately not a grand but a narrow vision, however, because it isolates the truths of Scripture, and the theologian, from the larger economy of salvation of which Scripture and its interpreters are a part.[19]

The Psalms are part of the solution to this problem because here the truth about God and his purposes is embedded in the life of the Messiah and his people. The sense to be made of life in this world is not always easily given – witness the reality of both agony and praise in Psalm 22. Too hasty a flight to a resolution will risk failing to

---

18. K. J. Vanhoozer, *The Drama of Doctrine: A Canonical Linguistic Approach to Christian Theology* (Louisville: Westminster John Knox, 2005), p. 88.
19. Ibid., pp. 87–88 (emphases original).

appreciate the proper intersection of the psalmist's struggle with that of the reader. The Psalms will not allow us to ignore the economy of salvation as we seek to understand who God is and what he has done.

Along with this challenge to a healthier vision of what systematic theology could be, the Psalms provide positive encouragements that point a way forward. The use of imaginative language and poetic devices encourage not only a careful attention to the word God has given us, in form as well as content, but a delight in the gift as well as the giver. Andrew Shead's comment about the words of Jeremiah could, with very little qualification, be applied also to the Psalms. Precisely because these are 'the particular words by which God has chosen to represent himself, one's delight in the Word [of God] must grow out of one's delight in the words'.[20] Systematic theology that appreciates this can itself engage the passionate and imaginative language of the Psalms in the service of its exposition of the gospel and its consequences. Why on earth should systematic theology be boring?

In the Psalms theology and doxology, confession and praise, are intertwined in a way that has deeply influenced the best of systematic theology over the past two thousand years. Once again we saw this played out in the brief case study of Psalm 22. It is a regular feature of the apostle Paul's writing in the New Testament (e.g. Rom. 11; Eph. 1). Augustine's *Confessions* are a classic instance from the early church. The point is made with just a little overstatement by John Goldingay:

> Doxology and theology are closely related. Doxology requires theology; glorifying God involves making many a statement about God. Conversely, theology finds one of its natural forms in doxology. There is a role to be played by dispassionate analytical theological statements, though I cannot remember what it is, but the natural way to make statements that do justice to God's nature is to make them in the form of praise. Dispassionate analytical statements about God deconstruct.[21]

---

20. A. Shead, *A Mouth Full of Fire: The Word of God in the Words of Jeremiah* (Nottingham: Inter-Varsity Press, 2012), pp. 288–289.

21. J. Goldingay, *Psalms*, vol. 1: *Psalms 1–41*, BCOT (Grand Rapids: Baker, 2006), p. 69.

Not always, but perhaps it is a matter of what is meant by 'dis-passionate'. Nevertheless, the Psalms make clear that theological truth is not simply another piece of information to be placed alongside others. There remains something to be said for Samuel Terrien's suggestion that 'doxology is the key to theology'.[22] Theological truth is deeply and inherently relational: it serves the proper relationship between God and those he has made and redeemed. As such it can both unsettle as well as encourage us. Perhaps from this perspective, then, there is more than one purpose for the imprecatory psalms. We should be unsettled if we find them too easy to say and if we cannot bring ourselves to say them. In both instances a piece of the puzzle may be missing.

The use of powerfully graphic and imaginative language in the Psalms is an encouragement to ask the questions that tease out the conceptual connections so central to the task of systematic theology. We saw this in the case study of Psalm 22. By asking how the beloved Son could be abandoned, a more careful examination of the text, with attention to genre and context as well as content, structure and the intertextual echoes, is encouraged. In this way systematic theology is able to play its role in assisting the Christian confession of the gospel by demonstrating the coherence of this message, exposing the consequences of misunderstanding and providing the resources for a better reading of the text.

Conclusion

Reading the biblical text well most certainly requires attention to the differences of genre. That is as true in the discipline of systematic theology as it is in Old and New Testament studies. Distortion is the almost inevitable result if the literary variety within the Bible is flattened out in the service of a preferred genre, whether that be analytical argument or even narrative. Instead this variety is part of what constitutes the richness of the canon, and in the case of the

---

22. S. Terrien, *The Psalms: Strophic Structure and Theological Commentary* (Grand Rapids: Eerdmans, 2003), p. 60.

Psalms its poetic and imaginative elements make a particular contribution that we would be impoverished without.

However, in the end, for all the distinctive character of the Psalms
as biblical literature, doing theology from the Psalms turns out to
be remarkably similar to doing theology from any other part of the
Bible. Responsible systematic theology is characterized by careful
attention to the particular biblical text under consideration in all its
dimensions – content, form and context. This ought to be a feature
not only of our engagement with the Psalms but with every other
part of the Bible as well. But perhaps the Psalms do remind us more
powerfully than most that the Bible comes to us not as an ethereal
word that needs to be translated into appropriate forms for proclamation and explanation but as the generous gift of a loving heavenly
Father given in the concrete conditions of human life. Since this is
the case, whatever theologies we draw from the Psalms ought to be
fit to be addressed to God – as so many of the psalms themselves
are – as well as to each other.

5. PATRISTIC PREACHING OF THE PSALMS: EXTRACTS FROM THREE SERMONS ON PSALM 45 (LXX PSALM 44)

Translated Seumas Macdonald

Translator's note

I have chosen three extracts from Basil of Caesarea, Augustine of Hippo and John Chrysostom. Each deals with the same psalm at different length. Basil's homily is much shorter, Augustine's much longer and Chrysostom is writing more in the style of a commentary. In each instance I prepared a fresh translation from the Greek or Latin, with the guidance of existing translations. I have aimed at readability, rather than a strictly oral style, as the latter would, in my opinion, carry us too far from the text, and I thought it best to preserve rather more of the strangeness of their style.

The extracts are not predominantly 'Christocentric' in the sense that they overwhelmingly show a typological or biblical-theological concern, but they do fit what one could call the patristic Christocentric approach. They demonstrate a number of fairly typical features – a concern to take poetry figuratively, and so to search for the meaning of each 'figure', sometimes in a strained manner; a ready movement to other parts of Scripture, especially the New Testament, in search of verses that cast light on the primary text; and application that takes the texts as directly relevant to the soul's 'life' of sanctification. However, each preacher does something quite different with the psalm, and draws on the parts of the psalm that lend themselves to his particular aim. Basil reflects on the two natures of Christ in a way that reflects the Nicene controversies of the day; Chrysostom, interested in grammatical 'exactitude', focuses on the power of God; and in the sermon that is perhaps least foreign to us today, Augustine preaches on the gospel of the kingdom.

LXX Psalm 44:2–10

My heart erupts with a goodly theme;
    it is I that address my works to the king;
    my tongue is a pen of a swift scribe.
Youthful in beauty, beyond the sons of men;
    grace is poured *out by* your lips;
    therefore God has blessed you for ever.
Strap your sword upon your thigh, O mighty one,
    in your youthfulness and your beauty,
and draw, and prosper, and become king
    for the sake of truth and meekness and righteousness,
    and your right hand will guide you marvellously.
Your arrows are sharp, O mighty one:
    peoples fall under you
    in the heart of the king's enemies.
Your throne, O God, is for ever and ever.
    A rod of directing is the rod of your kingdom;
you have loved justice and hated iniquity.
    Therefore God, your God, has anointed you
    with the oil of joy above your companions.
Myrrh and aloes and cassia waft from your garments,
    from ivory bastions, with which they made you glad;

Daughters of kings are in your honour;
    the queen stood at your right in gold-woven clothing,
    decked out in many colours.[1]

Basil of Caesarea (329–79): 'See the beauty and grace of Christ in his divinity and humanity'[2]

Youthful in beauty, beyond the sons of men. Grace is poured out by your lips [v. 3a]

The psalmist calls the Lord youthful in beauty, focusing on his divinity; he is not celebrating a worldly beauty. As Isaiah says, 'For we have seen him, and he had no form, no beauty, but his form was without honour, lacking alongside the sons of men' [Isa. 53:2–3 LXX]. It is clear then that the psalmist is looking upon, and being filled with, the Lord's brilliance, and is moved to a divine love of this spiritual beauty. When this divine love shines in the soul, all that once was loved is revealed as shameful and worthless. Therefore even Paul, when he saw the 'youthful beauty', 'reckoned all things excrement, that he might gain Christ' [Phil. 3:8]. People outside the word of truth call the proclamation of the gospel foolishness, and despise the simplicity of the Scriptures' verbal style.

But we who glory in the cross of Christ, we to whom the Spirit has revealed the gifts of God, we who were taught not by merely human wisdom, we know that the grace poured out in the words from God concerning Christ is *rich*. Therefore, in a short time, the message spread through almost the whole world, since the grace, rich and bountiful, was poured out in the heralds of the gospel, and the Scripture calls these heralds 'the lips of Christ'. Even in small, easily despised words, the preaching of the gospel is powerful to pull people towards salvation. Each soul is overpowered by unshakeable doctrines, confirmed through

---

1. The translation is taken from NETS, with some amendments; the corresponding section in the MT is Ps. 45:1–9.
2. Basil the Great, 'Homiliae in Psalmos 44,4–5', in PG 29.162–163, pp. 595–599.

grace to the unshaken faith in Christ. This is why the apostle Paul says, 'through whom we have received grace and apostleship for the obedience of faith' [Rom. 1:5].

Grace is poured out by your lips; therefore God has blessed you for ever [v. 3b]

In the gospel it says, 'They marvelled at the words of grace proceeding from his mouth' [Luke 4:22]. So the psalm, wishing to portray vividly the abundance of grace in the words spoken by our Lord, says, 'Grace is poured out by your lips', because of the abundance of the grace in the word. 'God has blessed you', he says, 'for ever.' Clearly these words refer to the humanity, since the humanity is that which advances 'in wisdom and maturity and grace' [Luke 2:52]. Going on, we understand grace to have been given to him even as a reward for his brave deeds. Just as later he says, 'You have loved justice, and hated iniquity; therefore God, your God, has anointed you, with the oil of joy above your companions' [Ps. 44:8 LXX]. Paul writes similarly in Philippians, 'He humbled himself, becoming obedient unto death, death on a cross, wherefore God has exalted him' [Phil. 2:8]. Evidently all these things are spoken concerning the Saviour as man. Or, since the church is the body of the Lord, and he is the head of the church, just as we have explained the lips of Christ to be those ministering in the heavenly word, and just as Paul considers Christ to be speaking in himself, and anyone equal in virtue, so also the remaining members of the body of Christ are we who believe. Therefore if you understand the blessing to refer to the Lord or to the church, both are correct, because of the unity. So the meaning of 'God has blessed you' is expanded into 'your members and your body he has filled with good things from himself for ever,' that is, 'time without end'.

Strap your sword upon your thigh, O mighty one, in your youthfulness and your beauty [v. 4]

Moving on, this verse refers figuratively to the living word of God being joined to the flesh, he who is 'active and sharper than any two-edged sword, and penetrating unto the division of soul and spirit, of joints and marrow, and is a judge of thoughts and intentions of the heart' [Heb. 4:12]. The thigh is a symbol of the activity of generation, as it says,

'For these are souls that came forth from Jacob's thighs' [cf. Exod. 1:5], and so refers to the flesh.

Just as our Lord Jesus is named Life, and Way, and Bread, and Vine, and True Light, and countless other things, so also he is a sword cutting through the passionable part of the soul, and mortifies the passions. Then, since God the Word was about to unite himself to the weakness of flesh, he masterfully adds 'O mighty one', since the fact that God is able to be born in the nature of Man is proof of the greatest power. For as great as the composition of heaven and earth, and sea, and air, and the origin of the greatest elements, and whatever else be known above the world and whatever beneath the earth, as great as they show forth the power of God the Word, they do not compare at all with the Dispensation regarding the incarnation, and the Condescension to the lowliness and weakness of humanity.

Chrysostom (347–407): 'God (Father and Son) has no need of the assistance of others'[3]

'Strap your sword upon your thigh, O mighty one' [v. 4a]. Another version has, 'Gird your sword upon the thigh', and another, 'Strap as with a sword upon the thigh.' *'In your youthfulness and your beauty' [v. 4b].* Another version says, 'Your praise and your dignity'; and yet another, 'In your glory, magnificence.'

What is the difference in the words? For at first he says 'Grace is poured out on your lips', but then he suddenly starts talking about the king like an armed warrior. And it's not the style of prophecy, but in the style of supplication. For he doesn't say, 'He *will* strap on his sword', but '*Strap* your sword'. Then he adds beauty to armour, first presenting him as an armoured warrior, then as a decorated one. He says 'in your youthfulness and your beauty'. Then he depicts him as an archer: 'Your arrows are sharp, O mighty one.' And then again he portrays him as conqueror and triumphant: 'Peoples fall under you in the heart of the king's enemies.' And he introduces the same person again anointed with

---

3. John Chrysostom, 'Expositiones in Psalmos 44,4–5', in PG 55.166–168, pp. 189–190.

unguents; warrior, king, archer, conqueror, he writes, 'myrrh and aloes
and cassia are from your garments'.

What do arms and unguents, ointment and sword, teaching and war,
bows and beauty have in common? Some are symbols of peace, others
of war and battle-lines. Who is peaceful and warlike together? Who drips
with myrrh and is armed to the teeth? Who looks out from ivory towers
and casts down countless enemies and wreaks slaughters? How shall we
solve this riddle? We will solve it only if we understand that all these
things refer to the Father. For the Scripture introduces him in another
place as armoured, when it says, 'If you do not repent, he will flash his
sword; he has stretched his bow, and prepared it, and in it has prepared
instruments of death' [Ps. 7:13–14 LXX (7:12–13 MT)]. In another place
it says, 'He will put on a breastplate, righteousness' [Isa. 59:17].

See here that he has absolute authority. For just as it says, 'He will
flash his sword', meaning that he is not commanded by anyone, but does
it from himself, so also in this text, 'the sharpened arrows of the mighty
one, peoples will fall under you in the heart of the king's enemies'. And
to show that he does all things from himself, it says, 'Your right hand will
guide you marvellously.' He doesn't receive his efficacy from another, but
is self-sufficient. But listen to the God of peace himself speaking to the
disciples: 'I did not come to bring peace to the earth, but a sword' [Matt.
10:34]. And again, 'I came to cast fire upon the earth, and what do I wish
except it were already alight?' [Luke 12:49]. He says this concerning him,
and concerning *how* he will come he says, 'He will descend like rain upon
a fleece, and like a drop falling upon the earth' [Ps. 71:6 LXX (72:6 MT)].

I am telling you this, so that you will be alert, and take note with
precision the things signified by the words, and so free yourselves from
the riddle of meaning. For all these terms are signifiers of God's works.
So when you hear in this passage, 'Strap on your sword upon your thigh,
O mighty one,' you will understand it to be talking about God's work;
also the bows and the arrows.

It is like when Scripture says that God gets angry, not to attach passion
to him; so too talking about weapons makes this plain to more dull-witted
people. For God wants to show his power for punishing, and so uses
terms known to us, not so that we think about God in terms of weapons
and armour, but that we hear of his punishment in more vivid terms.

Now some say this is harmful. They make this complaint vainly and
emptily and from their own foolishness. For especially when listening to

God, they need to understand that things are spoken more figuratively. Now Scripture has not neglected to teach them the impassibility of God through other words. Hear how in other places he shows how God holds this power of divine punishment: 'Let God arise, let his enemies be scattered' [Ps. 67:2 LXX (68:2 MT)]. No need of arms? No need of a sword? No, that God 'arises' is by itself sufficient. But this again is materialistic. Hear a more lofty way of putting it: 'All that he wished, he did' [Ps. 113:11C LXX (115:3 MT)]. It was enough for him only to will it. Consider how even in these more materialistic examples he shows God's freedom from need. For before he mentions weaponry, he called him mighty; and again when he lists the arms, he refers the whole victory to his right hand, that is, to God's nature and his power. Which is what another inspired writer makes clear when he says, 'His rule is upon his shoulder' [Isa. 9:5 LXX] – not so that you will be thinking about a shoulder (not at all!), but that you might know that God has no need of the assistance of others.

Augustine of Hippo (354–430): 'Let Christ be your king!'[4]

'Your throne, O God, is for ever and ever' [v. 7a]

However, the throne of the Jewish kingdom was temporal, pertaining to those who were under the Law, not to those who were under Grace: he came to liberate those who were under the Law, and constitute them under Grace. His 'throne is for ever and ever'. Why? That first throne referred to a temporal kingdom. Why now a throne for ever and ever? Because it is God's.

'Your throne, O God, is for ever and ever. A rod of directing is the rod of your kingdom' [v. 7]

It is a rod of directing, which rectifies human beings. They were crooked, they were distorted: they wanted to rule themselves, loved themselves, delighted in their own evil deeds. They did not submit their will to God, but sought to turn the will of God to their own carnal desires. For

---

4. Augustine of Hippo, 'Ennarationes in Psalmos 44,17–18', in PL 36, pp. 503–506.

example the sinner and transgressor is quite angry with God, because it
does not rain; but he does not wish God to be angry with him, because
he is ruinous.[5] And pretty much for this reason men sit down every day
to argue against God: 'He ought to do this, he did not do this well.' Do
you see clearly what he does, and he doesn't know? You are twisted, and
he is right. When will you join the twisted to the straight? They are not
able to be coaligned. Just as if you place a curved stick on a flat pavement:
it doesn't join, it doesn't stick, it doesn't fit the pavement. The pavement
is everywhere equal, but the stick is curved, it doesn't fit what is level. In
the same way the will of God is level; yours is curved. That's why the will
of God seems crooked to you, because you aren't able to be fitted to it;
straighten yourself to God's will, lest you seek to curve it to yourself.
Since you can't, you try in vain; it is at all times straight.

Do you wish to cling to it? Be corrected. He who rules you, his rod will
be a rod of directing. So too he is called 'king' from the act of ruling. He
does not rule who does not correct. For this is our king, a king of the
corrected. Just as he is priest by sanctifying us, so too he is king by ruling us.

'A rod of directing is the rod of your kingdom. You have loved justice, and hated iniquity' [vv. 7b–8a]

See the 'rod of directing'! Approach that rod, let Christ be your king:
let him rule you with that rod, lest it crush you. For that rod is iron,
unbending. And what does it say? 'You will rule them with an iron rod,
and as a potter's vessel you will crush them' [Ps. 2:9]. Some he will rule,
others he will crush: he will rule the spiritual, crush the carnal. Therefore
approach that rod. Why do you fear?

'You have loved justice, and hated iniquity: therefore God, your God, has anointed you' [v. 8]

For this reason he anoints you, that you might love justice, and hate
iniquity. See how he says it, 'Therefore God, *your* God has anointed you.'

---

5. Augustine plays on the contrast between *pluit*, 'it rains', and *fluit*, 'to flow'
(into dissolute living). There is also some wordplay here with *straight*, *correct*,
right, *rule*, etc.

God is anointed by God. Indeed in the Latin it appears as though the same case of the noun is repeated. In the Greek, however, the distinction is most evident, because one noun is the one addressed, the other the one who addressed: 'Therefore your God has anointed you, O God.' Take it and understand it in this way, that's how the Greek reads. Therefore who is the God anointed by God? Let the Jews tell us. These Scriptures are common to us. God is anointed by God: when you hear 'anointed', understand 'Christ'. For 'Christ' is from 'chrism'; this name that Christ is called is of anointing. In no other place were kings and priests anointed, except in that kingdom where Christ was prophesied and anointed, and whence would come the name 'Christ'. Nowhere in any other place, among no nation, in no kingdom, is this found. So then, God is anointed by God – with what oil, except a spiritual one? For the visible oil is in the sign, the invisible oil is in the sacrament, and the spiritual oil is internal. God is anointed for us and sent for us, and God himself was a man that he might be 'anointed', but he was man in such a way as to be God; he was God in such a way that he did not scorn to be man. True man, true God, in nothing deceitful, in nothing false, because he was everywhere true, everywhere truth. God then is man, and for that reason God was anointed, because God was man, and became 'Christ'.

PART 2

THE PSALMS IN THE
LIFE OF THE CHURCH

6. THEOLOGY IN POETRY: THE CHALLENGE OF TRANSLATING THE PSALMS[1]

Andrew G. Shead

> For me this is the essential challenge in translation:
> hearing, in the most profound way I can, the text in
> Spanish and discovering the voice to say (I mean, to write)
> the text again in English. Compared to that, lexical
> difficulties shrink and wither away.
>
> (Edith Grossman)[2]

The aim of this chapter is to consider some of the challenges involved in producing a translation of biblical poetry that can justly claim to be an equivalent of the original. Among other things, I would like to suggest that this cannot be done between the traditionally opposed poles of formal and functional equivalence, and I want to illustrate a possible way ahead by means of three newly translated psalms. Ultimately, translation can be completed only through exposition leading to obedience, and I will close with some suggestions about preaching poetry.

---

1. I would like to acknowledge the assistance of Dr Laurel Moffatt as I have wrestled with the poetry of the Psalms. Her ear for poetry and thoughtful criticisms were not enough to turn my translating into great literature, but they did manage to curb some of its worst tendencies.
2. M. Cervantes, *Don Quixote*, tr. Edith Grossman (London: Vintage, 2005).

Defining poetry

In the 1980s the Collins Dictionary defined poetry as 'literature in metrical form; verse'; today, Wikipedia's definition casts its net wider: 'a form of literary art which uses aesthetic and rhythmic qualities of language – such as phonaesthetics, sound symbolism, and metre – to evoke meanings in addition to, or in place of, the prosaic ostensible meaning'.[3] Either way, poetry is distinguished as a text in which the form of the words conveys meaning in and of itself.

Of course this is true to some degree in most types of speech – for example, the dry, detached tone of legal documents imparts a meaning quite apart from the contents of the words. However, what is an accidental feature of a legal document is intentional and significant in a poem. Jerome Walsh uses the analogy of physical dimensions to good effect, arguing that poetry cannot be reduced to the two prosaic dimensions of syntax and semantics. 'Here, then, is the third dimension in which poetry exists: the dimension of music and image, of metaphor and feeling. Grace of expression is ornamental to prose; it is constitutive of poetry.'[4] Umberto Eco terms these aesthetic features of poetry 'extra-linguistic substances'; his analysis may be represented as follows:[5]

Prosaic: Linguistic substance $\longrightarrow$ Content
Poetic: Linguistic substance + Extra-linguistic substance $\longrightarrow$ Content
Figure 6.1 Substance of expression in prose and poetry.

The more poetic a text, the more difficult it is to translate. '[P]oetic texts are a sort of touchstone for translation, because they make

---

3. <http://en.wikipedia.org/wiki/Poetry>, accessed Jan. 2013.

4. J. T. Walsh, 'מליצית פשעו בי: Theology and the Translation of Poetry', in *Translation of Scripture: Proceedings of a Conference at the Annenberg Research Institute May 15–16, 1989*, JQRSup (Philadelphia: Annenberg Research Institute, 1990), p. 240.

5. U. Eco, *Mouse or Rat? Translation as Negotiation* (London: Weidenfeld & Nicholson, 2003), pp. 134–137. 'Extra-linguistic' is used here narrowly to describe features of the text, not 'extra-textual' aspects of communication such as tone of voice, gesture, etc.

clear that a translation can be considered absolutely perfect only when it is able in some way to provide an equivalent of the physical substance of expression."[6]

The challenge of translating poetry

In the broadest sense translation involves taking a text from its place of origin – the original authors and readers in their particular time and culture – and transferring it ('translating' it), as intact as possible, to the receiving culture, which in our case is peopled by English speakers in the twenty-first century. The goal is to produce a text in the receptor language whose meaning is *equivalent* to the meaning of the text in its original language. When one examines translations of secular poetry, one finds that translators generally aim to represent not the words of the original, in two dimensions as it were, but its 'voice', that thought or impression or emotion the poem, taken as a whole, conveys by all three of its dimensions at once. This involves a movement away from the words and forms of the original to make space for the translator to create new forms of expression capable of capturing the genius of the original in a different tongue. To translate a poem one must make a new poem. David Rosenberg's translations of biblical poetry are examples of this.[7]

However, the translator of Scripture is presented with a text whose words are of peculiar importance, because the word they convey is secured as the same word in translation by ensuring that the original words are represented faithfully. For this reason Bible translations tend to remain much closer than other translations to the words of the original. Of course the English translator must use

---

6. Ibid., p. 144.

7. D. Rosenberg, *A Poet's Bible: Rediscovering the Voices of the Original Text* (New York: Hyperion, 1991). In John Dryden's noteworthy system of classification this sort of translation counts as 'imitation'. He calls word-for-word rendition 'metaphrase', and his preferred option of sense-for-sense translation is 'paraphrase'. See George Watson (ed.), *John Dryden: Of Dramatic Poesy and Other Critical Essays* (London: Dent, 1962), pp. 262–273.

the actual English that ordinary people speak and read (otherwise we have failed to translate), but without domesticating the text in such a way that its sense of place and time, its cultural context, is lost. A good Bible translation therefore values not only equivalence of *function*, so that the translation effectively carries forward and communicates the meaning of the original, but also values equivalence of *form*, so that where possible the translation faithfully and authentically reflects the words of the original. Translations are typically said to display 'functional (or dynamic) equivalence' when they orient themselves first towards the receptor language, mindful of clear communication, and 'direct (or formal) correspondence' when they orient themselves first towards the source language, mindful of authenticity.[8]

This picture is complicated when we bring poetry into it. For the translation of a poem to be truly equivalent to the original, it is necessary to find not only linguistic equivalents to its words, but *aesthetically* equivalent 'extra-linguistic substances'. This does not mean simply replicating the poetic forms of the original, any more than we simply replicate the original vocabulary. Once Hebrew words are replaced with English equivalents, the sounds and rhythms of the original are destroyed and must be replaced by forms in the receptor language that can stand as equivalents to the original forms by producing an 'equivalent' aesthetic effect. When the aesthetic dimension of a poem is ignored by translators, the result cannot be considered properly equivalent to the original. And the unfortunate reality is that English Bibles render Hebrew poetry as if it were prose. Jerome Walsh observed as much in the 1980s, but his hopes that change was in the air have not been realized.[9] Some versions, of course, do better than others;

---

8. For a recent survey of approaches see P. Kirk, 'Holy Communicative? Current Approaches to Bible Translation Worldwide', in L. Long (ed.), *Translation and Religion: Holy Untranslatable?*, Topics in Translation 28 (Clevedon: Multilingual Matters, 2005), pp. 89–101. Kirk points out that if one desires perfect authenticity, then one must return to the original languages, for a translation cannot achieve it, being a fresh work of authorship (p. 99).

9. Walsh, 'Theology', pp. 235–247.

the Jerusalem Bible of 1966 is a brave attempt.[10] More recent versions, however, are sadly uninspiring. It makes no difference whether the translation committee is pursuing direct or functional equivalence; by rendering poetry as prose they fall short of proper equivalence.

Before I go on to present some translations and raise possibilities for 'poetic equivalence', it is worth considering why translations have not taken this direction.

Why is biblical poetry translated so prosaically?

There is a long tradition of translating the psalms prosaically. In part this is because what makes a text poetic varies from language to language. For Hellenistic readers of the Psalms, for example, none of the rhythms that told an educated Greek he or she was listening to poetry was present in Hebrew. The Greek Psalms translation of the third/second century BC followed a strict interlinear approach in which the translator focused on individual words and ignored the context, with figurative language tending to suffer badly.[11] This reflects the overriding priority of the translators to bring their non-Hebrew-speaking Jewish readers as close to the ancestral Hebrew text as possible. Any attempt to give this foreign poetry Greek cadences was necessarily precluded.

The New Testament authors frequently cite psalms (in Greek), but as prophecy rather than poetry. Poetic considerations are set to one side in the face of the immediate task of showing that the Psalms prove Jesus to be the Christ. However, we must not forget that the apostolic writers also made use of the Psalms in the context of gathered worship (Matt. 26:30; 1 Cor. 14:26; Col. 3:16; Eph. 5:19). The Hebrew psalms, through regular singing, continued to speak to Jews and the earliest Christians *as poems*.

---

10. It attempts an acrostic for Ps. 119, for example, but suffers from unevenness of language and idiom: see David Frost, *Making the Liturgical Psalter*, Grove Liturgical Study 25 (Bramcote: Grove, 1981), pp. 20, 24.

11. A. Pietersma (ed.), *A New English Translation of the Septuagint* (New York: Oxford University Press, 2007), p. 543.

For most of the history of the church the Psalms, with the art of Hebrew poetry now forgotten, were translated prosaically in Bibles, but given free poetic adaptation in hymns and anthems. Psalms in plainsong and Anglican chant fall somewhere in between: with the help of a musical line the prose translation falls into a fluid but sturdy metre. With the Reformation the practice of making rhyming, metrical paraphrases of psalms for singing became widespread,[12] and by the seventeenth century numerous poets were taking up the challenge of turning psalms into English poetry, whether to sing as hymns or simply to read and enjoy.[13] It was not until the work of Hebraists such as Robert Lowth in the eighteenth century that distinctive forms of Hebrew poetry such as parallelism began to be appreciated once again;[14] and in due course English Bibles began to lay out psalms to make their poetic structure clearer to the reader. However, the artfully arranged words remained as prosaic as ever, and the situation today remains unchanged: prosaic biblical translations are read aloud in church, accompanied by 'translations of translations' by which scriptural psalms are turned into hymns for singing together.[15]

As long as the chanting of prose psalms was a staple of the Christian life, their prosaic nature was compensated for by music,

---

12. E.g. Thomas Sternhold, *Certayne psalmes chosen out of the Psalter of Dauid, and drawen into Englishe metre by Thomas Sternhold grome of ye kynges Maiesties roobes* (Edouardus Whitchurche, c. 1547); Zoltán Haraszti, *The Bay Psalm Book* (facsimile of the first edition, 1640; Chicago: University of Chicago Press, 1956); and many others.

13. E.g. Isaac Watts, *The Psalms of David: imitated in the language of the New Testament, and applied to the Christian state and worship* (London: Printed for C. S. Arnold, 1828 [1st ed. 1718]); see also the collection by Laurance Wieder, *The Poets' Book of Psalms: The Complete Psalter as Rendered by Twenty-Five Poets from the Sixteenth to the Twentieth Centuries* (New York: Oxford University Press, 1995).

14. R. Lowth, *Lectures on the Sacred Poetry of the Hebrews* (London: printed for J. Johnson, 1787).

15. On the two stages of translation involved in producing psalms for liturgical use, often in rhyme, see further Peter R. Ackroyd and Michael A. Knibb, 'Translating the Psalms', *BT* 17.1 (1966), pp. 2–4.

which is capable of infusing the most pedestrian of words with emotional resonance.[16] However, the dying out of psalms singing in many churches today has meant that the Psalms no longer feature in poetic garb except through such hymnic adaptations as remain in the repertoire, and the occasional contemporary song containing paraphrases – usually of just a few verses from the psalm in question. English Bible translations remain as prosaic as ever, committed to linguistic equivalence of one sort or another without much regard to the aesthetic dimension of meaning in the originals. They do not set out to engage us in three dimensions, and so for the first time much of the church finds itself untouched by the Psalms as poetry. There is, of course, a place for reviving hymns and songs based on Psalms. Yet, as Ackroyd and Knibb point out, when we work to a recognized metrical or musical pattern, 'there is real danger that less than justice may be done to the poetic quality of the Hebrew original'.[17] What is more, no matter how successful we are, we cannot turn back the cultural clock. For most modern Christians, most of the time, the book of Psalms functions as literature and not as lyrics. And as literature they cannot engage us as they should, as poems should, when they are not translated as poems.[18]

---

16. See the excellent treatment by Gordon Wenham, *The Psalter Reclaimed: Praying and Praising with the Psalms* (Wheaton: Crossway, 2013), pp. 13–35.

17. 'Translating the Psalms', p. 3. In recent years there has been a pleasing number of revivals of psalm singing of one form or another, ranging from traditional, such as Calvin Seerveld, *Voicing God's Psalms* (Grand Rapids: Eerdmans, 2005), to contemporary, such as the group Sons of Korah (www.sonsofkorah.com), to alternative, such as Isaac Everett, *The Emergent Psalter* (New York: Church Publishing, 2009). However, sung psalms have not yet entered the corporate life of the evangelical churches of my experience.

18. The use of committees to translate exacerbates this problem, and one of the most successful recent translations, the 'Liturgical Psalter', included in *An Australian Prayer Book* (Sydney: AIO, 1978) and *The Alternative Service Book 1980* (Colchester: Clowes, 1980), was worded by a single translator, David Frost. Compare the success of the Coverdale Psalter, which was preferred over the AV's group effort for the *Book of Common Prayer* (1662): according to Frost the essence of Coverdale's success was 'his ability to make the psalms his own' (*Making the Liturgical Psalter*, p. 4).

Towards 'direct poetic equivalence'

'Direct equivalence' is something of an oxymoron, with 'direct' suggesting identity with the original, and 'equivalence' suggesting non-identity. In practice it tends to indicate translation word by word rather than proposition by proposition, or thought by thought. An unfortunate corollary of this is the dubious aim shared by many English versions (but achieved by none) of lexical stereotyping, that is, of rendering the same Hebrew word with the same English word across the Old Testament. This devotion to distant parallels hinders the translator from choosing words that best enrich their immediate context. Fortunately, the English translator is blessed with a language rich with synonyms, and the task of finding equivalents for the aesthetic substance of a poem is not a hopeless one.

I have chosen to focus on six features of Hebrew poetry; the following observations about equivalence will then be illustrated through translations of Psalms 46, 111 and 93.[19]

Equivalence of sound

Hebrew poetry is a very frequent user of assonance, alliteration, wordplay, onomatopoeia, rhythmic echoes, and so forth, and these features set it strongly apart from more prosaic texts. Occasionally these features are tied to the meaning of specific words, such as harsh-sounding verbs of destruction. There are even cases, such as Psalm 40:3 (v. 4 in Hebrew), where a logical connection is forged through sound-play alone.[20] More often, though, the effects are general in nature, and the same effect can be created in English by finding other types of sound pattern to insert into the translation.

Equivalence of parallelism, enjambment and word order

The creative counterbalancing of ideas is fundamental to Hebrew poetry, which is therefore very sensitive not only to parallelism in

---

19. Ackroyd and Knibb, 'Translating the Psalms', pp. 4–10, provide some helpful observations along similar lines, though of a more general nature.
20. 'Many shall see [*yirē'û*] and fear [*yîrā'û*]' implies the meaning 'seeing, many shall fear'.

general, but to word order within lines, as well as to the effects of running a line over into the next one (enjambing it), without any verbal parallelism. English lacks the flexibility of Hebrew, and even the most direct of English versions, being stubbornly fixed in a prosaic register, make little or no effort to reflect Hebrew word order. However, English poetry permits much more flexibility of word order than does prose, and inversions of syntax are one of the surest ways of making a text feel poetic. Of course, too many inversions soon produce an archaic and stilted style, often foreign to the mood of the psalm in question. Finding the best equivalence of form here needs careful negotiation from poem to poem.

Equivalence of vocabulary

Hebrew poetry is full of rare words. We do not always know how rare they were, since the surviving body of biblical Hebrew literature is relatively small. But it is safe to assume that many words were literary and not in common spoken use. When translators aim for a text that communicates easily to their audience, this may be a feature they are reluctant to replicate, but nearly always the decision to use a small English vocabulary will drastically reduce the translators' ability to produce an appropriate texture of sounds and images without straying very far from the linguistic substance of the original. What is more, nobody writes as they speak, and we recognize about a third more words than we use in actual conversation.[21] I would love to see Bibles that use footnotes to explain difficult English words in the Psalms, just as books of poetry sometimes do today.

Equivalence of thrift

Robert Alter's translation stands out for its attempt to approximate a little more closely to the concise lines of the original.[22] It is remarkable how many unnecessary words are added to English translations simply because the source text is being treated like prose. It means that we lose the power poetry gains from distilling experiences into

---

21. According to research cited by Frost, *Making the Liturgical Psalter*, p. 22.
22. R. Alter, *The Book of Psalms: A Translation with Commentary* (New York: Norton, 2007).

as few words as possible, so that we pay closer attention to each one and consider the varied methods by which it conveys meaning to us.

Equivalence of metre

Hebrew metre is rhythmic but very fluid, more akin to plainchant than Greek-inspired Western poetry, and here the question of what counts as equivalent is especially acute. English versions from the sixteenth to nineteenth centuries either ignored metre or translated it into metres that were meaningful to their audiences. This ensured the poems were heard as poems by their modern listeners, but it also domesticated the texts, as if their authors had been ancient Greeks or even moderns. A generation ago most Anglican churchgoers were familiar with liturgical psalms in which each line accommodates itself with infinite flexibility into a single chant, not metrical but rhythmical with the rhythms of speech, moving forwards only when a musical cadence gives permission to do so. But today we translate for speaking.

In general I have tried to create metres that sound deliberate, but that do not always have the regularity of metrical poetry, so that while the poems, read aloud, feel like poems, they feel somewhat more Hebrew than European. Part of the success of the Jerusalem Bible lies in its recognition that a translator 'should not try to inject a rhetorical quality and an orotundity of cadence which belong more truly to the first Elizabethan age than to the Hebrew originals'.[23]

Acrostics, refrains and other frames

Acrostics are especially interesting because they often convey important meaning; but to create a corresponding English acrostic often forces us to be more creative lexically and syntactically than we might otherwise wish to be. We will have to decide whether the sacrifice of strict lexical equivalence, or one-to-one correspondence of words, results in a text that, taken as a whole, is more faithful to the original.

The strongest case for reproducing an acrostic scheme is probably

---

23. A. Jones, 'Editor's Foreword', *The Jerusalem Bible* (London: Darton, Longman & Todd, 1966), p. vi. See also Alter, *Book of Psalms*, esp. pp. xxix–xxxi.

the book of Lamentations. The American poet David Slavitt observes that Lamentations' acrostics are

> a serious assertion that . . . there is, beyond all the disaster and pain the book recounts, an intricacy and an orderly coherence the poetry affirms in a gesture that is encouraging and marvellous. The texture of the poetry is what lets us know that, somehow, the catastrophe is not total.[24]

Most English versions indicate in a footnote that these poems are acrostics in the original, and many mark the point where the next Hebrew letter enters the sequence. However, that is a commentary on an untranslated aspect of the poem rather than a translation of that particular formal feature. We can only ever imagine it, never experience it – and the result is a different message.

An example of 'direct poetic equivalence': Psalm 46

A comparison with a version such as the ESV or AV will immediately reveal the many departures from lexical fidelity in the following translation. Words are omitted, occasionally added, common words replaced by rarer ones, and the odd verb altered. In the comments that follow I seek to show that these departures facilitate an overall *increase* in fidelity to the original. Once we recognize that we are reading a poem, it follows that direct equivalence cannot be achieved by a simple lexical mapping exercise.

> For the music director. A song on the *alamot* by the sons of Korah.
> 1 *God's a mighty fastness for us,*
> *aid in plight he ever grants. So*
> 2 *we'll not fear though earth plummets,*
> *summits plunge beneath the sea;*

---

24. David R. Slavitt, *The Book of Lamentations: A Meditation and Translation* (Baltimore: The Johns Hopkins University Press, 2001). Slavitt's translation speaks with its own voice, abandoning the Hebrew metre altogether, but nevertheless achieves a close and beautiful fidelity to the original.

3   *its breakers boom, they boil,*
        the summits sway with its surging.   [Bridge]

4   *A river.*
    Its streams gladden God's city,
        holy abode of the Highest.
5   *God is there, she'll not sway;*
        God grant her aid at break of day.
6   *Nations boom,*
        kingdoms sway!
    He gives voice,
        earth gives way.

7   The LORD of Hosts is here with us;
        Jacob's God, our strong fortress.   [Bridge]

8   *Go, survey the deeds of the LORD*
        who lays desolations in the earth,
9   *shutting down battles to earth's end.*
    Bow he breaks and shatters spear,
        chariots he incinerates.
10 *Give up! Know that I am God:*
        exalted by nations, exalted on earth.

11 The LORD of Hosts is here with us;
        Jacob's God, our strong fortress.   [Bridge]

Psalm 46 is marked by striking sound patterns, such as the sound-plays in verse 2 (*nîrā'* . . . *hāmîr* . . . *hārîm* . . . *yammîm*) or the repeated consonants in verse 3 (*yeḥĕmû yeḥmĕrû mêmâw*). To create an English version whose sound patterns are similarly rich, some common word equivalents must be scrapped. To take just one example, the usual 'mountains' for *hārîm* has been replaced by 'summits'. This is a small loss, since the hope that consistent translation equivalents might enable meaningful word studies is elusive at best. On the other hand, in many places the psalms do use stereotyped language, and there will be a tendency for more colourful translations to move away from that, which is a real loss.

Much of the vocabulary of Psalm 46 is either very rare or peculiar to poetry, or both (in vv. 1–3, 'fastness', 'plummet', 'plunge', 'boom', 'boil', 'surging'). Overall, words are kept to a minimum: there are just sixteen Hebrew words in verses 2–3, which ESV takes thirty-four words to translate. Some expansion cannot be avoided, since Hebrew is a more concise language, but once a translator places a value on thrift of expression it is not hard to minimize the disparity. There is no need to translate one word ('plummets' in my version) as two ('gives way' in the ESV), or add a clarifying 'though' to both lines of verse 3 – the logic of the poem works through juxtaposition, not exposition. And while 'beneath' (v. 2) is less faithful lexically than 'into the heart of' (ESV), it is more faithful in every other respect: its two syllables, its assonance with 'sea', its sense of rhythm.

The final choice of words should not be determined by a simple desire for thrift, but by decisions about metre. In the case of Psalm 46 I was able to echo the original metre (the number of stressed beats in a line) fairly closely, but I tried to smooth out the rhythms to make them feel more poetic to English ears. On the other hand, I have avoided creating a regular hymnlike metre, lest the psalm's foreignness be unduly domesticated. The result preserves the shifts of metre that accompany transition points such as verses 4–5, though I have taken some liberties in verses 7 and 12 to mark the climaxes of stanzas. In the end it is important that we hear this as a poem, because it shapes, often unconsciously, the way one hears and understands what is being said.

The one point at which I have ignored thrift and Hebrew metre is in the refrain of verses 7 and 12, to which I have added words ('here', 'strong') in order to strengthen the couplet and give it the drive of a contemporary refrain or group chant. (I also rendered the cryptic *selâ* as 'bridge' to put readers in mind of the fact that this was written to be performed. The LXX translation 'interlude on strings' points in this direction.) The other point at which judgments of style affect the directness of the translation concerns word order. The lovely balance of verse 9, 'bow he breaks and shatters spear', cries out for retention; but to copy the word order of verse 1a, 'God's for us a fastness mighty', is to create something more affected and lopsided than its rather normal Hebrew parent, and out of keeping with the tone of what follows.

Who knows how the original hearers heard this poem? Which features resonated with them and in what way? We can make fairly safe assumptions about the music of the language based on the universal responsiveness of humans to mellifluous noises, and about the power of metaphor and juxtaposition based on its ubiquity in Hebrew poetry, but presumably many subtleties of the poetic craft and its performance are now lost to us. It therefore seems reasonable to take opportunities to allow poetic elements to creep in that are not present in the original (such as the play on the word 'give' in v. 6b), in the hope that some of the original impact, attenuated by the gulf of time and place, may be restored by other means – always supposing, of course, that these ornaments do not generate meanings foreign to the original.

The logic of Psalm 46 emerges from its elevated language, its synonyms, its repeated words and its contrasts of metre. It builds its argument viscerally, by juxtaposing images. It is immediate and sensuous rather than didactic and detached. For example, we see God making mountains sway; the city not sway; and kingdoms sway. This amounts to a theology, in pictures, of the presence of God. Does a prosaic translation teach us these things? Yes, but the impact of the poem is attenuated by the failure of the translation to be faithful to the aesthetic dimensions of the poem.

A second example of 'direct poetic equivalence': Psalm 111

Psalm 111 is a very different kind of poem. It is wise and cheerful, twenty-two measured lines of didactic praise. The psalm's acrostic scheme and equal line lengths convey the orderliness and knowable-ness of the God being praised, and suggests a teaching exercise by which the student systematically 'learns God'. The fact that most lines begin with Hebrew substantives strengthens the impression, as if a student could learn this as a series of topics, or even attributes, of God and his 'deeds' (a keyword). The psalm is not closely argued, but gains depth of meaning through simple juxtapositions and repe-titions of words and sounds within and across verses. The task of an aesthetically direct translation is therefore to create an analogous level and type of interconnectedness rather than always to replicate the particular cross-connections of the original. Our focus here, though, will be on the challenge of representing an acrostic in translation.

Judged by the standards of prose, what follows is a rather free translation, but as a poem I believe it is more directly equivalent to the original than a lexically precise rendition, because the overall effect of the poetry depends on its acrostic scheme. As we experience the acrostic form we feel the poet is trying to be clever, shaping a memorable collection of lines that take pleasure in their ingenuity and lead to the climactic statements about wisdom in verse 10. As a result, verse 10 seems to be warning the rest of the psalm not to get carried away with its cleverness, since it is fear of the Lord rather than clever theological one-liners that forms the ground of true wisdom. And yet at the same time the first nineteen lines are not trite, but take joyous pleasure in the God they catalogue; and they manage to paint a rich portrait of this Lord whom the truly wise person both fears and delights to praise.

1   *Hallelujah!*

   Applaud the Lord with all my heart;
   Blameless assembly, surround me with counsel.

2   *Colossal deeds the Lord has wrought,*
   Delved in by all who in them delight.

3   *Eminence and excellence stamp his work;*
   For ever, for ever his righteousness stands:

4   *Graven in memory his marvels he's fixed.*

   How gracious and merciful is the Lord, who

5   *Invited his fearers to feast on meat;*
   Jealously, always, his covenant recalls.

6   *Kingly deeds he declared to his people,*
   Lavishing on them the nations' estate:

7   *Meet and right are the deeds of his hands.*

   Nothing but truth in all his edicts:

8   *O'er all eternity they stand firm,*
   Performed in truth and blamelessness.

9   *Quittance – redemption – he sent to his people,*
   Required them for ever to keep his covenant:
   Sacred and terrible is his name.

10 *The beginning of wisdom is fearing the Lord:*
   Untarnished reward, for all who do it.
   Vaunted, his praise for ever prevails!

The Hebrew acrostic scheme is not interrupted by structuring devices, so that there is no clear subdivision of the poem into smaller units. Commentators have made a range of proposals, and I have ventured one of my own, but it is probably best to leave the poem to flow without interruption. This leaves a range of possible readings latent within its verses, to be brought out in the way a reader chooses to perform it. As an acrostic the psalm lends itself to memorization, and with the constant repetition this requires, reading possibilities will begin to unfold within a pupil's imagination. My subdivisions should therefore be taken as nothing more than one performance suggestion.

The original poet has gone to considerable effort to achieve the acrostic, in a number of cases choosing rare and unusual words that happen to start with the required letter. In verse 2b, for example, a common word ('to seek') is converted into the passive participle 'sought' (rendered 'delved' by me), which occurs in only one other place in the Bible. In verse 5a an unusual word for 'meat' opens the line, which normally refers to the prey of wild beasts, and has its present derivative meaning only half a dozen times. In a third example verse 8a uses the verb 'to lean' in a passive form meaning 'supported', found only twice outside this verse.

Beyond this highly contrived structure the poet's use of language is quite conventional,[25] marked by stereotyped word pairs and conventional phrases (e.g. v. 3a, 'glorious and majestic'; v. 4b, 'gracious and compassionate'; v. 7a, 'faithful and just'; v. 3b, 'his righteousness endures for ever'; v. 5b, 'he remembers his covenant for ever'; v. 9c, 'holy and awesome is his name' – all from the NIV translation). My translation has frequently been pulled away from the conventional by the constraints of the acrostic, and by the decision to imitate the regular lines by a constant four-beat metre; the unstereotyped feel this gives to the whole is probably the most significant betrayal of its source.

To create an English acrostic a lot of negotiation was required. Sometimes minor reshuffling sufficed, as in the opening colon

---

25. See Alter, *Book of Psalms*, pp. xx–xxviii.

where an imperative addressed to the self comes very close to the original cohortative, and the sign marking the speaker was shifted from start to finish. However, in verse 1b more had to be done, with the opening preposition replaced by a verb ('surround'), and 'me' carried over from the first line.[26] And to manage the acrostic new starting words sometimes needed to be contrived: 'invited' (for 'gave'), 'jealously' (a thought absent from the original, suggesting God's refusal to tolerate divided loyalties in his people), 'kingly' (instead of 'power') and 'vaunted' (meaning 'boasted about', and carrying a non-pejorative sense from its context).

To achieve a regular metre also required the occasional addition, such as the doubled 'for ever' in verse 3, or the explanatory 'redemption' in verse 9. Finding equivalents for sound patterns was not as disruptive, so that 'eminence and excellence', for example, is a direct rendering of *hôd wĕhādār* (v. 3). Overall, however, an acrostic will inevitably push a translation further from lexical equivalence than we have come to expect. One alternative is to create a less prominent acrostic pattern, such as the following:

> **A**pplaud the LORD with all my heart,
> in **B**lameless council congregated.
> **C**olossal deeds the LORD has wrought,
> sought by all who **D**elight in them (etc.)

Nevertheless, I chose to create a full acrostic to demonstrate that even when the extra-linguistic substance of a poem imposes large demands on the translation it is still possible to find a faithful linguistic equivalent for each phrase of the original. The result is no imitation (see n. 7), but a close translation. In fact, it sticks so closely to the original words that its effectiveness as a poem in its own right is noticeably diminished.

---

26. A direct prosaic translation might read, 'I'll praise the Lord with all [my] heart, / in the council of the upright assembly', taking *yĕšārîm wĕ'ēdâ* as a hendiadys.

An example of 'functional poetic equivalence': Psalm 93

To create poetry that carries forward the total substance of the original more faithfully into today's world, that is to say, that captures in English the unique meaning created by poetry's bringing together of language and form, requires a commitment to 'render sense for sense and not word for word' – an approach to translation that Jerome, patron saint of translators, adopted from the famed Roman translators Tully and Horace.[27] On the level of aesthetics this produces English psalms with more integrity as poems in their own right, such as the following translation of Psalm 100 by Francis Sullivan, which condenses the form but preserves the sense of each line, and leaves behind Hebrew formal features such as parallelism in favour of a more native idiom:

Break out shouting   *Chant at the door,*
joy to God, you earth,   *chant into the square*
reach God singing   *the name, Holy*
your summit of joy.   *God, thanks be, thanks be*

Know it is God   *to our good God*
who made us belong   *for a faithful love,*
to the flock, God   *life after life,*
who owns this people.   *no one can destroy.*[28]

I have already argued against taking this approach to translation in Bible versions, but its strengths should be noted. With the sacrifice of direct word-for-word equivalence a translation is free to find its own 'voice', to achieve a thrift of language and concentration of ideas that comes much closer to aesthetic equivalence than a more lexically direct rendition. Judged as prose, this would of course be an extremely loose paraphrase, but it is not prose, and

27. St Jerome, 'Letter to Pamachius on the Best Method of Translating', in Philip Schaff and Henry Wace (eds.), *A Select Library of Nicene and Post-Nicene Fathers of the Christian Church*, 2nd series, vol. 6, tr. W. H. Fremantle (New York: Christian Literature Publishing, 1893), p. 115.
28. F. P. Sullivan, 'Poetic Psalms', *Bible Today* 19.2 (1981), p. 126.

Sullivan achieves a type of equivalence that eludes every translation that is less poetic than the original. However, Psalm 100 is
a rather straightforward case. When it comes to imagery, and the
world view that generates it, the problem of equivalence is not
so tractable.

It is impossible for Psalm 93 to awaken in the mind of a modern
reader the mental images ancient readers would have shared, let
alone create an equivalent emotional response. 'Rivers' (v. 3;
rendered 'floods' by ESV and 'seas' by NIV) denoted the infinite
cosmic chaos within which we maintain our tenuous existence; they
had nothing to do with the large ponds we float across in cruise
liners and pollute with oil. According to ancient cosmology we live
on a world whose dry lands and airy spaces are surrounded on all
sides by an endless expanse of primeval waters (the notion that the
sky might not actually be a solid dome over our heads did not occur
to anyone as far as we can tell until the late Middle Ages). For every
culture other than Israel, the firmament of the heavens could only
keep the waters from crashing down and extinguishing all life as
long as the gods acted to keep them up, and placating these fickle
beings was a constant and nerve-wracking obligation. What translation of Psalm 93 can yield an even approximate equivalence of
response?

The following attempt wrenches us out of the ancient world;
technically one would say this is a 'domestication' of the original,
just as it is when we give our 'shirt' (rather than our tunic) to the
person who has taken our 'coat' (rather than our cloak).[29] It moves
the text towards the receiving culture rather than making the reader
travel back in time to the source culture. If one strays too far into
the receiving culture, the gospel can lose its historical moorings. And
yet the amount of work a source-oriented translation requires the
reader to do can sometimes be so great that he or she will never
understand what the text means without extensive footnotes, in
which case one might as well have provided a text that communicates
the theological message more directly, with footnotes provided to
achieve the required historical fidelity.

---

29. Luke 6:29 HCSB (compared with ESV).

1   The LORD reigns! in majesty robed
        Robed, the LORD is ringed by might
     Our steadfast earth – its orbit runs true
2   Steadfast your throne from aeons past
        You always were
3   Stars went nova, O LORD
        Stars sent out their waves
        Black holes devoured their frenzy
4   Above the swirling galaxies
        Nobler than the stars' bright fires
        Noble in highest height is GOD!
5   Your scriptures are entirely sure
        Your house, adorned by holiness
        LORD, for as long as time endures.

In my judgment the above translation fails the equivalence test, but
not because it has left behind the 'rivers' (v. 3) and 'sea' (v. 4) of the
original. The problem lies in what has replaced them. The cosmos
of modern science is a clinical place, a huge physics lab, a closed
system from which God is usually excluded, and even when he is
not, we conceive of the physical universe as just that – a big, imper-
sonal machine. What Psalm 93 does, if only we can learn to read it
untranslated into a twenty-first-century world view, is to present us
with a universe in radical contrast to the evidence of our eyes. And
so this version would not make it into my Bible. But it might be
good to sing.[30]

Achieving 'functional poetic equivalence' through preaching

A preacher is a translator before anything else, seeking to translate the
text into the world of the listener and the listener into the world of
the text. This is not an easy task when the original text communicates

---

30. On the pitfalls of translating images see Luis Alonso Schökel, *A Manual of
     Hebrew Poetics*, SubBi 11 (Rome: Editrice Pontifico Istituto Biblica, 1988),
     pp. 99–105.

its message in the form of poetry. While prophets once preached in poetry, a modern-day 'poet-preacher' is in danger of inducing embarrassment, even mirth, in his or her listeners (especially Australian ones!). Our challenge is to let the ancient text do its work, at all levels, within the formal artistic medium of the sermon.

At the very least this means slowing down to let the poetry do its work on us as a poem, to linger over its images and forms so that their power is not lost, and to strive to convey this power with immediacy. It will usually be preferable to *change* a foreign image for one with immediate impact, at the cost of blurring the original image, than to *explain* the foreign image, at the cost of blunting the original impact. The communicative goal of the psalmist should help the preacher set up a communicative goal that can serve as a guide in making these decisions.

As an aid to the preacher I offer the following grid, which is designed to help us consider how the aesthetic elements – sounds, shapes, rhythms and images – build across the poem into an emotional picture or journey, and how this journey supports the rational 'argument' conveyed by the meaning of the words, much as a musical score supports a motion picture. On both levels, the aesthetic and the rational, the poem conveys its message by aggregation, each element combining through similarity of sound or wording, or simply by proximity, to create the journey's successive stages.

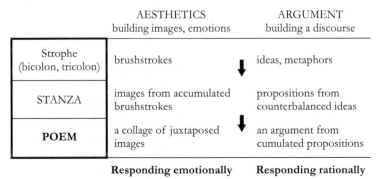

	AESTHETICS building images, emotions	ARGUMENT building a discourse
Strophe (bicolon, tricolon)	brushstrokes	ideas, metaphors
STANZA	images from accumulated brushstrokes	propositions from counterbalanced ideas
POEM	a collage of juxtaposed images	an argument from cumulated propositions
	Responding emotionally	**Responding rationally**

Figure 6.2 An analytical grid for biblical poetry.

As an example I have placed a second, and more direct, translation of Psalm 93 into the left-hand box (see figure 6.3). In the columns to its right I have tried to indicate, in the first place, the aesthetic

The poem as a whole:

Prosody: the emotional journey	**Argumentation**: the rational journey
Vertigo; a journey into awe; a guided tour of resurgent evil powers as seen from a safe height; and the excitement of discovering shards of divine majesty embedded in mundane words and gathered worshippers.	A psalm about the way in which God, incommunicably and infinitely noble, transforms our daily experience of death and life by communicating his eternal majesty through law and temple.
This psalm is like a small child in the park thrown high into the air, who lands back in her father's arms with leaves clutched in her fists.	This psalm describes Christ on the mount of transfiguration, the curtains of his flesh parted to reveal the nobility within. It describes the infinite God who is present among us by his words of Scripture, and the foolish message of the gospel.

Figure 6.3 Psalm 93 analysed as an emotional and rational discourse.

Strophe by strophe:

	Aesthetics: building images and emotions	Argumentation: building a discourse
1 *The LORD reigns! in majesty robed* *Robed is the LORD, self-girded in might*	Measured, balanced, confident. What does majesty look like? Raw glory – terrifying.	'Clothed in his attributes'; God is his own source of glory/power; majesty is how God is to us.

2 *How steadfast the world, unshakeable*
    Steadfast your throne from days gone by
        You are from ever
	Shift from radiant energy to immense mass, from pure presence to vast stretches of time, vertiginous.	Creation as the simile of God's immovable ruling presence; God's eternity is a corollary of his omnipotence.

3 *Oceans lifted up, O LORD*
    Oceans lifted up their sound
    Oceans lifting up their pound
	Hypnotic. Each time the waters surge higher, until the change of tense brings them down upon us.	Cosmic enemies from ancient times, threating our existence – a universe charged with life and purpose, good and evil.

4 *Above the sounds of many waters*
    Nobler than the sea's great breakers
        Noble in highest height is GOD!
	Repetitions continue to elevate us, and the delaying of God's name makes the climax: vv. 3–4 are one vast discomparison.	It is not righteousness, or goodness, or love, but God's imposing, heart-lifting *nobility* that the psalm projects.

5 *Your precepts are entirely sure*
    Your house, adorned by holiness
    LORD, for as long as days endure
	Back down to earth ... but with a bit of God which is like stable ground, and a house beautiful with his glory: transferred splendour!	The noble vision transforms our perception of law and temple: they bring God's majesty into our lives and secure them from every evil power.

'brushstrokes' painted by each of the poem's five strophes; and consequently, the ideas and propositions conveyed by means of them. I have treated the poem as a single stanza, so in the columns beneath these I have skipped over stanza-level analysis to reflect on the whole poem as an emotional and rational journey into God.

The practical suggestion I have just provided is nothing more than that. It exemplifies no rules or fixed principles, because, as Wilfred Watson observes, 'No poem worthy of the name "follows the rules".'[31] Poetry is designed explicitly to slow a reader down, to focus the attention and wake up the imagination, and one way of making sure the reader pays attention is to confound expectation. Whether translating a psalm or expounding it, there is nothing for it but to slow down. If there is one rule to follow, it is to be found in Luis Alonso Schökel's wise advice: 'What has been written with imagination, must also be read with imagination.'[32]

Conclusions

Translating poetry is not the same as translating prose, and even the most direct translations need to find ways of representing the aesthetic substance of the original if they are to remain faithful to it. Bible translation committees are conservative, and rightly so; however, my call to re-evaluate our translation technique does not amount to an argument for full-blown poetic translation. The psalms I have created fall well short of full poetic equivalence, for they are still bound so tightly to the original Hebrew words that the aesthetic substance of the poetry cannot be naturalized; instead, there is a piecemeal carrying over into English of aesthetic features of the Hebrew, half-digested. As Francis Sullivan remarks,

> Poetry is not the result of verbal techniques, a rhythm, a rhyme,
> a physical image. To translate a psalm accurately into the physical

---

31. Wilfred G. E. Watson, *Classical Hebrew Poetry: A Guide to Its Techniques*, 2nd ed., JSOTSup 26 (Sheffield: Sheffield Academic Press, 1986), p. 16.
32. Schökel, *Manual of Hebrew Poetics*, p. 104.

appearance of poetry won't do. It takes a poetic act to catch another poetic act. To translate a psalm as a poem requires a poet to create a poem which is a psalm. There is no chance for identity with the original. There is a chance for likeness, a poem like a psalm.[33]

My more modest aim has been to contrive translations that stay close enough to the original words to count as the enscripturated Word, prophecy as well as poetry. And within these tight restrictions I have attempted to show that a degree of genuine aesthetic equivalence is nevertheless achievable. While the versions of psalms currently printed in our English Bibles are recognizable as poetry by their layout, their density of imagery and their apostrophic tone, they are poor equivalents to the originals, and too often they neither sound nor feel like poetry – which is hardly surprising given the prosaic approach taken to translating them. For 'poetry is experience: a poet's experience made articulate in language hewn to engender experience in its hearer'.[34] The first step to capturing that experience must be taken by translators; to finish the journey, practised and attentive readers (or retentive hearers) must give themselves to the poem with patience and imagination.

As with prose, translations of poetry are susceptible to the so-called 'horizon of the translator', that is, the literary conventions of the day that influence a translator's choices and place a time stamp on the result.[35] More than prose, however, poetry is liable to feel occasional, of the moment, flavoured by the individuality of the translator. Given the aesthetic nature of poetry this cannot be helped, but if the result still sounds like poetry to our ears it will have done its job, which is to sensitize us to the poetic nature of the text, so that we start to listen to it as such, alert to the energies, the images, the layers of meaning and the emotional landscapes through which the words come to us, bursting with meaning.

---

33. Sullivan, 'Poetic Psalms', p. 121.
34. Walsh, 'Theology', p. 240.
35. Eco, *Mouse or Rat?*, p. 143.

7. SINGING WITH THE MESSIAH IN A FOREIGN LAND

Andrew G. Shead and Andrew J. Cameron

In many churches the Psalms are read or sung every Sunday, or even daily, in succession. These churches have preserved a priceless treasure, for only with daily use does one appropriate this divine prayer book. When read only occasionally, these prayers are too overwhelming in design and power and tend to turn us back to more palatable fare. But whoever has begun to pray the Psalter seriously and regularly will soon give a vacation to other little devotional prayers.

(Dietrich Bonhoeffer)[1]

Bonhoeffer's opening observation has become less and less true over the years. Today, many evangelicals are in congregations where the Psalms are heard less than they have ever been heard in the history of the church. When did they become optional? Did we drop them out of principle, or carelessness? Either way, we need to consider whether or not it matters that so few of our new songs are old.

In this chapter we will challenge that drift. We will consider how Christians can regard themselves as participants in what, after all, began as the literature of another time, place and people. We will

---

1. *Psalms: The Prayerbook of the Bible* (Minneapolis: Augsburg, 1970), p. 25.

offer some candidate explanations for why Christians often do not use the Psalms. We will consider how such diverse genres of psalm can all be regarded and experienced as 'praise'. We will propose some 'experiments' in how we may, in corporate settings, enact these 'praises'.

We have so many songs: why the Psalms?[2]

The Hebrew title of the book of Psalms means 'praises'. And perhaps more than in any other part of Scripture, we are conscious in the Psalms of the human voice of the authors, of men and women pouring out their hearts to God, giving expression to every conceivable emotion in every possible life situation.

But the Psalms are not just outpourings of human words. They are only in the Bible at all because they have become God's word to us, divine speech, and it is one of the things that makes these praise songs unique: they are, at one and the same time, human words to God and his words to humanity. Which 'humans' and which 'humanity', and whether we can include ourselves in that, pivots on our relationship to the psalms' Messiah, Jesus Christ.

We will return to that relationship shortly. But in the first instance what sort of words are they? According to Psalm 1:2, they are words of *law*, a word that here means something close to 'instruction'. The psalter is God's instruction book, whose words promise to sink into those who say or sing them (the word in 1:2 is 'speak', or 'mutter', *hāgâ*), and root them deeply in righteousness and fruitfulness of life.

As well as instructing us and making us wise for salvation, Psalms is a book of *prophecy*, a book that speaks of Jesus. As Jesus himself said, 'Everything must be fulfilled that is written about me in the Law of Moses, the Prophets and the Psalms' (Luke 24:44). It is significant that the New Testament writers left us so few psalms of their own. The way they use the Psalms suggests that they did not

---

2. The first part of this chapter is a slightly revised version of an article published in the magazine *Southern Cross* 17.5 (June 2011), pp. 18–19, and is reproduced with the permission of the publishers, Anglican Media Sydney.

think they needed to write many new songs – the Psalms as they stood were already a Christian hymnbook.

What happens when we use them together?

God speaks to us in the Psalms by giving us words with which to praise him, words that speak of what he is like and what he has done. The frequent appeals by the psalmists for God's people to join in (Pss 34:3; 35:27; etc.) are now addressed to us. Through Christ, who is our David, we are able to use the Psalms as our book of *praises*. And as we praise God with his own words, they penetrate deeply into us and become our words, helping to shape who we are.

This is why the Psalms have always played such a central role in the gathered worship of God's people. For Thomas Cranmer, who shaped the Anglican pattern of church during the Reformation, our gatherings are to be characterized by 'the continual course of the reading of Scripture'.[3] The foundational means by which God speaks to us should not be the sermon as such, but the systematic, public reading of Scripture. And it should principally be the public reading of that same Scripture by which we speak back to God in prayer and praise. In the Psalms God has given us a book full of his own words that we might say and sing back to him whenever we meet together.

No wonder Christians have felt they must justify using freshly composed songs. Songs are indeed justified, in the same way that expositions of Scripture are justified over and above simple Bible reading.[4] To sing 'songs' in church, but not the Psalms, is like having preaching but not Bible reading. Much of contemporary evangelicalism has abandoned orthodox practice at this point, and the fact that we are blind to this is hard to account for, except in terms of a cultural capitulation to the cult of musical entertainment.

What message do the Psalms proclaim?

In a word, they proclaim the gospel. Their main theme is the universal reign of God and his Messiah. In the words of Psalm 2:

---

3. From the preface to *The Book of Common Prayer* (1549).
4. For an example of the opposing case see Bruce C. Stewart, *Psalm Singing Revisited: The Case for Exclusive Psalmody* (Pittsburgh: Crown & Covenant, 1999).

Let me recount the LORD's decree:
> You are my son, he said to me,
> I did this day beget you.
Ask it of me and I shall make
> nations into your freehold,
> earth's ends your estate.
(Ps. 2:7–8, our tr.)

The Psalms paint a rich and complex picture of the Messiah.[5] Even psalms that are not particularly about him take on new meaning when read as part of a book whose main character is God's anointed king. Psalm 8, for example, permits reflection on the humanity of the Messiah. 'What is mankind that you are mindful of them?', asks the psalmist, yet 'you have made them a little lower than the angels' (Ps. 8:4–5). The way God incorporates humans into the heart of his creative purposes tells us something very profound about him, and ultimately it points to the most profound embrace of weakness God ever made: to clothe himself in the form of a suckling infant crying in a Judean stable. And so the New Testament uses Psalm 8 to reflect on Jesus' humanity:

---

5. The present brief sketch entirely omits a vast scholarly discussion of both the message of the Psalms and the proper way to read it as Christian Scripture, some of which is touched on in other contributions to this volume. On the message of the Psalms the reader may also like to consult J. Clinton McCann (ed.), *The Shape and Shaping of the Psalter*, JSOTSup 159 (Sheffield: Sheffield Academic Press, 1993); Walter Brueggemann, *The Message of the Psalms: A Theological Commentary* (Minneapolis: Augsburg, 1984); James L. Mays, *The Lord Reigns: A Theological Handbook to the Psalms* (Louisville: Westminster John Knox, 1994); Gerald Wilson, *Psalms*, vol. 1, NIVAC (Grand Rapids: Zondervan, 2002); John Goldingay, *Psalms*, vol. 1 (Grand Rapids: Baker Academic, 2008). On messianic reading of the Psalms, the following works represent a variety of approaches: James L. Mays, 'Old Testament Psalm, Cry of Jesus, and Christian Prayer: Psalm 22', in *Preaching and Teaching the Psalms* (Louisville: Westminster John Knox, 2006), pp. 97–106; Richard P. Belcher, Jr., *The Messiah and the Psalms: Preaching Christ from all the Psalms* (Fearn: Mentor, 2006); Gordon Wenham, 'Reading the Psalms Messianically', in *The Psalter Reclaimed* (Wheaton: Crossway, 2013), pp. 81–102; and chapters 1 and 2 in the present volume.

In putting everything under human beings, God left nothing that is not subject to them. Yet at present we do not see everything subject to them. But we do see Jesus, who was made lower than the angels for a little while, now crowned with glory and honour because he suffered death, so that by the grace of God he might taste death for everyone. (Heb. 2:8–9)[6]

The Psalms bring us a Messiah who is not only human, but who suffers. The untriumphant and distressed king in David's laments is at the centre of this portrait:

Show grace to me O LORD,
    for I'm distressed.
Wasted away with vexation are my eyes,
    my throat and my belly.
For exhausted in sorrow is my life
    and my years in sighing.
Failed in iniquity is my strength,
    and my bones, wasted away.
(Ps. 31:9–10, our tr.)

This weak, oppressed king, who trusts in God regardless, foreshadows the Son of Man whose triumph came through suffering and faithful death.

Gradually, however, we begin to encounter more psalms that point us not to Jesus in his past sufferings, but to Jesus in his present exaltation. The famous Psalm 110 points us to Jesus today, risen and ruling, seated at God's right hand. Its opening line is the New Testament's most-quoted Bible verse: 'The LORD says to my lord:

---

6. Scholars are divided over whether v. 8 refers to Jesus in particular (ESV: 'man'; so D. G. Peterson, *Hebrews and Perfection: An Examination of the Concept of Perfection in the 'Epistle to the Hebrews'* [Cambridge: Cambridge University Press, 1982], pp. 51–54), or to humans in general (NIV: 'human beings'; so P. T. O'Brien, *The Letter to the Hebrews*, PNTC [Nottingham: Apollos; Grand Rapids: Eerdmans, 2010], p. 96). Either way, the specific application of Ps. 8 to Jesus is clear; it is just a matter of whether it begins in v. 6 or v. 9. We hold to the former view.

"Sit at my right hand until I make your enemies a footstool for your feet."' It was this psalm that gave the apostles their teaching on Jesus' exaltation to the right hand of God and his eternal, royal priesthood. Colossians 3:1 is just one example of many allusions to it: 'Since, then, you have been raised with Christ, set your hearts on things above, where Christ is, seated at the right hand of God.'

How do they get their message across?

Each Psalm tells a gospel-shaped story about some aspect of who God is and what he has done; ultimately, what he has done in Jesus. And the Psalms tell us these stories in poetry. Poetry is not exactly an efficient way of communicating information, but it has two great benefits. First, it slows us down. It forces us to read and reread, to ponder, to use our imagination. And secondly, it has the power to engage our spirits and minds with great immediacy. It can create a world for us where we are challenged to see, feel and understand differently.

We do not have to sing the Psalms, because saying them – if the leader has thought long and lovingly about how to do it – can already be an expressive, a dramatic, even a musical, experience. Of course, singing them would be ideal, but the relatively few contemporary settings of the Psalms themselves (rather than songs based on Psalms) tend to be performed rather than sung together.[7] By all means, let our musicians write; but it is far more important that we think hard with our service leaders about what we might do to turn routine and plodding recital of the Psalms into adventures of the imagination, of creativity, of senses come to life. Our task is to bring the gospel alive through the Psalms so that the congregation can re-experience it together as we tell God what he has done – which is praise.

---

7. There is a growing amount of newly composed music on the Internet, such as http://www.sonsofkorah.com and http://www.mattsearles.bandcamp. com. For a good survey of available material in a variety of contemporary idioms see John D. Witvliet, *The Biblical Psalms in Christian Worship: A Brief Introduction and Guide to Resources*, Calvin Institute of Christian Worship Liturgical Studies (Grand Rapids: Eerdmans, 2007), pp. 116–120.

Shortly we will tease out this idea of gospel-shaped stories a little further, as it applies both to the book as a whole and to individual psalms. First, however, we pose a very practical question.

What is stopping us from using the Psalms?

The use of Psalms continues in many branches of the church, though even in churches that maintain a Daily Office less psalmody is set than used to be the case, and the ancient tradition of systematically reciting the whole psalter in a regular cycle is now very rare. In our own evangelical context the speaking, let alone singing, of Psalms is sporadic at best. Why is this the case? Why might people find the Psalms difficult to embrace?

Our personal experience suggests a number of reasons why we shun the Psalms. Experience has also shown that none of these is insurmountable.

1. Precisely because the Psalms are rarely recited, read or sung in our churches their conventions are new and strange. *However* – like any new thing, once one dives in, the strange becomes familiar. One of us (Andrew Cameron), indifferent and somewhat perplexed after years of exposure to drab recitals of Psalms in church, has found himself increasingly mesmerized as a result of coming back to them determined to engage and be engaged. An appetite has developed for more, and the strange is becoming familiar.

2. We hear of God's 'mighty acts' in the Psalms, but if we have internalized our neighbours' unbelief we find it hard to believe God acts mightily. *However* – unbelief in God's mighty acts sometimes simply evaporates when one remembers those acts, and points to them, and talks about them. Psalms are constructed in that way and for that purpose, as an antidote to unbelief.

3. Christians know that the Psalms have something to do with Jesus; but we do not always see what, or how. *However* – a good leader will find it easy to lead the congregation into an experience of the Psalms that is neither individualistic and private, nor aloof and unengaged. We can soon learn to sing with our Messiah as befits those who are brothers and sisters 'in Christ'.

4. We love different things than the psalmist. What the psalmist laments, we do not care about. What the psalmist delights in does not always move us. It is not always easy, or even possible, simply to jump in and sing a praise psalm with all one's heart. *However* – this should not be an issue, precisely because when we participate in the 'prescriptive liturgy' of each psalm, the psalmist shows us our broken imaginations and lost loves. Each psalm will diagnose false loves when we *do not want* to respond in praise. Each works a kind of 'heart surgery' to retrain our love.

5. When we do recite Psalms the occasion can easily be monotonous, routine and even apologetic. The routine of saying Psalms is boring in part because the psalms' ideas and expressions have little hold over us, and can seem only distantly connected to our life together. *However* – if a congregation learns to read psalms as gospel-shaped stories where we can participate through our union with Christ, then our experience will be transformed, and increased usage will slowly draw our imaginations into the thought world of the psalter.

Another cause of boredom is the prosaic way we go about performing the Bible's poetry. We read it efficiently, unimaginatively, superficially, rarely drawn into the world of the poet. Our imaginations are not engaged as they ought to be. *However* – if service leaders put even a fraction of the imagination it took to write the psalms into performing them together, boredom would soon become a thing of the past, as the distance between us and the Psalms began to close. As Brock observes, 'the poetic form (with its inherent linkage with music) expresses an immediacy before God via the text that is at root not critical . . . and hence is destroyed by critical distance'.[8]

In the remainder of this chapter we would like to encourage congregations to revisit the psalter by fleshing out our previous comments about the gospel-shaped stories, the journeys of praise, on which psalms take their readers, and give one or two practical examples of ways in which we can embark on these journeys in a spirit of imagination and discovery.

---

8. Brian Brock, *Singing the Ethos of God: On the Place of Christian Ethics in Scripture* (Grand Rapids: Eerdmans, 2007), p. 176.

Journeys of praise

As many scholars have shown, the anthology of poems that makes up the psalter has been carefully arranged.[9] Not all the principles of arrangement are concerned with the book's narrative scheme,[10] but if we step back far enough we see that this diverse material, a collection of many small collections from many periods of Israel's life, has been shaped at the 'macro' level to take the singer from lament to praise, a journey whose trajectory of descent followed by ascent is fundamentally gospel-shaped.[11] Nowhere is the gospel shape of this journey expressed better than in one of the few new psalms we find in the New Testament, the Christ hymn from Philippians 2:

> Being found in appearance as a man,
>   [Jesus] humbled himself
> by becoming obedient to death –
>   even death on a cross!
> Therefore God exalted him to the highest place
>   and gave him the name that is above every other name . . .
> (Phil. 2:8–9)

It is important not only to recognize that the book of Psalms traces this journey as it follows the career of God's Messiah and the people under his care, but also to recognize that each individual psalm engages with some part of this story in miniature. Psalms of *lament* occupy the descent into the humble regions of this journey, though most at least turn the corner and begin the final ascent. Psalms of *praise* (what Westermann calls descriptive praise[12]) inhabit the exalted

---

9. See the literature listed in n. 5 above, especially the works by McCann (ed.) and Wilson.
10. For example, at the smallest level psalms are often placed next to each other on the basis of shared vocabulary or shared musical style, and not to advance an unfolding plot.
11. For a more detailed account of this journey see chapter 1 in the present volume.
12. Claus Westermann, *The Praise of God in the Psalms* (Richmond: John Knox, 1965), pp. 22–30.

regions where God's faithfulness is celebrated in its fulfilment. And in between these, the psalms of *trust and thanksgiving* (Westermann's 'hymns' and 'songs of thanksgiving') are much more conscious of the corner they have just turned, and may spend equal time on either side of it.[13]

The perspective of the psalter is not limited to the immediate concerns of God's people, but looks to the nations and the creation itself, whose renewal is the purpose for Israel's calling in the first place, and this broader vision frequently shines through psalms of almost every type.[14] A few psalms, such as creation hymns and didactic wisdom psalms, are not caught up in the journey with such immediacy, but contemplate and celebrate the journey and the God of the journey from a thoughtful distance. Wisdom psalms, such as Psalm 1, seek 'to nurture the righteous life'[15] by exhorting the reader of the Psalms to know that Yahweh is God in and over every circumstance, and to live accordingly. As Gerald Wilson has pointed out,[16] these psalms can be found at the margins between the five books of the psalter, and they guide the reader into an appropriate use of the book as a whole.[17]

---

13. Examples of lament psalms include Pss 3 – 7; 11; 13; 30 – 32; 38 – 41; 51; 63; 71; 79; 91; 130; 137; praise psalms, Pss 8; 19; 29; 33; 47; 68; 96 – 100; 104 – 106; 111; 117; 134 – 136; 145 – 150; trust and thanksgiving, Pss 18; 30; 33; 40; 66; 100; 116; 118; 126; 135.

14. See further chapters 11 and 12 in the present volume.

15. W. H. Bellinger, Jr., *Psalms: Reading and Studying the Book of Praises* (Peabody: Hendrickson, 1990), p. 130.

16. 'The Shape of the Book of Psalms', *Int* 46 (1992), pp. 129–142.

17. Note that this analysis differs from the influential schema of Brueggemann (*The Message of the Psalms*), who begins from the same Philippians text (p. 10) but uses it to suggest three phases in the psalms: the celebration of God's graciousness in an initial time of *orientation*; the *disorientation* of suffering and lament; and the final *reorientation* that results from new acts of divine grace to restore the sufferer. A major difficulty with this schema, despite its descriptive power, is the difficulty of distinguishing between psalms of old and new orientation. Brueggemann concedes that this is often difficult and that, depending on the reader's life experience, a single psalm may function as one or the other (p. 22). Even more of a problem is that the psalter as an unfolding story leaves very little room for a time of orientation before the

The recognition that both the psalter as a whole, and the bulk of its psalms (whether of lament, thanksgiving or praise) reflect a gospel-shaped journey of death and resurrection, does not drive us to see each psalm on the lips of Christ; however, it does move us to seeing the psalter's prefigurement of Jesus as emerging from a bringing together of the untriumphant David and the triumphant Messiah, and even to see in the pattern of Israel's national life a Christ-shaped echo. (The example set by Heb. 2:5–9 provides further encouragement to read each psalm in this way.)

That this method of Christian reading is not a brute foisting of later material onto a reluctant text is well argued by Gordon Wenham, who shows that the editors of the psalter were not thinking of some spiritual realization of God's promises, but of a real Davidic kingdom in the future, and one that was to be ruled by a suffering David to boot.[18] The whole-Bible setting of the psalter points us in the right direction when we look for a place to stand as hearers and prayers of the psalms.

We will illustrate what it looks like to speak a psalm in solidarity with Jesus the Christ by thinking briefly about lament.

----

crisis of disorientation. Ps. 2 descends immediately into Ps. 3, and while a creation psalm such as Ps. 8 seems at first glance to be one of 'old orientation', its insight that God acts through weakness (v. 2) gives more than a hint of 'new orientation'. Most hymns that celebrate God's reliability, his creation or his governing law (p. 19) are similarly nuanced by their contents or their place in the psalter. Yes, there are psalms of unshaken confidence in creation 'as a mode of equilibrium, coherence, and reliability', and yes, these affirmations are acts of 'high faith' (p. 31) – but this last insight pushes the genre towards reorientation. It takes a righteous person to perceive the order of creation (Ps. 33:1; p. 36). In short, we believe the storyline of the psalter should have more of a controlling voice in creating a framework for interpretation, so that (for example) the acrostic Ps. 111 in Book 5 reflects not so much God's initial wise order, but the new order won by God for his people and the nations through the experience of Israel's death and restoration in an eschatological kingdom. Like the biblical story of the human race, no sooner are God's people made into a nation than they fall from grace; similarly, the starting point of the Psalms is not a static point but a dynamic movement – a downward slide into death.

18. 'Reading the Psalms Messianically', esp. pp. 94–101.

Lamenting with the Messiah

As soon as we step through the door of Psalms 1 – 2 we find not praises, but lament, or words spoken by those who seem to have lost God:

> My tears have been my food day and night,
> while people say to me all day long, 'Where is your God?'
> (Ps. 42:3)

Many of the psalms of lament arise from David's inner circle: Asaph, Heman, the Sons of Korah. But the Lord's anointed loses God too:

> Save me, O God,
>   for the waters have come up to my neck.
> I sink in the miry depths,
>   where there is no foothold.
> I have come into the deep waters;
>   the floods engulf me.
> I am worn out calling for help;
>   my throat is parched.
> My eyes fail,
>   looking for my God.
> (Ps. 69:1–3)

In Psalm 69 David fears the pit (v. 15, *bě'ēr*). The line between inner despair (vv. 3, 5, 7b, 20) and outward attack (vv. 4, 7b, 8, 11–12, 19) effectively disappears. Only after calling for God's wrath upon his enemies (vv. 22–28) can he imagine praising (vv. 29–36). While it is a psalm that may fit our experience from time to time, it becomes the New Testament authors' favourite psalm to refer to Jesus:

> They hated me without reason (v. 4, in John 15:25)
> I am a foreigner to my own family, a stranger to my own
>   mother's children (v. 8, in Mark 3:21–35)
> Zeal for your house will consume me (v. 9, in John 2:17)
> The insults of those who insult you fall on me (v. 9, in Rom. 15:3)
> They put gall in my food and gave me vinegar for my thirst
>   (v. 21, in Matt. 27:48)

It is also used to refer to those who rejected Jesus:

> May his place be deserted (v. 25, of Judas Iscariot in Acts 1:20)
> May the table set before them become a snare; may it become
>   retribution and a trap. May their eyes be darkened so they
>   cannot see, and their backs be bent for ever (vv. 22–23, in
>   Rom. 11:9–10)

This psalm, which might seem to fit us from time to time, turns out to be about the Messiah; and, in a sense, Jesus the Messiah then gives it back to whoever asks to be his. Jesus knows the pit. He lost God, and died alone. He goes before us, and knows our condition. Much later, Paul says, 'We always carry around in our body the death of Jesus, so that the life of Jesus may also be revealed in our body' (2 Cor. 4:10). Here he hints at a huge discovery the early Christians made: that our suffering can be a kind of sharing in what Jesus went through. That obviously applies to external persecutions, but it can also include inner despair, and even our struggles against sin (e.g. Heb. 12:1, 3; 1 Pet. 4:1–2) – in short, any kind of attack upon the life of faith. All of it is a kind of parallel to Jesus' suffering: he who suffered for the sins of the world, yet declares, 'you suffer with me'.[19] And so we may take his psalms of lament upon our own lips, to help us find God again. The penitential laments show this applying in a particular way to sin. The historical non-specificity of the enemies, of the assaults and of each pit means we can take them to ourselves. Even in our most despairing, God-doubting depressions, we are permitted to say, 'I suffer with the Messiah. He and I are alongside each other in suffering.' There is no greater gift, no greater dignity, no greater kindness to the sufferer. He gives to us his psalms of suffering, and his suffering begins our journey from death to resurrection.

Whatever a given psalm looks like – lament, instruction, thanksgiving, and so on – the act of taking it upon our lips becomes an act of praise. The aim of the rest of this chapter is to explore praise in

---

19. See further Andrew J. Cameron, *Joined-up Life* (Nottingham: Inter-Varsity Press, 2011), pp. 105–107.

its different guises, and to offer some suggestions as to how we might find our way back into these texts together, and train ourselves by them to be a people of praise.

Using the Psalms when Christians gather

The Psalms lend themselves to more varied use than any other book of Scripture. They may be prayed, read or sung together, proclaimed or performed by individuals, and preached on. In addition, their nature as pieces of response makes them perfect accompaniments to almost any other part of Scripture. Their poetic form and richness of imagery opens the door to the use of other media beyond speech and music, such as images and drama. However, in the words of John Witvliet, 'Thoughtful, prayerful use of the Psalms in both public worship and personal devotion requires theological poise, pastoral perception, and artistic imagination – all grounded in the texts themselves.'[20]

Witvliet has provided a valuable compendium of suggestions for how, when and why Christ's gathered people might read or sing psalms together. He offers suggestions for solo and choral readings, antiphons, chants, metrical singing, choral anthems, contemporary and popular musical settings, as well as guidance for prayers, sentences, sermons and translations from the psalms. Our aim here is not to replicate his work, but to supplement it with a few creative suggestions for corporate Christian appropriation of the Psalms.

Recovering communal lament: Psalm 44

Most laments are individual, but in about fifteen psalms the community stands shoulder to shoulder, calling upon God.[21] These communal psalms reveal most strikingly our individualism. We simply do not do this any more. We do mourn together at a funeral,

---

20. Witvliet, *Biblical Psalms*, p. 15.

21. Pss 12, 44, 58, 60, 74, 79, 80, 83, 85, 89, 90, 94, 123, 126, 129 are all candidates.

and process our collective grief by talking about our departed friend, but we do not lament in the manner of these psalms. And yet communal lament – lament by the people and for the people – is an essential part of reorienting to what matters. It calls us out of our own heads, and into the world together, the world that should know the Lord's anointed King, but is yet enslaved to his raging, mocking opponents.

- We may lament together for the people in our own *congregation*: the tradesman or mother or doctor or high-school student who is mocked and oppressed for following the Christ.
- We may lament together for *other Christians* we know: the pastor, the footballer, the politician, who are pilloried for their faith in Christ.
- We may lament for the *Christians we do not know*: the North African, the Subcontinental, the Scandinavian, the Indonesian, who follows Christ and brings down very tangible and violent enemies.
- We may lament for *all those people among fallen humanity* who are ground down by tyrants; for the widows and children who know no Messiah, and know no peace; for the victims of natural disaster and war and greed who do not 'know that I am God'.

The example we have chosen involves the interpretation of a lament psalm by projected images. Visual images can be a dangerous addition to spoken words, because they can so easily convey un-intended messages. However, in a psalm filled with verbal images Christian readers are invited to reimagine in the light of their fulfil-ment in Christ; visual images can be as powerful an interpretative instrument as a sermon. The following version of Psalm 44 (from the NIV) divides the psalm into captions the congregation reads out together, placed under images designed to reposition the psalm hermeneutically. Even a single well-chosen image per stanza would work. The specific images in our example reflect an Australian context.

Table 7.1 A visual reinterpretation of Psalm 44

Psalm 44 text, projected as captions . . .	. . . *beneath a series of images*

1 We have heard it with our ears, O God;
   our ancestors have told us
what you did in their days,
   in days long ago.
2 With your hand you drove out the nations
   and planted our ancestors;
you crushed the peoples
   and made our ancestors flourish.
3 It was not by their sword that they won the land,
   nor did their arm bring them victory;
it was your right hand, your arm,
   and the light of your face, for you loved them.
	Billy Graham crusades, churches packed with people in 1950s clothing, politicians in suits praying, other signs of a culture penetrated by the gospel.

4 You are my King and my God,
   who decrees victories for Jacob.
5 Through you we push back our enemies;
   through your name we trample our foes.
6 I put no trust in my bow,
   my sword does not bring me victory;
7 but you give us victory over our enemies,
   you put our adversaries to shame.
8 In God we make our boast all day long,
   and we will praise your name for ever.
	Contemporary images of successful evangelism: a pair of university students reading the Bible, a preacher, a hospital or military chaplain at work.

9 But now you have rejected and humbled us;
   you no longer go out with our armies.
10 You made us retreat before the enemy,
   and our adversaries have plundered us.
11 You gave us up to be devoured like sheep
   and have scattered us among the nations.
12 You sold your people for a pittance,
   gaining nothing from their sale.
	A half-empty church service, a fashionable couple relaxing in an expensive house overlooking water, a church building closed up with people from many cultures walking past.

13 You have made us a reproach to our neighbours,
   the scorn and derision of those around us.
14 You have made us a byword among the nations;
   the peoples shake their heads at us.
15 I live in disgrace all day long,
   and my face is covered with shame
16 at the taunts of those who reproach and revile me,
   because of the enemy, who is bent on revenge.
	An atheist apologist attacking a Christian spokesman, a comedian mocking the church, a priest arrested for child abuse.

17 All this came upon us,   *A family reading the Bible together,*
   though we had not forgotten you;   *our own congregation singing joyfully.*
   we had not been false to your covenant.
18 Our hearts had not turned back;
   our feet had not strayed from your path.
19 But you crushed us and made us a haunt for
       jackals;
   you covered us over with deep darkness.

20 If we had forgotten the name of our God   *Someone kneeling in prayer . . .*
   or spread out our hands to a foreign god,
21 would not God have discovered it,
   since he knows the secrets of the heart?
22 Yet for your sake we face death all day long; *. . . at the foot of the cross.*
   we are considered as sheep to be slaughtered.

23 Awake, Lord! Why do you sleep?   *(dark)*
   Rouse yourself! Do not reject us forever.
24 Why do you hide your face
   and forget our misery and oppression?
25 We are brought down to the dust;
   our bodies cling to the ground.
26 Rise up and help us;   *The empty tomb.*
   rescue us because of your unfailing love.

An example of communal trust: Psalm 126

A less adventurous way to reposition a psalm in the readers' theological imagination is to interpret it by juxtaposition with New Testament texts. In the following example – an interleaving of Psalm 126 with words from 1 Corinthians 15 – an individual voice delivers Paul's text to shape our theological imagination as we perform the psalm.

If only for this life we have hope in Christ, we are of all people most to be pitied. But Christ has indeed been raised from the dead, the firstfruits of those who have fallen asleep. (1 Cor. 15:19–21)

When the LORD restored the fortunes of Zion,
    we were like those who dreamed.
Our mouths were filled with laughter,
    our tongues with songs of joy.
Then it was said among the nations,
    'The LORD has done great things for them.'

The LORD has done great things for us,
     and we are filled with joy.

Listen, I tell you a mystery: We will not all sleep, but we will all be
changed – in a flash, in the twinkling of an eye, at the last trumpet.
(1 Cor. 15:51–52)

Restore our fortunes, LORD,
     like streams in the Negev.
Those who sow with tears
     will reap with songs of joy.
Those who go out weeping,
     carrying seed to sow,
will return with songs of joy,
     carrying sheaves with them.

A thanksgiving drama: Psalm 118

Apart from hearing it in Christian accents, the challenge of a psalm
like this is that, on our own, we are notoriously poor at reminding
ourselves of what God has done, and our default mode is thankless-
ness. Admittedly, any mention of a formula or anything prescriptive
takes us right back to our earlier objections: 'This is telling me to
feel something I don't feel: it's inauthentic.' But Psalm 1 promises
us that to love and take refuge in the Lord and his anointed is to
become our true righteous self.

Because the thanksgiving psalms often push us beyond where we
are comfortable to be, the following performance suggestion is
designed to give us a Christ-shaped structure by which to enter into
the action of the poem. It is fairly elaborate, and would probably be
for a once-only occasion, assuming the congregation was well
disposed to such experimentation. It might work best after a sermon
on the psalm. The following paragraph could serve as an explanation
to the congregation.

'We have turned Psalm 118 into a script for the dramatic re-
enactment of Jesus' resurrection. Humans love to relive a great win,
blow by blow. So we are going to relive the triumphant resurrection
of our Lord Jesus together – in fact, we are going to re-enact it in
a victory ceremony. The speaker representing the solo voice of

Table 7.2 A theatrical reinterpretation of Psalm 118

Psalm 118, marked for dramatic reading	Performance directions

1 Give thanks to the LORD, for he is good;
  His faithfulness is for ever!
2 Let Israel now say,
  His faithfulness is for ever!
3 Let Aaron's house now say,
  His faithfulness is for ever!
4 Let those who fear the LORD now say,
  His faithfulness is for ever!
	Call and response, leader to (shouting) **people**.

5 *From narrow straits I cried to GOD;*
  GOD answered me with spaciousness.
6 *The LORD is for me; I'll not fear.*
  What can people do to me?
7 *The LORD is for me as my helper,*
  and I will stare my foes down.
	Solo voice at the rear, with a travelling mike so she can speak thoughtfully when called for.

8 It is better to shelter in the LORD
  than to trust in a human being.
9 **It is better to shelter in the LORD**
  than to trust in leaders.
	Leader, then **people**, but not shouting.

10 All the nations surrounded me;
  with the name of the LORD I cut them
    down.
11 They did surround me, yes, they surrounded
  me;
  with the name of the LORD I cut them
    down.
12 They surrounded me like bees;
  they burned up like a fire of thorns;
  with the name of the LORD I cut them
    down.
	Distant drums accompany vv. 10–12, and during their recital the *soloist* processes to next stopping point. After 5 seconds of drums the call and **response** begins, with drums stopping before v. 13.

13 *You shoved me hard to make me fall,*
  but the LORD – he helped me.
14 *The LORD is my strength and my song;*
  He has become my salvation.
	Solo voice, by now stopped a third of the way to the front.

15 There are shouts of joy and victory
  in the tents of the righteous:
  'The LORD's right hand strikes with power!
16 'The LORD's right hand is raised!
  'The LORD's right hand strikes with power!'
	Drums again, perhaps other instruments, accompanying the call and **response** of vv. 15–16; *soloist* processes as before to stop at next point.

17 *I will not die, but I will live*
  and proclaim what the LORD has done.
18 *The LORD disciplined me severely*
  but did not give me over to death.
	Solo voice, two-thirds of the way forward.

19 Open for me the gates of the righteous;
  **I will enter through them
  and give thanks to the LORD.**
20 This is the gate of the LORD;
  the righteous may enter through it.
21 **I will give thanks to you
  for you answered me;
  you have become my salvation.**
22 *The stone that the builders rejected
  has become the cornerstone.*
23 **This came from the LORD;
  it is marvellous in our eyes.**
24 **This is the day the LORD has made;
  let us rejoice and be glad in it.**

25 *LORD, save us!*
  LORD, please grant us success!
26 *Blessed is he who comes in the name of the LORD.*
  From the house of the LORD we bless you.
27 *The LORD is God and has given us light.*
  **Bind the festival sacrifice with cords
  to the horns of the altar.**
28 *You are my God, and I will praise you;*
  you are my God, and I will exalt you.

29 *Give thanks to the LORD, for he is good;*
  His faithfulness is for ever!

As well as drums etc., a barrier at the front row of seating could be drawn back, or arms stretched into the aisle lifted to make an arch to allow the *soloist* to mount a podium at the front.

Solo voice, from the front.

The climax. Perhaps sing a version of v. 24.

From this point on, the **people** are addressed by the **leader** and the **soloist** together.

End with the same call-and-**response** that began the Psalm.

Jesus (we suggest a female, to underline that she is not pretending to be Jesus, but is one of us, a "re-enactor") will start at the back of the room, in the grave, and gradually move to an elevated place of resurrection at the front. Each stage of her progress will be accompanied by drums and a "chorus" of onlookers. The chorus (i.e. the congregation) observes her progress and takes Jesus' words onto their lips in a triumphant reliving together of his victory.'[22]

Singing the praises of God: Psalm 146

According to its Hebrew title the entire book of Psalms is a book of 'praises' (*těhillîm*), but it is only because of the way it ends that

---

22. The translation has been somewhat modified from the NIV, with the help of Robert Alter.

we can characterize the often painful journey as a journey of praise. By the same token, the praise that fills the psalms at journey's end (Pss 145 – 150) derives its character from the descent into death that preceded it.

These final psalms are places where all is right in God's world: where God is near to all who call on him (145:18), where he feeds the hungry and frees the prisoners (146:7), where he gathers the exiles of Israel (147:2), where all creation praises its God (148) and all opposing powers are shackled (149:8). How can we sing these songs in a foreign land, with the shadow of death still hanging over us?

By the end of the journey we know the answer. Even in our darkest times we have found God's faithfulness and love so all-sufficient that we now 'get it': to have God is to have all his goodness and joy and blessings as well. Of course there will come a day when death really is defeated and creation really will be renewed, but the psalmist does not need to wait for that day, because everything that really matters about heaven he has right now: the presence of his precious Lord. In the words of Psalm 73:28, 'the nearness of God is my good'.

We do not always feel God's nearness, but there is a very real sense in which praise brings God near. Praise has the power to release us from the fears and frustrations of a fallen world, and to make us notice God afresh, and marvel in him anew, and exult in what he has done. Praise can make the invisible God visible to us in any and every place.

And more than this, praise draws us into the life of God himself. Remember that this is the praise of the Messiah; this is the new song our Saviour sings as he praises his Father for bringing him through his sacrificial death to sit down at his right hand. This is the purpose of our existence, to be drawn up in Christ into the eternal praise of God. There is nothing more important, nothing more perfect, nothing more precious, nothing more glorious, than to come before God and praise him!

Some of the examples we have provided are fairly elaborate, and so we finish with a 'bread-and-butter' suggestion, which could easily be made into a weekly staple with the help of a sympathetic musician. First, rather than having everyone speak the psalm (which can grow rather mundane), or chant it (an activity culturally alien to the present generation), let a well-prepared reader speak the psalm over a musical accompaniment. Then, have the congregation sing a brief chorus, technically known as an 'antiphon', after each natural break. The antiphon is typically a verse from the psalm that distils its message, but our preference is to give it a Christological twist, to help the congregation recognize that they sing in and with Christ our Lord. The antiphon should be simple enough to learn in thirty seconds, before the reading begins.

> *Antiphon: Christ reigns for ever, your God, O Zion, for all generations.*
> Hallelujah!
> Praise the LORD, my soul.
> I will praise the LORD all my life;
>> I will sing praise to my God as long as I live.
> *Christ reigns for ever,*
>> *your God, O Zion, for all generations.*
> Do not put your trust in princes,
>> in human beings, who cannot save.
> When their spirit departs, they return to the ground;
>> on that very day their plans come to nothing.
> *Christ reigns for ever,*
>> *your God, O Zion, for all generations.*
> Blessed are those whose help is the God of Jacob,
>> whose hope is in the LORD their God.
> He is the Maker of heaven and earth,
>> the sea, and everything in them –
>> he remains faithful for ever.
> *Christ reigns for ever,*
>> *your God, O Zion, for all generations.*
> He upholds the cause of the oppressed
>> and gives food to the hungry.
> The LORD sets prisoners free,
>> the LORD gives sight to the blind,
> the LORD lifts up those who are bowed down,
>> the LORD loves the righteous.
> *Christ reigns for ever,*
>> *your God, O Zion, for all generations.*

The LORD watches over the foreigner
   and sustains the fatherless and the widow,
   but he frustrates the ways of the wicked.
The LORD reigns for ever,
   your God, O Zion, for all generations.
Hallelujah!
(Ps. 146)

Conclusion

As we read and absorb the whole variety of the psalms, they catch us up into the life of the Messiah, and by accompanying him on his journey of suffering and glory we enthrone God on our praises. That we sing together is very profound, for as we praise God using the words he has given us to praise him with, we join the Son in his praises, and they accompany our praises into the Father's presence. We gather together in church to be met by God, and to meet him together, shoulder to shoulder, bound together in the unity of the Spirit into one body, drawing near to the Father through his Son, our human and divine king. Songs do not get much newer than that.

8. THE PSALMS OF LAMENT IN THE EXPERIENCE OF SUFFERING CHRISTIANS

Tara J. Stenhouse[1]

Pain and suffering are part of the reality of life in this world as we wait for Jesus to return. As believers, how are we to cope with this pain? How are we to lament well? Throughout history the Psalms have played an important part in ministering to suffering Christians. We could say that they are a handbook for Christian lamenting.

This chapter will discuss the experience of fellow-believers – in their suffering, their reading of the Psalms and their service of those who are suffering. These observations are based on quantitative and qualitative studies, gathered from surveys and personal interviews.[2]

---

1. With the editing help of Emma Little, student at Moore College.
2. An anonymous online survey was sent out to a selection of the Moore Theological College community, my own church and my wider Christian community. Fifty-four people responded (65% women, 35% men; average age 37, age range 19–73; 75% attending Anglican churches; 95% currently living in Australia; 80% born in Australia). A follow-up survey had 38 people respond. The surveys were a mix of quantitative and qualitative responses. I also interviewed three contacts who have experienced significant pain and testify to the importance of the Psalms as they suffer.

We will learn from these experiences something of the reality of pain, people's responses to pain and the nature of the Psalms, focusing on the psalms of lament in particular as a healing balm and comfort to suffering Christians.[3] We will also learn of the confusion some have had as they read the Psalms and times when the psalms of lament are not as comforting as we think. Lastly, we will reflect on some implications for ministering personally and publicly to Christians in pain.[4]

My hope is that we will see the real healing balm of the Psalms as we ourselves suffer and serve those who suffer. We will be encouraged to be more proactive in teaching and using the psalms of lament in our churches, ministries and our own lives, realizing what we miss if we neglect them.

The reality of pain

'We were in a pit that we couldn't get ourselves out of.'[5]

Many others shared their experiences along the way. I am thankful for all those who have contributed their experiences and wisdom.

3. Almost half of all 150 psalms are psalms of lament (either personal lament, corporate lament, lament of repentance or lament of imprecation). The most common format is usually complaint ('a cry for help and description of distress') in the first person, petition ('an appeal to God and reasons for divine intervention') and praise ('ends on note of certainty that the prayer has been heard and a vow to praise God for deliverance'), with many variations to this – as described by Terry L. Smith, 'Darkness Is My Closest Friend: Using the Psalms of Lament to Address Grief Issues', North American Association of Christians in Social Work (NACSW) Convention 2007 <http://www.nacsw.org/Publications/Proceedings2007/SmithTDarkenessClosestFriendE.pdf>, accessed 8 Apr. 2012. Claus Westermann's work on the forms of lament has been influential in this (*Praise and Lament in the Psalms* [Atlanta: John Knox, 1981], pp. 52–55, 64–71).

4. While my own reading of the Psalms and secondary readings has contributed to this chapter, its focus is on how experientially the Psalms (especially the psalms of lament) minister to suffering Christians.

5. In an attempt to capture the reality of the experience of fellow-believers, their actual words will be quoted throughout.

There is no doubt that pain is real, and we do not have to look too far to realize this, in our own lives or in the lives of those around us. Suffering is real and pervasive; very few people are untouched by it. The figure below shows responses to the occurrence of pain and suffering that the people surveyed (the respondents) have experienced.

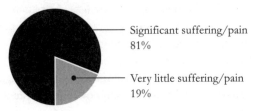

Significant suffering/pain
81%

Very little suffering/pain
19%

Figure 8.1 The experience of suffering/pain.

Eighty-one per cent of respondents had experienced significant suffering and pain at some time in their lives, while only 19% reported that they had experienced very little suffering or pain.[6] No one reported that they had experienced no pain or suffering.

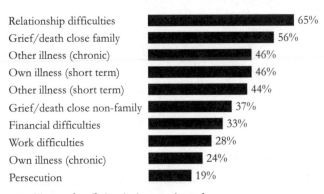

Relationship difficulties	65%
Grief/death close family	56%
Other illness (chronic)	46%
Own illness (short term)	46%
Other illness (short term)	44%
Grief/death close non-family	37%
Financial difficulties	33%
Work difficulties	28%
Own illness (chronic)	24%
Persecution	19%

Figure 8.2 Types of suffering/pain experienced.

The pain and suffering of respondents took many different forms, from personal illness and health difficulties to the illness or death of others, which in itself brings grief and its own share of difficulty.

---

6. Those who experienced little pain or suffering were 45 years old or younger (average age = 34).

The most common pain experienced was relationship difficulties (65%), followed by the death of a close relative (56%). There were significant levels of illness (of self and others, including chronic illness such as depression, suicidal tendencies, infertility), as well as financial difficulties. Nineteen per cent of respondents had experienced persecution for being a believer – a reminder that we live in a world opposed to God and critical of us as Christians.

The following quotes show how some of those people surveyed felt during times of pain and suffering.

'It was an intensely emotional time.'

'I experienced the full spread of emotions – numb, raging against God and against the situation, to a kind of dull acceptance, a desire to resolve things emotionally.'

'I didn't have the energy to go to God during that time.'

'I felt very distant from God.'

'It was a source of distress in terms of our viewing God as good, gracious and faithful to us.'

'It was hard to focus and concentrate on anything.'

'It was nearly impossible to get work done.'

'Life was in slow motion.'

'I became quite distant from everyone.'

'It was very isolating; I felt very alone, as though no one quite understood what I was going through; I couldn't make sense of what I was experiencing and feeling and express that to others.'

'I felt helpless.'

'We were in a pit that we couldn't get ourselves out of.'

Pain is clearly real and devastating, but how do we respond to this pain, in ourselves and others?

Responding to pain

'We rob grieving people of being able to grieve.'

Usually we do not know what to do; it is paralysing and overwhelming, so we often withdraw and hide our pain, trying to deal with it by ourselves with a stoic attitude. We compare our suffering to someone else's and realize they are worse off, or we try to cheer

ourselves up with our strong theology – things are all right because
God is in control, he loves us, and one day there will be no pain.

Why do we respond in this way? Why do we largely deny our
pain? There is a strong cultural element to this. It is what most people
in our society, including Christian circles, do. Personally and publicly
we deny pain and suffering, pretending they do not exist. We do not
say much about suffering because we do not want to see it in people
and we do not want to hear about it. Catherine[7] shared her observations about this, after the death of her son from leukaemia a few
years before. As she and her family went through the suffering of
leukaemia and then the ongoing grief over the loss of her son, she
was struck by the way Christians and others responded (and continue
to respond) to her. She feels that as a society we want to eliminate
all pain. We want to medicate everything and find 'quick-fix'
solutions, ways to take control. Christians and churches fall into a
similar trap. We use platitudes or quote verses meant to make people
feel better. We try to fix people, answering the 'why' questions, trying
to bypass the pain and rushing to a happy ending.

It is not surprising that those in pain respond by withdrawing or
denying it. Catherine's major observation is that we do not give
people permission to really feel what they are feeling: we do not
allow people to be real. We rob a grieving person of being able to
grieve, and this only rubs salt into the wound. For a person already
going through pain and suffering it is worse when they are around
Christians, because we will not let them be real. Everyone seems to
be happy. Our songs, prayers and sermons are safe, our prayers
polite, controlled and unemotional.

Catherine's experience is far from unique. It has long been
observed that we have lost the ability to lament in our churches.[8]
We will not give permission for people to find life difficult. Failure

---

7. Names have been changed.
8. E.g. Walter Brueggemann, *Spirituality of the Psalms* (Minneapolis: Fortress,
   2002), pp. 25–27; Michael Jinkins, *In the House of the Lord: Inhabiting the
   Psalms of Lament* (Collegeville, Minn.: Liturgical Press, 1998), p. 36; Paul
   Bradbury, *Sowing in Tears: How to Lament in a Church of Praise* (Cambridge:
   Grove, 2007), pp. 3–7.

to cope with life is seen as weakness; questioning God and complaining to God about one's pain is often taken as a lack of faith.

How, then, can we respond more adequately to the pain of those around us?

The lament psalms as healing balm for suffering Christians

'They are often the only source of comfort when I'm suffering.'

The Psalms, and especially the psalms of lament, can provide great comfort to believers. What is more, they can help us to lament well. The majority of those surveyed testified to the Psalms' ability to minister to them during their suffering.

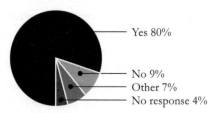

Figure 8.3 Have the Psalms ministered to you during your suffering/pain?

When respondents benefited from reading the Psalms during their suffering it was mainly during their own personal Bible reading, often with the encouragement of a friend (in a letter, email or conversation). Many have listened to the Psalms in song and read them with a friend. One person has even created artworks inspired by the Psalms.

Suffering Christians testify to the ministry of the Psalms to them during their pain. Catherine speaks of them as 'healing balm'; for Alison, they are the only source of comfort when she is suffering. Many others also used the word 'comfort' to describe the ministry of the Psalms.

What is it about the Psalms that provides such comfort to those in pain? How does one go about lamenting well from the Psalms? What does God's handbook of Christian lament say to his people? The responses of those I surveyed can be grouped into seven areas,

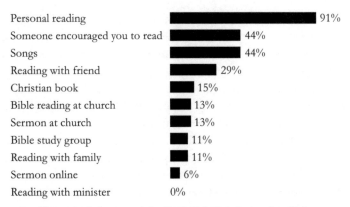

Personal reading	91%
Someone encouraged you to read	44%
Songs	44%
Reading with friend	29%
Christian book	15%
Bible reading at church	13%
Sermon at church	13%
Bible study group	11%
Reading with family	11%
Sermon online	6%
Reading with minister	0%

Figure 8.4 How people have read the Psalms during times of suffering.

seven ways the Psalms, especially the lament psalms, offer healing, comfort and help.[9]

The psalms of lament acknowledge the reality of suffering and pain

'The honesty of the psalmist – expressing dismay and anger as well as joy – is real and relatable.'

The lament psalms acknowledge the reality of suffering and pain. They speak of agony (Pss 13:2; 48:6),[10] desperation (88:15), abandonment (38:21; 71:9; 88:5), being afflicted (10:2, 9, 12; 25:16, 18; 70:5) and consumed (31:10), feeling weak (79:8; 102[title]; 143:4), helpless (10:14; 72:13; 116:6), overwhelmed (55:5; 88:7) and stuck in a pit (40:2; 57:6; 88:6). As one respondent said, 'Every life situation and human emotion is expressed'; another spoke of 'a display of raw and real emotions that people can relate to'. We identify easily with the Psalms because they match the reality of our lives. They speak of life in the real world, which is full of death, pain and hardship.

---

9. The categories used here are particularly influenced by Smith, 'Darkness Is My Closest Friend'.

10. The terms in this list come from HCSB; other versions contain a similar set of words.

The Psalms acknowledge that life is hard; here there is no pretence that life is easy. They are honest about how terrible life can be, that there will be times when we cannot cope. In the lament psalms suffering and pain are acknowledged as normal and to be expected: 'The Psalms are respectful of our situation and realistic about it,' says Catherine; for another respondent 'they are unapologetic in their expectation that life won't be easy'.

This validates and normalizes the pain people are experiencing. Catherine continues, 'They give us permission to be real and to feel awful, when others often don't let you be real or negate the pain.' This is a pain from which God himself is not removed – Christ Jesus entered our world and experienced the reality and horror of pain and suffering.

The psalms of lament give a voice to this suffering

> 'They helped me to express my feelings and thoughts to God when I didn't have the strength to do it myself.'

In the lament psalms we have permission to be real with God and to cry out in pain, something we might not otherwise think we were allowed to do. It is often seen as sinful to question God, to accuse him, to say that God has abandoned us, but that is how it feels for many people, and if we cannot tell God how we feel, where else can we go? 'The lament psalms remind me that I am, as a child of God, able to express the sorrow of my heart candidly and at length.' Jesus shows this on the cross: he was real with God, crying out in pain, and he articulated his suffering by taking on the agonized words of Psalm 22:1, 'My God, my God, why have you forsaken me?'

So not only do the lament psalms give us permission to be real with God and cry out in pain, but they give us a language to do so. Often those who are in pain and trying to express their feelings find that they do not have the words. Many respondents testified to this: 'They give words to difficult situations where we feel unable to pray or to voice our discomfort.'

Why do we not have the words to express our pain? Part of the reason seems to be that there is an absence of talking about and expressing pain in our society and the church, as mentioned earlier, but also – and more deeply – because pain is inherently language shattering. It takes our words away. Pain and suffering suppress us at the deepest level, including our voice. There is much evidence that when people go through trauma, pain and suffering, they lose their words. Elaine Scarry, a doctor whose research on pain has a particular focus in the area of torture, finds that those in great pain are left unable to communicate.[11] In his summary of Scarry's findings William Cavanagh says that 'pain does not merely resist language but actively destroys it'.[12] Torture is about unmaking persons so that they cease to exist as identifiable agents.[13] Part of unmaking people includes taking away their speech, for 'if pain destroys language so too it destroys the world of the prisoner, for it is through language that a person's world is constructed'.[14]

It follows that in the midst of pain and suffering there is a need for the reality of our pain to be expressed. In order to let people grieve, they need a language to do so, words by which to work through their suffering. As Brueggemann reflects, 'the only counter to torture is speech. As torture unmakes persons, so speech makes persons.'[15] This is why 'therapy for torture victims is centered on recovering their voice, allowing them to conceptualize and verbalize their anguish'.[16] 'It is speech which lets us discover the power, depth and intensity of the hurt,'[17] and the lament psalms can help us do that. As one respondent said, 'They express what I want to feel, even when because of distress I'm not there yet.' It is greatly comforting to have the words of the psalm to help one understand what one is feeling and thinking.

---

11. Elaine Scarry, *The Body in Pain: The Making and Unmaking of the World* (Oxford: Oxford University Press, 1985).

12. William T. Cavanagh, *Torture and Eucharist: Theology, Politics, and the Body of Christ* (Cambridge: Cambridge University Press, 1997), p. 34.

13. Walter Brueggemann, 'Voice as Counter to Violence', *CTJ* 36 (2001), p. 23, again summarizing Elaine Scarry.

14. Cavanagh, *Torture and Eucharist*, p. 36.

15. As discussed in Brueggemann, 'Voice', p. 23.

16. Cavanagh, *Torture and Eucharist*, p. 42.

17. Walter Brueggemann, *Praying the Psalms: Engaging Scripture and the Life of the Spirit* (Eugene, Oreg.: Cascade, 2007), p. 66.

Solidarity in suffering

*'Reading the Psalms is like having other people join me in my Christian walk. I'm
not alone.'*

One of the biggest problems with grief and pain is that people feel
so alone and abandoned. The nature of pain means that only you
can experience it and so in this way it is isolating; only you can grieve
in the way you do. But the lament psalms remind us that we are not
alone. They show us that God is with us in our suffering; he understands our afflictions and entered into suffering for us. Jesus prayed
these prayers as he suffered, and we are reading the same psalms
Jesus read.[18]

In the end Jesus was alone in his suffering, abandoned by his
followers, even his closest friends, and in some way abandoned
by God the Father at his death. Ultimately, however, he knew that
God would vindicate him, that God was with him – hence Jesus'
use of Psalm 31:5 in Luke 23:46. In taking psalmists' words on his
lips Jesus showed himself to be in solidarity with the suffering
people of God in the past. Jesus knew that he was not alone in his
suffering.

So we have companions with us in our suffering. We are not the
only ones who have ever suffered: we are reading the words of those
who suffered before us, especially our Lord Jesus, and we are in
concert with a long line of sufferers. This reduces the sense of
isolation. 'We have fellowship with the Psalm writers in crying
out in distress,' said one respondent; another, 'The Psalms are our
common voice with saints across the span of time.'

Most importantly of all, the psalms of lament remind us that
God is with us in our suffering. Even if we do not feel it or if we
feel abandoned, the Psalms testify that God sees and hears everything (Pss 11:4; 139:1); he hears our cries and prayers (6:9;
94:9); he cares and is concerned (27:10; 95:7); he is our helper
(10:14; 46:1; 54:4; 118:7), rock (18:2, 31, 46; 31:2–3; 62:2), stronghold (18:2; 27:1; 46:7, 11), protector (121:3–4) and refuge (9:9; 31:4;

---

18. E.g. Ps. 22:1, in Matt. 27:46 and Mark 15:34.

46:1; 57:1; 62:8). God is powerful, strong, mighty (Pss 62:7; 89:8; 140:7) and he is in the dark pit with us when we feel helpless. The Psalms speak of God's holding our hand (Pss 37:24; 63:8; 73:23; 139:10); he will ultimately bring us through these things. 'He will not let our foot slip,' said one person, remembering Psalm 121:3.

An invitation to turn to God

'The Psalms helped me to cling to God at all times'

Suffering Christians love the fact that the lament psalms invite them to turn to God and call on him in prayer. They draw people out of themselves and into a lively communion with God. In the words of one respondent, 'They keep God in the centre of one's complaint when enduring suffering rather than pushing him to the side or ignoring him completely.' And again, 'They invite us to call out to God in prayer, becoming the voice and words of my prayer.'

Expressing our pain, crying out to God in agony and questioning God can be seen as a lack of faith, but in fact the reverse is the case. The lament psalms cultivate a robust and bold faith in the midst of suffering. One respondent put it this way: 'The picture is of an extremely raw and deep relationship where the believer has such a deep faith they really expect the work of God in their lives.' For another, 'They helped me to channel my anger into prayer, to teach me the patience to wait on the Lord, and not to act on his behalf.' In this way we are following our Lord Jesus, who turned to God in prayer with great vigour, pleading that he would not need to die and entrusting himself to God (Matt. 26:39, 42; Mark 14:36; Luke 22:42).

In short, the lament psalms acknowledge that God is our only hope – there is no one else to turn to (Pss 33:17, 22; 62:5, 10; 71:5, 14; 131:3). These psalms are relational and personal. They are about genuine conversation with God, encouraging a real relationship with him. Catherine said, 'They remind us of the most important relationship, . . . [showing] that our relationship with God is intact, regardless of the circumstances.'

Hope amid suffering

'They show that human frailty and hopelessness is overwhelmed by God's eternal faithfulness and love.'

The lament psalms give us enormous hope in the midst of despair: 'They steady our heart, nourish our faith, and restore our soul because they give us a big and eternal perspective,' said Catherine. What kind of hope do they give? They show that we have the security of relationship with God in the midst of the pain. Life might be dark and difficult, an emotional roller coaster, but the God of the Psalms is King (Pss 10:16; 24:7–10; 29:10; 47:2), and because of Jesus we can safely call him our God. In the Psalms God is with his people. 'He is mighty and personal and will set things right,' wrote one respondent. Catherine shared that the Psalms remind her that 'there is something more important than our pain that can't be taken away', that is, relationship with God – which in Christ is eternally secure by faith. The Psalms provide a picture of God's protectiveness and stability. He is a shelter (Pss 119:114; 121:5; 142:5), a stronghold, and under his wings we find refuge (17:8; 36:7; 57:1; 61:4; 63:7; 91:4).

The Psalms also minister to suffering Christians by giving a magnificent picture of the future, the perspective of eternal salvation. Catherine had much to say about this magnificent picture of the future: 'It doesn't negate the pain, but puts it in perspective, so that you can get your bearings straight.' Other respondents affirmed this: 'They remind me of the bigger picture than my immediate situation'; they 'lifted my eyes above the situation'. With the perspective of Jesus as the Christ and God's plans centring on him, we see in the Psalms the promise that one day God will rescue us and get rid of all sin, enemies, illness and suffering. There is a sure hope of rescue, because God promised it and in the Psalms we see God's faithfulness to his promises everywhere. Because of all of this Catherine said, 'There is no reason ever to abandon relationship with God.'

The lament psalms remind us of what we know to be true about God and the world but find hard to express because of the pain. We need these reminders. As one respondent shared, 'They remind me to take refuge in God, to see things from his perspective and point me to Jesus and God's sovereignty.' The Psalms encourage us to wait patiently for the Lord (Pss 27:14; 33:20; 37:7, 34; 40:1; 130:5–6). For another, the Psalms show that 'things are bigger than my troubles and that God does answer us, even if his timing is different to ours. God does keep his promises and he will help me through the tough times.'

Guidance on the journey of grief

'They move through the experience of suffering to an affirmation of trust in God in the midst of pain.'

Suffering Christians have valued the shape of the lament psalms in providing a structure for the process and journey of grief itself, giving guidance about how to go about one's journey through the ups and downs of life.

In the midst of suffering we often do not know what to do or where to turn; we do not have the energy or capacity to work through the pain. So the shape of the psalms of lament is a gift from God, showing us how to suffer and grieve, as Jesus did. The lament psalms usually move from complaint to petition to praise. 'They refuse to allow us to rush to a happy ending,' as Catherine put it. They allow one to go through the normal process of grief. Andrew testified quite strongly to this: the lament psalms 'gave us words to shape our grief and walk us through the journey, under the umbrella of God's care and our trust of him'. In particular, Andrew found 'especially helpful . . . the Psalms where there is a metaphoric journey through the pit, because that's exactly how we felt – that we were in a pit that we couldn't get ourselves out of and needed to appeal to God'. Another respondent commented that 'they are a container, a form, that acknowledges and gives critical voice to the reality of our pain and which drives us on towards a reassertion of the goodness and the fidelity of God'.

One implication of this is that the psalms of lament prepare us for suffering beforehand. We want to read them before we suffer, so that they become familiar friends with us during any suffering. One respondent reported, 'Often the Psalms ministered indirectly and I have not always felt the full direct force during actual suffering, but it is more that any familiarity with the Psalms before encountering suffering prepares me for it and for reflecting on it when it has passed. The Psalms have helped me to process that experience and dwell on it helpfully.'

Help in the form of Psalms

'When I don't have the strength and mental and emotional energy to think deeply, I read Psalms to keep hearing God speak.'

Suffering Christians have found that the form of the lament psalms (not just their content) is key to their healing and comfort. But what is it about the form of the lament psalms that is so helpful and accessible?

First, they are short and self-contained. For those who cannot read anything else they are manageable. They are 'often short enough so people think they can read a whole one, even if they are feeling overwhelmed'. One woman shared her experience of the Psalms during a period of suffering: 'I couldn't sit and concentrate, but I could sit and read a short psalm and this was quite manageable – it might take five minutes but five minutes each day adds up and got me thinking about God and put helpful thoughts into my mind.'

Secondly, they are poetry and songs, with a richness of imagery, metaphor, rhyme and repetition that speak to the heart and are not just abstract theological truths in isolation. The richness of imagery in the Psalms connects deeply with the human heart; one may find oneself dwelling on an image for years. Respondents were aware of this dimension of the Psalms: 'The visual imagery can capture ideas that people are finding hard to express.' 'They connect with the emotional side of us, speaking to the heart, not just the mind, stirring the affections.' Because of the poetry and repetition there is a slow-motion aspect to the Psalms, so that we are drawn to take more time to dwell on them.

The innate music of the poetic rhythms has a similar effect. As some respondents testified, 'Poetry is like music and speaks to the heart in a way that plain knowledge can't.' 'Sometimes just the rhythm of the language is soothing.' That the Psalms were written to be sung is also highly significant, in view of the power of music to heal. According to the non-profit organization Able Australia Services, 'Research has shown that music provides a range of therapeutic benefits in the areas of psychological, physiological, social, emotional and cognitive function, . . . [providing] an outlet for expressing frustrations or grief.'[19] Music has profound effects on the brain, including the capacity to trigger the release of endorphins, which reduce pain.[20] Music is processed in a different part of the brain from speech, so it can reach those for whom words have become difficult.

Thirdly, their imagery, language, rhythm and brevity also make psalms easy to remember and recall. One respondent shared that 'they are easy to recall in hard times. Songs stick in your mind better than slabs of prose.' Lastly, they are extensive in number and breadth, and one can feed on them for many years and find nourishment for a vast array of emotions and life situations.

In the light of all of this, then, how does one go about lamenting well? How do the psalms of lament minister to suffering Christians such as those I surveyed and interviewed? We have seen that nearly all the difficult aspects of pain and suffering are ministered to by the Psalms. They acknowledge the reality of pain and include the full spectrum of emotions as they do so, allowing us to express our pain when this is sometimes frowned on and our speech is silenced. In the midst of the darkness of suffering, light and hope are found in God. God is there with us in the pit – we are not alone – and he will one day rescue us out of the pit.

When the psalms of lament do not comfort (but confuse) the suffering person

Sometimes the psalms of lament are not as comforting as the above testimony suggests. One quarter of those surveyed have experienced

---

19. Able Australia Services, 'Music Therapy' <http://www.ableaustralia.org.au/ ourservices/musictherapy?format=pdf>, accessed 4 Sept. 2012, p. 1.

20. M. Boso, P. Politi, F. Barale and E. Emanuele, 'Neurophysiology and Neurobiology of the Musical Experience', *Functional Neurology* 21.4 (2006), pp. 187–191.

a time when the Psalms were hard to read during their suffering. 'I found it hard to read the Psalms that speak of God's goodness, love and protection, etc. It was hard to believe this when I was suffering, so when I read them, or used them as prayers it just felt fake.' For another respondent, 'Sometimes crying out in anguish seems to elicit nil response in God. He is listening, is powerful to act, and yet remains seemingly unmoved at times.' We need to acknowledge that this can hurt. In the midst of the deep comfort the lament psalms bring, it is important to realize that there will be difficult times. This requires patience with ourselves and others, as well as prayer and sensitivity.

There is also some confusion about the ministry the Psalms ought to be having. Some respondents had significant questions about how to read the Psalms as Christians, and whether they have any direct relevance for us in our suffering. Of the people surveyed, 11% had questions of this nature. 'What is the hermeneutical key for deciding when the psalm is about Jesus and when can it also be read as our experience?' 'How can we avoid misapplying the Psalms?' Others reported that they are hesitant about using the Psalms in an overly anecdotal way as they suffer and care for suffering Christians. On the one hand, this reflects a proper hesitancy regarding careless handling of God's Word, and a desire to read the Psalms faithfully as Christians, rather than simply reading ourselves and our suffering into them. On the other hand, this does mean there is confusion about how we can let the Psalms minister to suffering Christians.

Contributing to this confusion is the fact that there is not a lot of exposure to the Psalms in our churches.[21] We do not appear to be teaching people how to read the Psalms, which are neither taught nor read aloud very often in our churches. This is especially true of the lament psalms. This is quite different from the past when Psalms would have been read or sung every week in church, especially the Anglican churches from which 75% of respondents came.

---

21. That is, in the churches represented by this survey.

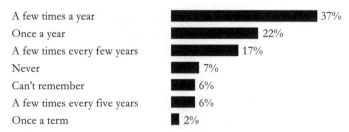

Figure 8.5 How often have you heard a psalm preached at your church?

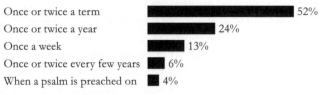

Figure 8.6 How often have you heard a psalm read out loud at your church?

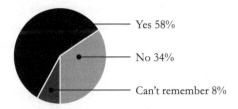

Figure 8.7 Have you heard a psalm of lament preached?

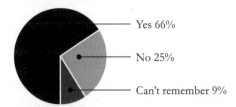

Figure 8.8 Have you heard a lament psalm read out loud in church?

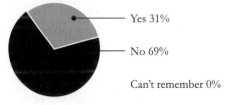

Figure 8.9 Have you studied a lament psalm in a Bible study group?

Figure 8.10 Have people been taught how to read the Psalms?

The survey showed that only just over a third of people have been taught how to read the Psalms in an explicit way, and this occurred mostly at theological colleges and conferences.

Many have understood that they should not simply apply the Psalms directly to themselves, but read them first as fulfilled in Jesus the Christ; my suspicion, however, is that this biblical-theological framework sometimes means that people limit their application of the Psalms to their fulfilment in Jesus. This does not allow the Psalms, specifically the psalms of lament, to minister to us as broadly as they can, in all of our life, and especially during our suffering.

Yes, the psalms of David are first about the Christ, and are fulfilled in Jesus, the Christ; he embodies the Psalms in his righteous life, suffering, death and resurrection. Jesus read the Psalms as words about him and for him; they were his prayers and pleas, as he entrusted himself to God his Father in the midst of his pain and suffering, with the firm hope that God would vindicate him one day. However, as those united to Christ, chosen by him and belonging to him, the Psalms really do apply to us. They teach us to follow Christ and suffer alongside him, entrusting ourselves to God in the midst of that suffering. We live in the same world Christ did, a world opposed to God, filled with affliction and awaiting full restoration. We turn to the same God with great confidence, as our refuge and strength, our rock and salvation, and we wait for the glory to come that we will share with Christ, the Lord and Saviour of the whole world, who will bring perfect justice and healing.[22]

It is clear, then, that although many Christians find the Psalms to be a wonderful healing balm and comfort during their suffering, there is significant confusion about how to apply them to themselves (as well as hesitation and guilt in doing so). I believe we need to work

---

22. For a more detailed discussion of the Psalms as Christian Scripture see
    chapter 2 in this volume.

more proactively at teaching people how to understand and apply the Psalms.

Ministering to Christians in pain

I conclude with a few reflections on the implications of these testimonies for personal and public ministry to Christians experiencing pain and suffering, mostly drawn from the testimonies of those I have listened to.

Ministering personally

As we serve someone who is in pain, one of the key implications of this survey is to let people grieve. As Catherine put it, we need to 'sit with people, shut up and listen!' A lot of what follows draws on her experiences and wisdom.

We must ensure that we stand alongside the suffering person and acknowledge their pain and suffering. We must give them permission to feel awful. We must acknowledge that 'This is horrible; I'm really sorry.' It is important to take cues from the people in pain to ascertain whether they want to talk about their trouble or not, as they often can take in nothing beyond 'I'm sorry you're hurting.' Being there with people is important, to care, to listen, to pray. Many of those surveyed testified to the importance of 'having family and friends just be there', of 'friends who don't demand anything of me during that time', of 'knowing friends are praying for me', of 'having friends pray with me and then ask how I'm going at future occasions'.

Our biggest mistake is often saying too much. We will usually be tempted to do this because we feel awkward and want to fix their problem. These are Kate Bradford's reflections: 'Whatever we would like to say is usually too big a leap for people at this moment in time. . . . The person suffering feels that they are in a pit below, with a dark cloud above. The sufferer is unable to see things from God's point of view. As we serve them we can compassionately choose to be below with them, limiting our field of vision to what they can see; to be beside them, not running ahead of them; and to be present "now" with them, because they are unable to escape this moment. Unless we first stand with them, we cannot go forward with them.

We want prayerfully to help them realize eventually that the sun is still shining above, but for now they can only see the cloud.'[23]

Other common mistakes made by those ministering to someone in pain, as experienced by Catherine and others, give rise to the following list of 'don't' statements:

- Don't ignore their pain and suffering just because you do not know what to say, or feel awkward, and don't try and jolly people out of their distress.
- Don't do the comparison game ('I know how you must feel'), as this robs the grieving person of being able to grieve.
- Don't offer a solution or try to fix them: it is not our responsibility to get people out of the pit, but rather we are helping them not to be alone.[24]
- Don't just dump Bible verses on people as platitudes or sticking plasters as though that will make them feel better or fix the problem.
- Don't expect people to get over their pain and grief quickly – or perhaps ever.
- Finally, don't try to answer the question 'Why' ('it could be cold comfort when actually people need to be listened to'), and do not rush to a happy ending.

When it comes to the Psalms, can we use them in pastorally sensitive ways as we care for those who are in pain? A number of respondents were positive about this. They appreciated 'people reminding me of the truths of the Bible beyond my emotions and even beyond my current experiences', 'people sharing Bible verses via text messages' and 'God's people getting alongside you and reminding you of truths when you are tempted to forget'. One person appreciated a friend who texted her a psalm each day. Respondents also gave advice from their experiences of

---

23. Kate is an Anglicare hospital chaplain and Moore College chaplain.
24. This last insight comes from Jill McGilvray. Jill has written a wonderful and very practical book to equip people for caring for others in a church context, including those who are suffering: *God's Love in Action: Pastoral Care for Everyone* (Victoria: Acorn, 2009).

helping other sufferers. One suggested the gentle approach: 'I just asked them if I may share a psalm with them, and only the psalm, not advice or even talking more about the suffering.' However, 'Don't go to the Psalms too quickly as if that's definitely the cure or what the other person needs.' But rather, 'Have a few psalms locked away in your head that can speak to a person where they are, particularly those that cry out to God in distress, whilst still acknowledging his goodness.' One person has a list of psalms in the back of her Bible, so that she does not need to remember them when she is suffering, or when she is caring for others who are suffering.

Some respondents found it comforting and manageable to pick one psalm to be their psalm for this period of suffering, to meditate on it, memorize it and cling to it for an extended period of time. 'I love reading the Psalms slowly and have done this a lot and found it helpful.' One member of the Moore College community wrote about her experience as follows:

> I read Psalm 23 every day. I memorized it and pondered its words and let the kernels of its truth feed me. It was an amazing and eye-opening experience. I discovered that taking time to read God's word slowly and savouring its truth was what fed my soul . . .
> Reading God's word has revived me time after time.[25]

The same person has also valued books that meditate slowly on one psalm.[26] By contrast, Catherine read through the book of Psalms in a continual loop with her son when he was diagnosed with leukaemia. They read about five a day, completing a tour through the psalter each month, so that every night her son went to sleep with a psalm running through his mind, with its comforting truths of God's presence and care. Catherine has continued doing this after his death, as she grieves his loss.

---

25. Sarah Condie, 'He Restores My Soul', *sarahspostcards* <http://www.sarahspostcardsnaps.blogspot.co.uk>, accessed 28 Aug. 2012, paras. 6, 11.

26. Paul David Tripp, *A Shelter in the Time of Storm: Meditations on God and Trouble* (Nottingham: Inter-Varsity Press, 2009); *Whiter Than Snow: Meditations on Sin and Mercy* (Wheaton: Crossway, 2008).

Almost half of those surveyed (44%) value greatly the way the Psalms minister to them as music. Alison loves the band Sons of Korah. 'When I went through a time where I couldn't read the Bible or pray, this was all I could manage.'[27]

Publicly (in our churches)

If the lament psalms can be used to minister personally to those in pain, how do we encourage our churches more publicly to benefit from the healing balm of the lament psalms, especially when they are largely absent from our churches? Bradbury suggests that the minister and leaders need to teach a new language – the language of lament:

> The minister is to act as a linguist, the teacher of a new language. The absence of lament in our life together has reduced to a dearth the speakers of its language. As ministers we now bear the heavy responsibility of learning this language ourselves and then seeking to teach others. When people are introduced to the language of lament in the psalms there is a connection, an excitement and a release, because suddenly here is a language that can give expression to how I feel and what I am experiencing. . . . The minister must then encourage this language to be used . . . the minister may enable people to move on from the raw expression of pain to the teasing out of the complaint . . . the minister, being faithful to the given-ness of the lament form, just encourages people to reengage with the God of faithfulness and justice.[28]

What might it look like to teach this new language of lament? There are implications for our Bible readings, our preaching series, our prayer times, our singing, our leading of church, our interviews, as well as our Bible study groups, training courses, weekend away or conference topics, and so on. Here is a suggestion for our intercessory prayer, again from Paul Bradbury:

---

27. E.g. Sons of Korah, *Resurrection* (Victoria: Wordsong Artists, 2005); Sons of Korah, *Redemption Songs* (Victoria: Wordsong Artists, 2000) <http://www.sonsofkorah.com>.

28. Bradbury, *Sowing in Tears*, pp. 11–12.

It is easy for those who lead intercessions to slip into using a language that is felt to be appropriate – polite, inoffensive, and dispassionate. . . . God is the one who invites us to speak plainly. . . . The psalms of lament offer us a language that we can borrow and appropriate. . . . Something as simple as using that language in a response, such as 'Lord we cry out to you, Hear our cry' . . . It may not be just with selected verses that we pray but with the deeper structure of the lament form. It encourages us to speak directly to God, to form our protest, to petition that he act, to invoke his character and covenant as a motive for him acting, and to acknowledge with praise that he is a God of faithfulness and endless mercy.[29]

Each church will look different as we seek to acknowledge the reality of pain (including our own), help people have a voice to express their pain, and give opportunities to turn to the God of hope and comfort. Here are some reflection questions to help us apply these things in our church life:

- How well are we teaching the psalms of lament in our churches? Are the psalms of lament missing? What does it cost the church to be without a language of lament?
- How are we preparing people for suffering?
- How does our church life connect with the experience of those who are suffering? Have we asked any of those who have suffered what they think?
- How can we teach people to read the psalms of lament as Christians – as fulfilled in Jesus and often on the lips of Jesus, but also as their prayers since we belong to Christ?
- How can the psalms of lament shape our corporate worship? How can we acknowledge and embrace the pain people are going through and offer a journey from one to the other?
- What might be some implications for our preaching programme, application in our sermons, Bible readings, corporate prayers, songs/hymns, interviews/testimonies, Bible study groups, and so on? Could we have a service of

29. Ibid., pp. 16–17.

lament, in response to a particular circumstance, or, more generally, acknowledge that many are suffering, getting people to share their story of pain and grief?

We have seen what a blessing the book of Psalms is as God's gift to us, his handbook for suffering, his hymnbook and his book of prayer. The Psalms reveal his steadfast love and righteousness in his worldwide salvation plan through his promised Christ. Christ suffered in every way for us, praying these same psalms; these psalms help us turn to Christ in our suffering, with genuine hearts, acknowledging the pain, but turning to him. He is our refuge, our rock, our comfort, under whose wings we find refuge, and so we wait patiently for Jesus to return and to put all things right.

It has been a humbling experience for me to hear stories of Christians who have turned to God in the depths of their suffering by using the Psalms. I am thankful to all those who shared their experiences and wisdom both with me personally or through the surveys. The Psalms, especially the lament psalms, are indeed a healing balm. Let us continue to read them, teach them in our churches, teach others how to read them and let them shape our pastoral ministry and our church gatherings. Let us continue to work at lamenting well.

Further reading

Capps, D., 'The Use of Psalms and Grief Counselling', in *Biblical Approaches to Pastoral Counselling* (Philadelphia: Westminster, 1981), pp. 47–97.

Kaiser, W. C., *Grief and Pain in the Plan of God: Christian Assurance and the Message of Lamentations*, 2nd ed. (Fearn: Christian Focus, 2004).

Peterson, E. H., 'The Pastoral Word of Pain-Sharing: Lamentations', in *Five Smooth Stones for Pastoral Work*, 2nd ed. (Grand Rapids: Eerdmans, 1992), pp. 113–148.

9. PSALMS OF THE POWERLESS: A THEOLOGICAL INTERPRETATION OF IMPRECATION

Kit Barker

The imprecatory psalms have been a continual source of confusion and debate. Readers have found it difficult to understand how the psalmist could express such hatred, let alone explain how this hatred 'fits' within the Christian canon. It is the burden of this chapter to offer a theological interpretation of the imprecatory psalms by offering an explanation of how these psalms function as the Word of God.[1] I will argue that such an interpretation supports their

---

1. The practice of 'theological interpretation' or 'TI' has witnessed renewed interest in recent years. See Daniel J. Treier, *Introducing Theological Interpretation of Scripture: Recovering a Christian Practice* (Grand Rapids: Baker, 2008). While a concise definition is elusive, TI regards biblical interpretation as a canonical, creedal and cultural practice (ibid., p. 201). It seeks a return to many of the 'pre-critical' methodologies that were shaped by Christian beliefs and practices. While this is certainly a helpful description of the endeavour, I would suggest that the definition be focused more specifically as the practice of reading Scripture in order to understand what God was and is doing with the text.

continuing use and demonstrates that an a priori rejection of imprecation is unjustified.[2] To this end, I will first review various approaches
to the imprecatory psalms; then consider the imprecatory psalms in
the contexts of both the psalter and the broader canon; next, offer
speech-act theory as a tool for understanding how the psalms
function in these contexts – in particular, how they function as the
Word of God. Finally, I will present a brief theological interpretation
of Psalm 137.[3]

Various approaches to the imprecatory psalms

The various approaches to the imprecatory psalms have been
outlined elsewhere and do not require a detailed presentation here.[4]
They can be categorized as follows.

Dismiss them as irrelevant
The first approach is to excise these psalms or parts thereof and
ignore them completely. This move, reflected in various liturgies,
clearly does not account for how these psalms can be considered
Christian Scripture.[5]

---

2. I do not aim to present a comprehensive defence of the contemporary use
   of imprecation, which would require a more detailed discussion.
3. Of the imprecatory psalms, Ps. 137 is notorious. Responses to it are typical,
   making it an appropriate focus of discussion.
4. See John N. Day, *Crying for Justice: What the Psalms Teach Us About Mercy and
   Violence in an Age of Terrorism* (Leicester: Inter-Varsity Press, 2005), pp. 9–35;
   Eric Zenger, *A God of Vengeance? Understanding the Psalms of Divine Wrath*
   (Louisville: Westminster John Knox, 1996), pp. 13–24; Joel M. LeMon,
   'Saying Amen to Violent Psalms: Patterns of Prayer, Belief, and Action in
   the Psalter', in Rolf A. Jacobson (ed.), *Soundings in the Theology of the Psalms:
   Perspectives and Methods in Contemporary Scholarship* (Minneapolis: Fortress,
   2011), p. 102.
5. The 'Notes on the Pointing' that introduces the Psalms in *An Australian
   Prayer Book* states in n. 7, 'The following verses may be omitted in the public
   service at the discretion of the minister: 17.14; 54.5; 55.16–17; 58; 59.6,14;
   68.21–23; 69.24–30; 79.10,12; 83.17; 101.6,9; 109.5–19; 137.7–9; 139.19–22;

Admit they are canonical, but do not accept them as appropriate for Christians[6]

This position has three variants. First, there are those who believe imprecatory psalms to be expressions of an Old Covenant faith based on Old Covenant promises that are no longer appropriate for the people of God in the church age.[7] In other words, they are consistent with the Psalms and the Old Testament but at odds with the teaching of the New Testament.

Secondly, there are those who believe they reveal the ugly reality of sinful humanity, in any era, and are to be rejected. C. S. Lewis is famous for his numerous comments to this effect: 'we must face both facts squarely. The hatred is there – festering, gloating, undisguised – and also we should be wicked if we in any way condoned or approve it or (worse still) used it to justify similar passions in ourselves.'[8]

Thirdly, others suggest that imprecatory psalms (and subsequently those who appropriate them) 'incite hatred' and are never appropriate for Christian use.[9] New Testament theologian Francis Watson remarks, 'The implied reader is expected to acquiesce in this judgment, and the text may therefore be said to perform the speech–act of inciting hatred – hatred of a particularly intense and extreme kind . . .'[10]

These positions at least recognize the canonical status of the psalms, but consider them to be either abrogated in much the same way as the Levitical cult or to be counter-examples of a righteous response. In either case, little defence is offered for these conclusions.

140.9–11; 143.12' (*An Australian Prayer Book* [Sydney: Anglican Information Office, 1978], p. 306). For a discussion of psalms that have been omitted by the Roman Catholic Liturgy of the Hours see W. L. Holladay, *The Psalms Through Three Thousand Years* (Augsburg: Fortress, 1993).

6. This summary is taken from Kit Barker, 'Preaching Imprecation, Inciting Hatred' (unpublished paper; AA–CC, 2009), p. 4.

7. See Carl J. Laney, 'A Fresh Look at the Imprecatory Psalms', *BSac* 138 (1981), pp. 35–45.

8. C. S. Lewis, *Reflections on the Psalms* (London: Geoffrey Bles), pp. 22–23.

9. Francis Watson, *Text and Truth: Redefining Biblical Theology* (Edinburgh: T. & T. Clark, 1997), pp. 120–121.

10. Ibid., p. 120.

Accept them as a necessary but unrighteous response

Brueggemann epitomizes this more accepting position when he suggests that they are a useful and necessary way for us to engage with our rage and move our way through it. Ultimately though, in Brueggemann's estimation the prayers of these psalms are not authorized places to 'remain':

> My hunch is that there is a way beyond the Psalms of vengeance, but it is a way through them and not around them. And that is because of what in fact goes on with us. Willy-nilly, we are vengeful creatures. Thus these harsh Psalms must be fully embraced as our own. Our rage and indignation must be fully owned and fully expressed. And then (only then) can our rage and indignation be yielded to the mercy of God. In taking this route through them, we take the route God 'himself' has gone. We are not permitted a cheaper, easier, more 'enlightened' way.[11]

> There is no or little slippage between what is thought/felt and what is said. The Psalms are immediate.[12]

> The cry for vengeance is a powerful part of disorientation . . . There is nothing pious or 'Christian' about his prayer. But (as psychotherapists know), our deep disorientation is not a time when we are able to be genuinely humane toward others because we are singularly attentive to the lack of humanness in our own life.[13]

---

11. Walter Brueggemann, *Praying the Psalms: Engaging Scripture and the Life of the Spirit* (Eugene, Oreg.: Cascade, 2007), pp. 80–81. See also Zenger, *God of Vengeance?*, p. 74.

12. Brueggemann, *Praying the Psalms*, p. 53.

13. Ibid., p. 34. These statements are consistent with Brueggemann's conviction that the psalter presents a pattern of life moving from orientation to disorientation and then to reorientation. Brueggemann believes that this movement is necessary, in part, because of the flawed nature of humanity's responses to life. Responses reflecting disorientation, represented in the imprecatory psalms, are evidence of this.

    However, while Brueggemann on the one hand argues that there 'is nothing pious or Christian' about these prayers, on the other hand he elsewhere recognizes the mature spirituality involved in such a response

Brueggemann does not appear to have grappled, at this point, with how the canonical formation and presentation of the psalter affect the way these psalms now function. The textuality of the Psalms allowed the editors of the psalter to consider and reflect carefully upon the appropriate inclusion of imprecations. Furthermore, their presence in the psalter encourages a careful meditation on the one hand, and an impassioned appropriation, when appropriate, on the other. That these psalms represent a passionate, raw and uncensored response is not in question. However, these prayers are more powerful when it is recognized that they have subsequently been studied, authorized and utilized. Passionate response and theological depth are not mutually exclusive qualities.

Against sin, not the sinner

An alternate interpretation accepts the psalms as canonical and accepts their appropriation, but does not accept that we can direct these prayers at people (i.e. 'love the sinner and hate the sin'). The imprecatory psalms are thus understood as prayers that God would judge sin or spiritual forces of evil.[14] Since he has done so in Christ, the psalms point us to the cross and to forgiveness.[15]

For this position to be valid, one would need to demonstrate that it is possible to separate evil and sin from the morally capable beings that commit it. Such a demonstration is not convincing and additionally does not do justice to the specificity found in many of the psalms or in their reappropriation in the New Testament.

----

and thus displays an element of contradiction in his own thinking: 'The Psalms (and the entire Bible) are clear that vengeance belongs to God . . . It is a liberating assertion that I do not need to trouble myself with retaliation, for that is left safely in God's hands. The Psalmist seems to know that. The venomous words show that the reality of vengeance is present. But that these words are addressed to God shows a recognition that this is God's business and not ours' (ibid., p. 70).

14. John Shepherd, 'The Place of the Imprecatory Psalms in the Canon of Scripture', *Chm* 111.2 (1997), pp. 110–126.

15. Eric Peels, '"I Hate Them with Perfect Hatred" (Psalm 139:21–22)', *TynB* 59 (2008), pp. 35–51. Dietrich Bonhoeffer, *Psalms: The Prayer Book of the Bible* (Minneapolis: Augsburg, 1970), pp. 58–60.

A righteous response

The remaining position is the one I will be defending here. It accepts the imprecatory psalms as canonical and as appropriate (even righteous) responses in commensurate situations.[16]

A brief introduction to speech-act theory

In order to understand the terminology and argument of the hermeneutic offered below, it will be helpful to provide a brief description of speech-act theory and its usefulness in theological interpretation.[17] Speech-act theory, a subdiscipline of the philosophy of language, was founded by J. L. Austin and his student John Searle.[18] Austin's central idea is that the act of speaking performs other actions. He isolated three types of linguistic actions that can occur when we communicate verbally: the locutionary act – the uttering of the words; the illocutionary act – what we do in uttering the words (understood as the meaning of the sentence); and the perlocutionary act – what effect this has on the audience.[19]

The following example may be helpful. The locution 'It's after 10 o'clock' can be used to perform a number of actions and, consequently, can take on an equal number of meanings. It may be an assertion (in response to a question regarding the time). It may be

---

16. Day, *Crying for Justice*, pp. 10–11. See also Zenger, *God of Vengeance?*; Kit Barker, 'Divine Illocutions in Psalm 137: A Critique of Nicholas Wolterstorff's Second Hermeneutic', *TynB* 60 (2009), pp. 1–14.

17. For a fuller treatment see Kit Barker, 'Speech Act Theory, Dual Authorship, and Canonical Hermeneutics: Making Sense of Sensus Plenior', *JTI* 3 (2009), pp. 227–239.

18. J. L. Austin, *How to Do Things with Words*, 2nd ed. (Cambridge, Mass.: Harvard University Press, 1975); J. Searle, *Speech Acts: An Essay in the Philosophy of Language* (Cambridge: Cambridge University Press, 1969); *Expression and Meaning: Studies in the Theory of Speech Acts* (Cambridge: Cambridge University Press, 1979).

19. Austin, *How to Do Things*, chs. 8–10. Though these distinctions are sometimes contested, most scholars are willing to speak in terms of these three components: locution, illocution and perlocution.

a question (e.g. 'Where are you?'). It may be a request (e.g. 'Where's my coffee?'). It may be a command (e.g. 'Your talk needed to finish by now so sit down'). Therefore, the locution 'It's after 10 o'clock' could mean any number of things, since the meaning of the locution is determined by the context or background in which it occurs.[20]

Interpreting the locution, therefore, requires attending to this background and understanding what illocutionary act(s) the speaker (or author) performed.[21] In relation to theological interpretation this has significant implications. First, interpreting a biblical text requires understanding the illocutions of the human author or editor. Secondly, it requires understanding the illocutions God was and is performing by way of that same text.

Method

In order to explain how the imprecatory psalms function as God's Word, the hermeneutic will progress along the following lines of inquiry:

1. The 'fit' of the imprecatory psalms within the illocutionary stance of the psalter.[22] The question at this point is how the

---

20. This is a summary taken from Barker, 'Speech Act Theory', pp. 227–239.
21. For detailed discussion see Nicholas Wolterstorff, *Divine Discourse: Philosophical Reflections on the Claim That God Speaks* (Cambridge: Cambridge University Press, 1995); Kevin J. Vanhoozer, 'The Semantics of Biblical Literature: Truth and Scripture's Diverse Literary Forms', in Donald A. Carson and John D. Woodbridge (eds.), *Hermeneutics, Authority and Canon* (Leicester: Inter-Varsity Press, 1986), pp. 53–104; *Is There a Meaning in This Text? The Bible, the Reader, and the Morality of Literary Knowledge* (Grand Rapids: Zondervan; Leicester: Apollos, 1998); *First Theology: God, Scripture and Hermeneutics* (Leicester: Apollos, 2002).
22. The 'fit' of the imprecatory psalms within the rest of the Old Testament lies outside the scope of this chapter. Though it represents another basic line of inquiry, to sustain the thesis of this chapter, the validation of imprecation within the psalter and within the New Testament is all that is necessary.

imprecatory psalms are presented in the psalter. It will be argued that the illocutionary stance of the psalter is not only consistent with the illocutions of the imprecatory psalms, but that the psalter endorses their use.

2. The 'fit' of the illocutionary stance of the psalter with that of the New Testament. Particular attention will be given to possible central (or supervening) illocutions that could change the conditions in which the psalter originally performed its illocutions (e.g. the call to forgive one's enemies).

3. The ways in which the imprecatory psalms continue to function as the Word of God. It will be suggested that the primary way in which this can be construed is by attending to illocutions formed at the generic level (i.e. at the level of the psalm in its entirety).

Imprecation fits within the psalter

It has already been noted that some regard the imprecatory psalms to fit within the psalter either as examples of an outdated Old Testament spirituality or as an authorized concession to the human condition. In contrast to these views I wish to argue that the imprecatory psalms not only fit within the psalter but that they are presented as righteous responses to their particular circumstances.

The imprecatory psalms 'fit' by inclusion

To argue that the imprecatory psalms are being presented by the psalter in a manner different from the other kinds of psalms incurs the burden of proof. C. S. Lewis who, as has been noted, suggests these psalms are reflective of our sinful nature, concedes that imprecation 'will not come away clean'.[23] In the absence of literary markers it must be assumed that all of the psalms within the psalter are offered to the reader in a similar manner.

Furthermore, it is superfluous to suggest that the imprecatory psalms are consistent with the psalter as they themselves contribute

---

23. Lewis, *Reflections on the Psalms*, pp. 24–25.

a large percentage of its content. David Firth comments, 'the editorial process may have ensured that only psalms that operated within a given set of theological assumptions remained within the collection, whilst those variations that remain are themselves an intentional element within the instruction of the book'.[24] By their very presence within the psalter, the imprecatory psalms 'fit'. In speech-act terms the illocutionary acts of the psalter as a whole (i.e. its generic illocutions) are, in part, shaped by the illocutions of the imprecatory psalms. It is not surprising then, that illocutions of the psalter are not only consistent with imprecation but that they also encourage their appropriation.

The imprecatory psalms 'fit' the reading strategy

The introduction to the psalter performs a number of generic illocutions that reveal its intended reading strategy. Specifically, Psalms 1 and 2 present the psalter as *tôrâ*.[25] Brueggemann suggests that the psalter thus presents itself as a book to be read 'through the prism of torah obedience'.[26] The shaping of the psalter into five books, the repeated presence of *tôrâ* psalms and the introduction provided by Psalms 1 and 2 are evidence the psalter is to be read as divine instruction.[27] Mays comments:

24. David Firth, 'The Teaching of the Psalms', in Philip S. Johnston and David G. Firth (eds.), *Interpreting the Psalms: Issues and Approaches* (Leicester: Apollos, 2005), p. 162.

25. See Ps. 1:2; Gordon J. Wenham, *Psalms as Torah: Reading the Biblical Song Ethically* (Grand Rapids: Eerdmans, 2012); Michael LeFebvre, 'Torah Meditation in the Psalms', in Johnston and Firth, *Interpreting the Psalms*, p. 225. LeFebvre also argues that genres of wisdom and *tôrâ* are inappropriate because hope, rather than obedience, is the primary goal. He also argues that *tôrâ* is a strict reference to the Mosaic Law and does not justify Ps. 1 or the psalter being classified as 'instruction'.

26. Walter Brueggemann, 'Bounded by Obedience and Praise: The Psalms as Canon', *JSOT* 50 (1991), pp. 63–92; repr. in P. D. Miller (ed.), *The Psalms and the Life of Faith* (Minneapolis: Fortress, 1995), pp. 189–213.

27. The presence of divine illocutions at the generic level will be addressed in later discussion.

> As introduction to the book, Psalm 1 invites us to expect and receive *torah* from the psalms, that is, to read them as Scripture. The reader will come upon two other great witnesses to *torah* piety in Psalms 19 and 119 … Indeed, Psalm 1 wants the whole to be read as instruction – instruction in prayer, in praise, in God's way with us and our way under God.[28]

Psalm 1, with its invitation to blessing and life through a meditation on *tôrâ*, is implicitly an invitation to meditate on the contents of the psalter. It is here that blessing will be found through an engagement with God and his instruction. The many literary and thematic connections of Psalm 1 with Psalm 2 are widely acknowledged and affect the overall function of the introduction. Through this connection to Psalm 2, the invitation to righteousness and blessing in Psalm 1 becomes an invitation to be loyal to the king and an invitation to take refuge in him. The psalter thus begins with an eschatological and existential focus, reminding the reader of Yahweh's sovereignty, the reality of divine judgment and the question of whether the readers will find themselves 'standing' at the end. It is a reminder of the ever-present conflict in Yahweh's kingdom due to the presence of rebellious subjects and that Yahweh will, inevitably, exert his rule and vindicate those who remain loyal to him. Already, the illocutions performed in this introduction are commensurate with the illocutions of imprecation. I have argued elsewhere for this consistency:

> all of the imprecatory psalms are consistent with the themes found in Psalm 2, particularly the warning to 'Kiss the Son' or suffer his wrath. As Psalm 2 arguably functions as a type of introduction to the Psalter, the presence of the imprecatory psalms is hardly surprising.[29]

Therefore, Psalms 1 and 2 offer a reading strategy for the psalter by providing a number of its generic illocutions.[30] Fundamentally,

---

28. James L. Mays, *Psalms* (Louisville: John Knox, 1994), p. 42.
29. Barker, 'Divine Illocutions', p. 11.
30. This list is not meant to be comprehensive; rather, the most significant generic illocutions are highlighted along with those important for the subsequent discussion of imprecation.

as mentioned above, the psalter *invites*. It is an invitation to meditation, to blessing, to life, to submission to Yahweh and his
king,[31] and to refuge. The fact that most of the psalter comprises
prayers and songs directed to Yahweh indicates that it *invites imitation*.
It *offers* these responses as appropriate, even 'righteous' (Ps. 1:5–6),
responses to readers who find themselves in similar situations.[32]

The imprecatory psalms 'fit' theologically

While the imprecatory psalms can be defended on the basis of their
very presence within the psalter, further support for their appropriation is found in their fit within the broader themes or primary
illocutions of the psalter. A number of these primary illocutions
were just mentioned vis-à-vis the introduction of the psalter and
include the declaration that Yahweh is King and the corresponding
invitation to remain loyal to him and his anointed. 'Yahweh reigns'
is a central theme, occupying significant structural locations within
the psalter, that appears to be cogent.[33] The location of the *yhwh
mālak* (the LORD reigns) psalms and the inclusion of this theme
throughout the psalter at key literary moments, suggests that this
declaration be categorized as a primary illocution. The illocutions
of imprecation are consistent with the declaration of Yahweh's
kingship in the following ways:

---

31. Note Gerald Wilson's influential claim that the psalter both criticizes the
    limits of the Davidic king and at the same time affirms that only Yahweh is
    king. For Wilson, this assertion is the climax and centrepiece of the psalter
    (G. H. Wilson, *The Editing of the Hebrew Psalter*, SBLDS 76 [Atlanta: Scholars
    Press, 1985], p. 215). For additional discussion in support of this thesis see
    James L. Mays, *The Lord Reigns: A Theological Handbook to the Psalms*
    (Louisville: Westminster John Knox, 1994).
32. Implicitly, and through its connection with the ensuing prayers, the
    introduction performs a generic illocution asserting that Yahweh will be
    listening.
33. Gerald. H. Wilson, 'The Structure of the Psalter', in Johnston and Firth,
    Interpreting the Psalms, pp. 229–246; Mays, *Lord Reigns*; Jamie A. Grant, 'The
    Psalms and the King', in Johnston and Firth, *Interpreting the Psalms*,
    pp. 101–118.

- Imprecation is directed to Yahweh, acknowledging him as ruler and rightful judge over all creation. In so doing, it 'surrenders retribution' to Yahweh and precludes any acts of personal vengeance.
- Imprecation is based upon a desire for Yahweh to be glorified, recognizing that his reputation is at stake if injustice remains unpunished.
- Imprecation recognizes Yahweh's place as covenant Lord and cries out on the basis of his covenant promises.
- Imprecation is an act of loyalty as the psalmists seek refuge in Yahweh and distance themselves from the wicked.

The imprecatory psalms are thus offered to the reader as righteous responses to such situations. They are consistent with the psalter's primary illocutions regarding the reign of Yahweh and model a response that honours him as King in the midst of violent oppression.

Imprecation fits within the canon

The previous section outlined the illocutions of imprecation and argued that they both support and are supported by the generic illocutions of the psalter. This section will focus the discussion on whether these illocutions remain 'in play' within the context of the Christian canon. The New Testament undoubtedly performs central (and supervening) illocutions that, by definition, change the conditions in which the earlier locutions of the psalter now function. The question, however, is whether these central illocutions change the conditions in such a way that the previous illocutions of the psalter vis-à-vis imprecation are no longer performed. It will be argued that this is not, in fact, the case and that the central illocutions of the New Testament are not incommensurate with the psalter's illocutions of imprecation. Moreover, it will be argued that the illocutionary stance of the New Testament reveals its own attitude towards imprecation, which supports that of the psalter.

Admittedly, there are a few New Testament illocutions that seem, at first glance, to be at odds with the illocutionary stance of the psalter. Of particular note are the calls to love your enemy, to bless and not curse, and to forgive. Due to necessary constraints, the scope of this discussion will focus on the call to forgive one's enemies. This seems like a natural choice as it offers a seemingly contrasting response to situations of injustice, oppression and violence. If the call to forgive is unqualified, then the psalter's original illocutionary stance inviting the reader to imitate imprecation becomes infelicitous. The two calls cannot coexist. However, if it can be demonstrated that the New Testament's call to forgive one's enemies is qualified in some way, then it is possible that the illocutionary force of the psalter regarding imprecation *and* the illocutionary force of the New Testament regarding forgiveness could both remain 'in play'.

Forgiveness is a 'strong' speech act requiring a context of penitence

The argument of this section is that forgiveness is an example of a strong speech act that requires a particular context for it to be enacted. Subsequently, there are circumstances where this context is absent and forgiveness is not possible. It is clear from the New Testament that when forgiveness is possible, forgiveness is required. Conversely, it will be argued that when forgiveness is not possible, forgiveness is clearly not required. Finally, in some cases where forgiveness is not possible (and so, not required), then imprecation could be appropriate.

Forgiveness is a 'strong' speech act. Performing the speech act of forgiveness alters the reality in which people live.[34] While forgive-

---

34. 'Strong' speech acts differ in a number of ways from standard illocutions such as 'Please pass the salt.' Standard illocutions require little context and do not significantly change the world of those involved. Conversely, strong speech acts both require a high level of established context and have a significant effect on the lives of those involved. Furthermore, standard speech acts may or may not result in the desired effect (perlocution). In the case of strong speech acts the performance of the illocution ensures the perlocution. The relationship between the two is consequential, so that once the illocution is uttered, a change occurs in the reality of the persons involved. For example, a declaration by a judge that a defendant is 'guilty' is a strong speech act: because a high level of context has been established, the declaration has the desired effect on the defendant irrespective of his or her consent.

ness has been defined in many ways,[35] the definition offered here is as follows: to forgive is to declare that the offending party no longer owes you a debt with respect to the offence in question. In forgiving, you have noted that their debt outweighs any form of restitution, accepted their apology, and, at cost to yourself, have decided to treat the offender as though they owe you nothing more in this regard.

Like all 'strong' speech acts, forgiveness requires a very specific context in which it can occur: one can utter the words 'I forgive you,' but unless a number of other conditions are already satisfied, then the action is at best benign and at worst offensive. In the absence of these conditions it is an infelicitous speech act. It has not worked. This is obvious in many instances. Perhaps the person uttering the words is doing so to provoke the other person, who in reality has not committed any wrong against them. Or perhaps the person uttering the words is doing so in order to gain some advantage over the offender. In either case, forgiveness is not actually being offered.

There is yet another situation where the words 'I forgive you' do not work, and it is this situation that has a direct bearing on the possibility of imprecation. If a person utters the words 'I forgive you,' and the offender has not repented of his offence, then the words have not worked. Wolterstorff asks the question

> Can I forgive Hubert if I believe that he is not contrite? . . . I doubt it. I can be *willing* to forgive him – when he repents. I can have a forgiving disposition toward him. But it appears to me that no longer to hold against someone the wrong he did one while believing that he himself continues to stand behind the deed, requires not treating the deed or its doer with the moral seriousness required for forgiveness; it is to downplay rather than to forgive. 'I suppose he did wrong me; but it's not worth making anything of it.'[36]

---

35. For a review of the various conceptions of forgiveness over the last century see Nigel Biggar, 'Forgiveness in the Twentieth Century: A Review of the Literature, 1901–2001', in Alistair McFadyen and Marcel Sarot (eds.), *Forgiveness and Truth* (Edinburgh: T. & T. Clark, 2001), pp. 181–219.

36. Nicholas Wolterstorff, *Justice in Love* (Grand Rapids: Eerdmans, 2011), p. 173 (emphasis original).

The speech act of forgiveness requires a context of interpersonal communication where the offender has acknowledged her wrongdoing and repented of it. A Japanese proverb captures this reality: 'Forgiving the unrepentant is like drawing pictures in water.'[37]

Unconditional forgiveness?

That forgiveness is dependent upon repentance is not widely accepted. Worthington, Sharp, Lerner and Sharp state a standard position on forgiveness:

> Interpersonal forgiveness is meant to be unilateral, not contingent on or waiting for the offender to accept responsibility, confess, apologize, make restitution, ask for forgiveness, and completely turn from the sinful and harmful acts (Luke 23:34; 1 Samuel 25:23–25 . . .). Divine forgiveness is linked to human repentance (Luke 7:33–50; Exodus 32:32 . . .), but interpersonal forgiveness is not.[38]

This position states that forgiveness is always required, irrespective of the attitude of the offender. However, it is recognized that this is not the case when God forgives. Divine forgiveness happens in the context of penitence. It is 'linked to human repentance'. Worthington states elsewhere:

> Interpersonal forgiveness, within the Scriptures, is unconditional, whereas Divine forgiveness is conditional. Divine forgiveness is based on Divine truth, justice, mercy, and love, which are granted from an omniscient, merciful, and just God. Because God knows people's hearts, God can condition forgiveness on people's repentance. Non-omniscient humans are called to forgive unconditionally.[39]

---

37. Quoted in David W. Augsburger, *Helping People Forgive* (Louisville: John Knox, 1996), p. 29.
38. Everett L. Worthingon, Jr., Constance B. Sharp, Andrea J. Lerner and Jeffery R. Sharp, 'Interpersonal Forgiveness as an Example of Loving One's Enemies', *Journal of Psychology and Theology* 34 (2006), p. 32.
39. Everett L. Worthington, 'Just Forgiving: How the Psychology and Theology of Forgiveness and Justice Inter-relate', *JPC* 25.2 (2006), pp. 155–168.

There seems to be little justification for drawing such a sharp distinction between divine and human forgiveness. Worthington suggests that God can conditionally forgive because he alone knows if the offender is truly repentant, whereas we are always called to forgive because we cannot be sure if the offender is ever truly repentant. However, it would seem obvious that if someone is impenitent, then it is hardly necessary to second-guess his intention. Alternatively, if he claims penitence, then granting him the 'benefit of the doubt' would be the appropriate response (Matt. 18:22). Worthington's position, however, is a common understanding of Christian responsibility: God forgives only when we repent, yet we are called to forgive unconditionally, irrespective of repentance and even in the face of continued oppression.

'Unconditional forgiveness' is not supported in Scripture. There is no explicit command to forgive offenders who remain unrepentant. There are many commands to forgive, but they either mention repentance explicitly as a condition, or require that it be implied on the basis of (1) those passages where it is explicit and (2) divine forgiveness, where we see the mechanism of forgiveness more clearly.[40]

An example of this is found in Matthew 18, where repentance is not mentioned explicitly with the call to forgive. However, the preceding verses explain how one is to deal with a brother who is repeatedly *unrepentant* with respect to a matter serious enough to be brought before the whole community. The end result of his stubborn impenitence is exclusion, not forgiveness.[41] Furthermore, while Matthew's account is not explicit with respect to repentance, Luke's account is explicit: 'If your brother or sister sins against you, rebuke them; and if they repent, forgive them. Even if they sin against you seven times in a day and seven times

---

40. See Craig L. Blomberg, 'On Building and Breaking Barriers: Forgiveness, Salvation and Christian Counseling with Special Reference to Matthew 18:15–35', *JPC* 25.2 (2006), pp. 144–145.

41. Matt. 18:15–18. Blomberg also argues that the loosing and binding of v. 18 are references to forgiveness and the denial of forgiveness respectively and summarize the previous teaching on community discipline (ibid., p. 139).

come back to you saying "I repent," you must forgive them' (Luke 17:3–4).

Luke 23:34 is often referred to as an example of divine (and human) forgiveness that is performed in the absence of penitence. While a detailed examination of this text is relevant to the current discussion, it is not possible to accomplish it here. However, a number of features suggest that this text does not promote unconditional forgiveness: (1) Jesus does not pronounce forgiveness. While this is something that he often did, in this case, he requests that God forgive the offenders; and (2) Jesus' request is quite specific. He asks that they not be held accountable for the *gravity* of the offence, as there was no way they could comprehend this. Rather than understanding this as a request that they be forgiven of all wrongdoing connected to his execution, Jesus appears to be requesting that their culpability be limited to what they thought they were doing. In the light of the above, it seems unlikely that one can build a theology of forgiveness upon this text that describes such a unique event and does not present forgiveness as occurring.

For the purposes of this chapter it is also important to consider how this scene contributes to an understanding of imprecation. After all, Jesus requested forgiveness, not judgment. It may be helpful at this point to reflect upon the uniqueness of Christ's crucifixion. In the moment of crucifixion, Jesus did not imprecate but requested a limited culpability. He did not ask for deliverance, but willingly suffered punishment for all humanity. In this climactic moment, when the triune God accomplished his eternal purposes for creation, Christ's death was not primarily the fault of the Roman soldiers or the Jewish Sanhedrin. At this point, Christ willingly took the place of all humanity in their rebellion against God. To imprecate against the soldiers present would trivialize the staggering scope of its significance and wrongly attribute guilt to a select few. To imprecate in this moment would also have overplayed the significance of the suffering the soldiers inflicted. Christ willingly submitted himself to the wrath of the Father, a fate far worse than the soldiers could inflict.

Furthermore, because of his atoning work, Christ himself would see that justice is done for all those present. He knew that all things would be placed in his hands and that He would be the one ultimately to bring justice.[42] In the light of these unique features we would not expect a response of imprecation on the lips of Christ. Nor would we expect to find a theology of unconditional forgiveness (one that precluded penitence). Christ will punish all those who reject his kingship and atoning work. The crucifixion and resurrection make forgiveness and reconciliation with God possible, not automatic. It is here we discover the basis for forgiveness that requires all people to respond in faith and penitence.

The possibility of imprecation

The New Testament illocutions calling for forgiveness do not supervene in such a way as to negate the possibility or appropriateness of imprecation. Forgiveness is a complex interpersonal activity that requires the offending party to set the context in which it can occur. In particular, it is a strong speech act that requires a context of penitence for it to be performed. This does not preclude the victim's *offering* forgiveness, but the actual act of forgiveness is only possible in the presence of penitence. Forgiveness, therefore, is one response to wrongdoers, but it is not the only possible response. The reality of impenitence and the impossibility of forgiveness in this context opens up the possibility for the victim to respond in other ways, including imprecation.

Forgiveness and imprecation are mutually exclusive actions. This is due to the fact that imprecation is a speech act with different contextual requirements. In the context of a penitent wrongdoer, imprecation is clearly inappropriate and forgiveness is demanded. Alternatively, in a context of impenitence, forgiveness is an inappropriate response and, in fact, an impossible one. Whereas, in this same context, imprecation, though not a necessary response, could be warranted.

The New Testament invitation to imprecation

Examples of imprecation are found throughout the New Testament

---

42. That Jesus is both the model of a righteous sufferer and the one to whom righteous sufferers commit themselves represents one of the many mysteries of the incarnation.

and it will suffice, as they have been discussed at length elsewhere, simply to present them here.[43]

Jesus himself employs imprecation on a number of occasions. Day comments:

> Certainly in extreme circumstances, Jesus did not hesitate to pronounce imprecation (e.g. Mark 11:12–14, 20–21), and he uttered excoriating woes against hardened unbelief (e.g. Matt. 11:20–24; 23:13–39). Now although woes may be generally distinguished from curses, they are closely related. They bear a large measure of similarity and partial semantic overlap.
>
> This does not mean that Jesus acted out of accord with his own radical dictum. By Christ's own witness and example, this enemy-love is the attitude of readiness to show sustained and indiscriminate kindness. If, however, the enemy's cup of iniquity has become full to overflowing, this love is overtaken by the demands of justice and divine vengeance. Jesus' approach in this regard is strikingly similar to that of the psalmists who penned harsh words. David, for example by his testimony in Psalms 35:11–17 and 109:4–5, demonstrated habitual kindness toward enemies, only to receive abuse in return. His was an example of extreme love – and a love that finally and fittingly met its extremity.[44]

On several occasions Paul expressed his imprecatory prayers to the audiences of his letters. In the letter to the Galatians Paul desires that those who preach a 'false gospel' be *anathema* (Gal. 1:8–9). Later in the letter he expresses his desire that those who are undermining the gospel by demanding circumcision would have an 'accident' with the knife and emasculate themselves (Gal. 5:12).

Against those who would argue that the Pauline examples are all cases that exclude his personal enemies, is the prayer of the souls of the martyred saints who appropriate the imprecation of Psalm 79.

---

43. See Shepherd, who notes that this area warrants further research ('Place of the Imprecatory Psalms', p. 121). See also Day, *Crying for Justice*; Jace Broadhurst, 'Should Cursing Continue? An Argument for Imprecatory Psalms in Biblical Theology', *AJET* 23 (2004), pp. 63–89; Robert L. Thomas, 'The Imprecatory Prayers of the Apocalypse', *BSac* 126 (1969), pp. 123–131.

44. Day, *Crying for Justice*, pp. 89–90.

God's response to such request is that they must be patient, but that he will ensure their vindication (Rev. 6:9–11).

Perhaps less obvious, yet more poignant, is the invitation to all believers to imitate the Lord's Prayer. This prayer begins with the declaration that God deserves honour and voices a desire that his will be done throughout the heavens and the earth (Matt. 6:9–13). This opening declaration is calling for the kingdom of God to be fully realized, which requires that all his enemies be shamed and honour him. Implicit in the request for personal deliverance later in the prayer is the destruction of all opposition to God's people. This prayer is fundamentally a prayer calling for the Day of Yahweh.[45] Broadhurst concurs:

> The martyred saints continue to cry before God's throne, 'How long, O Lord, holy and true . . .' (Rev 6:10). Do we not ask for the same thing? Many churches announce implicit curses on the enemies of God every Sunday in the unison statement of the Lord's Prayer. In quoting the words of Christ, 'Thy kingdom come,' we are asking for the consummation of an era. This consummation brings about the destruction of our enemies and God's enemies. This petition involves the complete overthrow of Satan's kingdom and all his followers. There is really no difference in praying this than there is in praying an imprecatory psalm and so I suggest we should continue singing these psalms with all the fervour of the martyred saints.[46]

It is apparent that the New Testament performs the two illocutionary acts in parallel. On the one hand, there is the call to forgive one's enemies, and, on the other, the invitation to call for justice and for God's kingdom to be realized. The presence of imprecation throughout the New Testament, therefore, supports the illocutionary stance of the psalter.

---

45. Barker, 'Divine Illocutions', p. 14.
46. 'Should Cursing Continue?', pp. 84–85. Broadhurst's labelling of the Lord's Prayer as a 'curse' is inaccurate, as the prayer is directed to God and is not understood as efficacious in and of itself. Despite this unfortunate confusion of terminology, his broader thesis remains sound.

A theological interpretation of Psalm 137[47]

By the streams of Babylon,
   there we sat,
   more so, we wept,
as we remembered Zion.
On the poplars in its midst we hung our lyres.
For there our captors asked us for words of song,
   our mockers,[48] (words of)[49] rejoicing,
   'Sing to us from a song of Zion.'
How could we sing a song of Yahweh on foreign ground?

If I forget Jerusalem,
   may my right hand forget (how to play).
May my tongue stick to my palate,
If I do not remember you,
If I do not lift up Jerusalem above my greatest[50] joy.

Remember, O Yahweh, the sons of Edom on the day of Jerusalem,
those who were saying,
   'Strip (her)! Strip (her)! to her foundation.'
Daughter of Babylon, the one who is destroyed,
   Blessed is he who pays you back[51] your reward,
   exactly as[52] you rewarded us.
Blessed is he who seizes and smashes your infants on the rock.

Responses to Psalm 137 are typical of the responses to imprecation. Perhaps it receives greater attention due to the horrific nature

---

47. My tr.
48. 'Tormentors' is a hapax legomenon.
49. Ellipsis assumed.
50. Lit. 'head, chief'.
51. There is a possible play on words with 'Jerusalem'. Alternate translations
   could include 'brings you to completion' and, perhaps ironically, 'brings
   you peace'.
52. See BDB, p. 980.

of its request in the concluding lines. Watson concludes that this psalm has no place in Christian worship:

> Christian victims of oppression could never legitimately appropriate this psalm in its entirety, however extreme their sufferings; and its use in Christian liturgical contexts can in no circumstances be justified. Although the psalm as a whole belongs to Christian scripture, it is not permitted to enact its total communicative intention: for all communicative actions embodied in holy scripture are subject to the criteria established by the speech–act that lies at the centre of Christian scripture, the life, death and resurrection of Jesus as the enfleshment and the enactment of the divine Word.[53]

Similarly, Psalms commentator Robert Alter suggests that 'No moral justification can be offered for this notorious concluding line. All one can do is to recall the background of outraged feeling that triggers the conclusion.'[54]

A theological interpretation of Psalm 137 presupposes that this psalm has a contemporary function (i.e. that this psalm continues to function as God's Word). Such an interpretation will investigate how the psalm functioned in the context of the psalter and how it now functions in its canonical context. In particular, uncovering 'what God is doing' with the psalm in these contexts is definitive for such an interpretation. In speech-act terminology, the goal can be described as uncovering which divine illocutions are currently 'in play'. In response to Watson and Alter, it is not enough simply to assert that imprecation is at odds with the New Testament and 'the speech–act that lies at the centre'. Rather, it needs to be demonstrated how the illocutions of the New Testament have affected the context within which the illocutionary acts of the psalter now exist.

It was argued above that the stance of the New Testament supports the stance of the psalter vis-à-vis imprecation such that the illocutions of the psalter inviting imitation are not abrogated.

---

53. Watson, *Text and Truth*, p. 121.
54. Robert Alter, *The Book of Psalms: A Translation and Commentary* (New York: Norton, 2007), p. 475.

Subsequently, many of the divine illocutions in play in the context of the psalter currently remain in play. In addition to these original illocutions, there may now be new divine illocutions produced by the intertextuality of the psalter and the New Testament.

Elsewhere I have argued that the most obvious way in which divine illocutions are performed in the Psalms is at the generic level (how the psalms are presented as a whole).[55] Examples of such generic illocutions include the *offering* of the Psalms as examples of a righteous response and the *invitation* to imitate this response in commensurate circumstances. At this level the divine illocutions and the generic illocutions are congruent. God appropriates the generic illocutions of the psalter and *offers* these psalms to his people, *inviting* their appropriation in similar circumstances. This makes sense of the difficult problem of how the words of God's people directed to God can be counted as God's words directed to God's people.

Moreover, as God is offering the psalm as an example of a righteous response, he is also affirming the stance of the psalmist *within* the psalm. In the case of Psalm 137, and commonly in the imprecatory psalms, God is affirming the loyalty of the psalmist, the anger of the psalmist and the psalmist's desire that God's name and his people are vindicated.

Far from being at odds with 'the speech–act that lies at the centre of Christian scripture, the life, death and resurrection of Jesus as the enfleshment and the enactment of the divine Word',[56] the illocutions of Psalm 137 gain a new focus through their relationship with the canon. The New Testament provides a vision of reality and of the future where all of God's enemies, and so the enemies of his people, will be destroyed by his Son (Rev. 4; 5; 19:1–21). The prayers of loyalty to Zion become prayers for God's kingdom and the rule of Christ to be fully realized. The prayer for vindication is performed with the knowledge of God's wrath being satisfied in the One to whom the prayer is now offered. This One now has the right and the role of bringing God's judgment upon all who reject him.

---

55. Barker, 'Divine Illocutions', p. 14.
56. Watson, *Text and Truth*, p. 121.

It was noted earlier that some claim this psalm 'incites hatred', and so can never be appropriated by Christians.[57] In contrast to this view it was suggested here that God's offering of Psalm 137 to his people is an invitation to respond likewise in similar situations. As such, he offers this psalm to his people as a righteous response to extreme violence. However, there is an important sense in which the text also 'incites hatred'. In offering this psalm to his people, God is inviting them to imitate its content, its pathos, its faith . . . its hatred. In a world where injustice, violence and oppression are rampant and God's people are being afflicted at the hands of the wicked, Psalm 137 confronts an apathetic and ambivalent people and incites them to hate, incites them to side with God, his Son and his people and to hate all those who will not give him glory. At the same time, imprecation precludes human vengeance and calls for the oppressed to surrender retribution to the God who will justly judge.

What remains is for Christians to consider what counts as a 'similar situation'. I have argued that imprecation is a justified response in the face of continued violence and impenitence. However, it is not always a necessary response. Wisdom is required in judging what counts as 'commensurate' with the setting of the psalms and of their New Testament appropriation. A context of direct violence against God's people by an implacable enemy is an obvious candidate for imprecation. However, I have intentionally used the broader language of 'extreme violence'. Direct attacks against God's people and God's purposes are not the only contexts where God's rule is rejected and his just punishment is required. Developing a vision of the world that matches God's vision is foundational to Christian maturity and will shape our responses to injustice.

Conclusion

This chapter has offered the outline of a theological interpretation of imprecation. It has demonstrated that the imprecatory psalms are consistent with (and in fact comprise a key aspect of) the illocutionary

---

57. Ibid., p. 120.

stance of the psalter, which offers them to the reader as righteous responses to similar circumstances. Furthermore, it has argued that the New Testament illocution calling readers to forgive their enemies has not altered the conditions under which the original illocutions of the psalter now function. In addition, the illocutionary stance of the New Testament reinforces that of the psalter by encouraging a response to violence and oppression that cries out to God for vindication. Therefore, the psalter's invitation to imprecation and the New Testament's call to forgive are concurrently 'in play'.

I suggested that a theological interpretation should attend to the way in which a text functions as God's Word. With respect to the imprecatory psalms, this is most clearly seen in their generic illocutions. At this level, God is inviting their appropriation, while, at a lower literary level, God is affirming the stances of the psalmist. In the case of Psalm 137, God offers the psalm as a righteous response to extreme violence. He affirms the loyalty of the psalmist, the anger of the psalmist and the psalmist's desire that God's name and his people be vindicated. It remains for us to consider what counts as a similar situation today and how these psalms might shape our response.

10. THE PSALMS AND PERPLEXITY: MEDITATING WITH THE PSALMIST ON THE PUZZLE OF EXISTENCE

Dan Wu

The pastoral edge: the 'search for certainty' and fascination with mystery

The shift from modernity to postmodernity has brought with it sweeping changes in the cultural psyche of Western society. Modernity, with its foundations of certainty firmly set in the primacy of human reason and progress, has given way to postmodernity, with its attendant loss of an overarching metanarrative upon which to hang our understanding of life and our place in the world. In many ways this has been a welcome and necessary change. In a fallen world 'truth' *is* often simply an exercise of oppression, a tool for those in power to impose their will upon others and thus maintain their own privileged position.[1]

---

1. William Golding's fictional account *Lord of the Flies* and George Orwell's semi-fictional *Animal Farm*, for example, explore this idea in various ways.

On the other hand, while postmodernism has proved quite effective in critiquing modernism, it has failed rather spectacularly to provide, in turn, any satisfying answers to the problems of human existence. Instead of simply exposing the ways in which the truth may be distorted and twisted, postmodernism has launched an all-out attack on the entire notion; there is no longer 'the Truth', there are only 'truths' – 'my truth' and 'your truth'. Furthermore, without any external, objective measure, 'your truth' becomes simply what you prefer, and if that is all it is, then you have no right to suggest that someone else has any less right to define for themselves what 'their truth' is.[2] The result, unsurprisingly, is the epistemological and ethical mess that characterizes the contemporary West. We live in a world that is thoroughly perplexed, and this is particularly evident for those who are involved, for instance, in ministering to youth in Sydney as I do – on the whole young people have more choice, opportunities and freedom than ever before, and yet the overwhelming impression is that they are, on the whole, utterly lost regarding the direction of their lives.

This is the world in which Western evangelicals find themselves ministering the gospel, and the pressure to modify and shift our theology and practice 'with the times' is unrelenting. The postmodern ideology that entered the world of academic biblical and theological studies some fifty or sixty years ago has filtered through into pulpits and pastorates, and into the minds of those to whom we minister. It has become commonplace to dismiss foundational evangelical doctrines such as assurance of faith and the inerrancy of Scripture, and to ridicule those who continue to stand by them. This has taken concrete form in two related phenomena.

The first is the accusation that evangelicals are obsessed with a naive 'search for certainty', burying their heads in the sand of the

---

2. Although the dismissal of an authoritative, universal notion of truth in favour of a pragmatic one is common to most postmodern writers, the work of Rorty stands out as a sustained critique of the metaphysicality of truth. See Richard Rorty, *Philosophy and the Mirror of Nature* (Princeton: Princeton University Press, 1980); Richard Rorty and Pascal Engel, tr. William McCuaig, *What's the Use of Truth?* (New York: Columbia University Press, 2007).

modernist desire for security, and trying desperately to find comfort in a world of black and white that simply does not exist.[3] The second phenomenon, which breathes the air of postmodernism deeply, is the logical end point of the first: a fascination with 'mystery' – as if chaos is kept at bay by attempting to participate in the process.[4] Perhaps it is such impulses that have led to the rise in popularity of such theological movements as Open Theism and Process Theology, with their emphasis on divine mutability, passibility and the idea that God does not know, or at least cannot determine, the future.

In the light of all this the Psalms are a great resource for ministry and the Christian life. Perplexity and bewilderment form sustained themes in the psalter, a fact that allows us to acknowledge and appropriate the categories into our preaching and understanding of life. Critically, however, the themes also appear in a manner that is firmly grounded in assurance of salvation and the trustworthiness of God's Word, which in turn is grounded in God's sovereignty and his goodness.

Nothing new under the sun: perplexity in the ancient world

It should come as no real surprise that postmodernism is actually nothing new. As a personal illustration, a friend of mine at university once decided to 'try out' different religions every few months, to work out which one 'worked best' for him. He 'became' a Buddhist for a few months, then a Muslim, then a Hindu and so on. Several

---

3. E.g. Peter Enns, *Inspiration and Incarnation: Evangelicals and the Problem of the Old Testament* (Grand Rapids: Baker, 2005); Kenton Sparks, *God's Word in Human Words: An Evangelical Appropriation of Critical Biblical Scholarship* (Grand Rapids: Baker Academic, 2008); *Sacred Word, Broken Word: Biblical Authority and the Dark Side of Scripture* (Grand Rapids: Eerdmans, 2012).

4. This tendency is pronounced in some branches of Christian mysticism. Perhaps the most prominent text in this tradition is Evelyn Underhill, *The Book of Contemplation the Which Is Called the Cloud of Unknowing, in Which a Soul Is Oned with God* (London: Watkins, 1922).

months later when asked how it was going he said something akin to, 'Well, I'm just trying to cover as many bases as possible and find the one that helps me get my life under control.'

Compare my friend's approach to, for example, the ancient Assyrian *Prayer to Any God*, and the parallel is striking. Here is a brief excerpt from the prayer:

1. May the anger of the lord's heart relent.
2. May the god whom I do not know relent.
3. May the goddess whom I do not know relent.
4. May whichever god relent.
5. May whichever goddess relent.
    . . .
38. I am distressed; I am alone; I cannot see.
39. I search constantly for my merciful god (and) I utter a petition.
    . . .
51. Humanity is deaf and does not know anything.
52. Humanity – by whatever name – what do they know?
53. Whether (a person) does wrong or good they are ignorant.
54. Lord, do not turn away your servant.[5]

The basic idea behind the prayer is that if anything has gone wrong in life, then one must have done something to offend the gods. However, one can never really be sure what crime was committed, or which god/goddess was offended, so the prayer attempts to cover as many bases as possible. A pronounced perplexity dominates the prayer; it is quite chaotic, as the supplicants fire off as many shots in the dark as they can manage, in the hope of getting some sense of control in life.

This perspective was widespread across the ancient world. Thus it is striking that, in the midst of all this, Israel was the one people who claimed to belong to a transcendent God, completely other to his creation, and completely in control. This explains Israel's prohibition on idolatry, something that would have been quite unthinkable

---

5. Translated by Charles Halton. Cited online at <http://awilum. com/?p=1730>, accessed 24 Dec. 2012.

in ancient times (cf. Deut. 4:15–20; 5:7–10).[6] It is also (at least in part) why early Christians were accused of being atheists, because their worship involved no idols or images.[7] This unique perspective derives from the unique understanding of a God who is not just 'in the mix of things', towards whom we grope through the darkness, or whose power we manipulate through talismans or magic. Rather, he is above and beyond his creation, is in control, and in fact has reached through the fog of the fallen world and revealed himself to us clearly in his Word.

---

6. The issue of Israel's 'monotheism' has been hotly debated at least since the 1960s, when the consensus view established by Bright and Albright, that Israelite religion was established as monotheistic (or monolatrous), but slowly degenerated into syncretism, was challenged by several 'newer' scholars, including F. M. Cross and Mark S. Smith. These scholars argued that the direction ought to be reversed, and that 'monotheism' was the end product of an evolutionary process from polytheism. Smith, for example, has mounted a strong argument for Israel's polytheistic Canaanite origins, whose various gods were converged into the figure of Yahweh during the monarchy, eventually being distilled down to monotheism during the exile. While such research has led to a more accurate understanding of the polyvalent nature of 'Israelite religion', its basic premise stands at odds with the presentation of Israel's covenant relationship with God in the canon. Furthermore, if an evangelical doctrine of inspiration is accepted, such that the one true God reveals himself to his people through Scripture, then the evolutionary view stands fundamentally at odds with the biblical presentation. See further M. S. Smith, *The Origins of Biblical Monotheism: Israel's Polytheistic Background and the Ugaritic Texts* (New York: Oxford University Press, 2001). For a review and critique of the evolutionary model suggested by Cross and Smith, see B. T. Arnold, 'Religion in Ancient Israel', in D. W. Baker and B. T. Arnold (eds.), *The Face of Old Testament Studies: A Survey of Contemporary Approaches* (Grand Rapids: Baker Academic, 1999), pp. 391–420.

7. Dio Cassius, *Epitome* 67.14, in *Roman History, Epitome of Books LXI–LXX*, tr. E. Cary, LCL (Cambridge: Harvard University Press, 1995); *Martyrdom of Polycarp* 3.2, 9.2, in Paul Foster and Sara Parvis (eds.), *Writings of the Apostolic Fathers* (London: Continuum, 2007); Justin Martyr, *First Apology* 1.5–6, in *The First and Second Apologies*, tr. L. W. Barnard, ACW 56 (Mahwah: Paulist, 1997); Athenagoras, *Embassy for the Christians* 1, 3, in *Embassy for the Christians, The Resurrection of the Dead*, tr. J. H. Crehan, ACW 23 (Mahwah: Paulist, 1956).

Perplexity in the Psalms

The Psalms as the word of man?

Israel's unique perspective is made clear throughout the psalter, even in the psalms of perplexity. Postmodern approaches have given rise to a spate of studies on the psalms of lament (of which perplexity is often seen as a subcategory), and the impression gained from such studies is that the main purpose of such psalms is to affirm and explore 'mystery' and 'uncertainty' as endemic to the human condition and our relationship to God. It needs to be said that such studies do resonate at some level with the honest reader of the Psalms; it *can* be difficult to see how the psalms that express perplexity and distress are *theology* – words from God about God and his plans and purposes. Instead, they are filled with doubt and dissatisfaction, accusing God in ways that sometimes border on blasphemy. They seem to speak with a voice that sounds all too human, and not divine, and this is often the way they are primarily understood.

Crenshaw, for example says of the psalms of lament, 'Unlike much biblical literature, these psalms originated from below. They constitute human praise and requests for help, in short, prayers . . . Most other books purport to present God's revelation to humanity or give an account of divine action as understood by the authors.'[8] Likewise, Paul Hewson: 'Explaining belief has always been difficult. How do you explain a love and logic at the heart of the universe when the world is so out of kilter with this?'[9] For Hewson, the Psalms capture this tension most in their perplexed cries to God: 'That's what a lot of the Psalms feel like to me, the blues. Man shouting at God – "My God, my God, why hast thou forsaken me? Why art thou so far from helping me?"'[10]

What are evangelicals to make of all this? What do we do with the psalms of perplexity, which seem to clash with our clear

8. James L. Crenshaw, *The Psalms: An Introduction* (Grand Rapids: Eerdmans, 2001), p. 14.

9. Hewson is better known by his stage name Bono, and is the lead singer of the band U2.

10. Paul Hewson, *Book of Psalms* (Edinburgh: Canongate, 2004), no page (ebook).

theological formulations of God's goodness and sovereignty in all of life? One popular answer is to give in to the postmodern impulse, and see such psalms as critiquing and attacking 'calcified' orthodox formulations – man shouting at God, indeed. On this reading the Psalms, as a microcosm of Scripture, contain many discordant, clashing voices. Crenshaw, for example, following Brueggemann, sees Psalm 73 as attempting to 'correct' the naive view of God's sovereignty and justice expressed in Psalms 37 and 49. Whereas the latter expresses a rather simplistic 'cause and effect' view, where the righteous prosper and the wicked are cut down, Psalm 73 'suggests that the issue has been stated falsely . . . [and therefore] flew in the face of traditional teaching'.[11]

Pushing even further, Ellington, following Fretheim and Moltmann,[12] urges that a proper appreciation of the prayers of lament means abandoning the 'perfect' God in favour of one who has 'opened himself up' to being affected by his creation, and therefore suffering. As Ellington puts it, 'God opts consistently for the uncertainty of relationships over the kind of perfection that is only possible in isolation and through manipulation.'[13] The resulting difference to our understanding and experience of God identified by Ellington is striking: 'we meet a God who is not above the chaos, but in it with us'.[14] As disturbing as this may seem, Ellington contends that this is the only option for us:

> Only by risking the death of the perfect God can we take Israel's lament on our lips and make their prayers our own. The prayer of lament does not find in God's distance, silence, and hiddenness marks of his perfection . . . The prayer of lament rages against a God who pretends to be impassive and immutable, knowing intuitively that

---

11. Crenshaw, *Psalms*, pp. 114–115; cf. W. Brueggemann and P. D. Miller, *The Psalms and the Life of Faith* (Minneapolis: Fortress, 1995), pp. 16–25.

12. T. E. Fretheim, *The Suffering of God: An Old Testament Perspective* (Philadelphia: Fortress, 1984); J. Moltmann, *The Crucified God: The Cross of Christ as the Foundation and Criticism of Christian Theology* (Minneapolis: Fortress, 1993).

13. S. A. Ellington, *Risking Truth: Reshaping the World Through Prayers of Lament* (Eugene, Oreg.: Pickwick, 2008), p. 54.

14. Ibid.

these are the qualities of idols, and therefore wholly alien to the God of Israel.[15]

The Psalms as the Word of God

As stated previously, evangelicals can be helpfully challenged and enriched by such studies. However, we must also be discerning, or else we risk being led astray from the God who reveals himself to us in the Scriptures. For the arguments of the scholars above include a subtle hermeneutical sleight of hand: *a false dichotomy has been introduced between the Psalms as the Word of God and as the word of man.* Indeed, this is critical to the discussion. Of course the psalms of lament are the word of man, and transparently so. However, so is the rest of Scripture. And as with the rest of Scripture, 'men spoke from God as they were carried along by the Holy Spirit' (2 Pet. 1:21). The words of the psalms of lament are thus first and foremost God-breathed, and so we need to approach them from this fundamental perspective.

In fact, a closer look at the case for 'clashing theologies' and seeing the psalms of lament primarily as man's word to God rather than God's word to us shows that it is overstated. On closer inspection, both Psalm 37 and Psalm 49 are written, like Psalm 73, in the *present* context of injustice, with a view to the future justification of the righteous.[16] What Psalm 73 makes explicit to a greater degree is simply the experience of the challenge to trust in God that this presents, while Psalms 37 and 49 emphasize God's faithfulness to the righteous and confidence in his deliverance. However, despite the different emphases, all three psalms address the same cluster of concepts: the current prosperity of the wicked, the hope of deliverance, and the summons to trust God's promises and live by them.

---

15. Ibid., p. 58.
16. The eschatology of the Psalms has been hotly debated in OT studies, and addressing the issue goes beyond the scope of this chapter. The point I am making holds, whether one takes the deliverance to be temporal, eschatalogical, or both (as in a biblical theology framework). For further on this topic see Philip S. Johnston, 'Psalm 49: A Personal Eschatology', in K. E. Brower and M. W. Elliott (eds.), *Eschatology in Bible and Theology* (Downers Grove: InterVarsity Press, 1997), pp. 73–84.

In other words, the psalms of lament are consistent with so-called traditional, orthodox theology. Rather than contradicting, they enrich and enhance our appreciation of it, by giving a profound account of the mysteries and frustrations of life.[17] But the bottom line is that these psalms are, then, first and foremost, *theology*: words from God, about God and life under him. Thus, in approaching the Psalms, we may agree with Bono's suggestion, but we also need to recognize that it is not a sufficient description. More than 'man shouting at God', and more even than 'God inviting us to do so',[18] these psalms are primarily about God's revealing himself and his purposes to humanity, even as he gives us the words to shout at him. As such, the psalms of perplexity touch on some very important theological themes that lead to the gospel, deepen our doctrinal reflections and are pastorally powerful. To them we now turn, looking first at the 'positive' side of perplexity in Palms 8 and 139, and then the 'negative' side in Psalm 73.[19]

The two faces of perplexity

'Positive' perplexity: how majestic is your name!

Cutting right against the grain of modern epistemology (that knowledge must be 'objective' and exhaustive to be legitimate), the Psalms express the limits of our being and understanding in remarkably positive ways. There is a clear sense in which perplexity is a

---

17. I believe this is also the case in the wider body of OT wisdom literature. Against the common portrayal of discordant theologies in wisdom literature, whereby Proverbs expresses a neat 'cause and effect theology', which is progressively undermined by Job and Ecclesiastes, it is better to see them, again, as complementary perspectives of life with a faithful God, but in a fallen world, of which the different books emphasize different aspects.

18. John P. Dickson, *If I Were God, I'd End All the Pain: Struggling with Evil, Suffering and Faith* (Kingsford: Matthias Media, 2001), p. 36.

19. I put 'positive' and 'negative' in quotes because I want to make sure they are understood in a qualified sense, and not as absolute, opposite or contradictory categories.

good and appropriate response to the majestic complexity of our God, which leads to humility and joy before him. We will explore Psalms 8 and 139 for what they have to say in this regard.

Psalm 8

Psalm 8 contains some important and positive aspects of perplexity. First, and most obviously, the psalm begins and ends with the declaration 'LORD, our Lord, how majestic is your name in all the earth!' (vv. 1, 9). This confession of the unfathomable glory of God then forms the foundation for reflection on the nature and place of humanity before him. It leads, for example, to an appropriate humility before him: 'What is mankind that you are mindful of them?' (v. 4). However, there is also wonder and delight; the description of the night sky (v. 3) juxtaposes *majesty* – the vast canopy of the heavens – with *intricacy* – God has carefully crafted and placed each star with his fingers.

Reading the psalm gives the unavoidable impression that it is beautifully overwhelming that this is the God who calls us his own. Unfortunately, this sense of awe and wonder can be under-emphasized in an evangelical theology that rightly focuses on the atonement, but misses the wider context and ultimate purpose of the cross – that God glorifies and is glorified by his creation.[20] Appropriating this aspect of perplexity into evangelical theology and ministry would mean ensuring that we are not content simply to teach how the cross works and what it achieves, or that salvation is by grace alone, but seek to move people to marvel at the God of such things. Perplexity in the Psalms teaches us that in our ministry we want people to think great thoughts of God, but also to be joyfully perplexed at how God is bigger than all our thoughts can contain. In short, perplexity ought to draw theology into doxology.

A further aspect of positive perplexity revolves around God's establishment of humanity as rulers of creation. 'What is mankind?'

---

20. The most sustained reflection on this topic is by Jonathan Edwards, most recently republished in J. Piper, *God's Passion for His Glory: Living the Vision of Jonathan Edwards: With the Complete Text of* The End for Which God Created the World (Leicester: Inter-Varsity Press, 1998).

(v. 4) casts the mind of the reader back to Genesis 1 – 2 for the answer: we are but dust; and yet God has ordained that we should bear his image and rule creation under him; a perplexing paradox indeed! In recalling the early chapters of Genesis, the psalm draws us to reflect on the details of its narratives. As such, when Psalm 8 is taken together with the Genesis 1:26–28 mandate to 'fill the earth and subdue it', it perhaps implies that part of the purpose of our limitations and ignorance is to give us impetus towards that commission – driving us to discovery, to work out what 'mastery' of the world looks and feels like. If this is plausible, it could contribute to an evangelical doctrine of aesthetics and creativity.[21]

We must, of course, take into account that these are relativized by the gospel and the judgment of God on this fallen creation and, further, the fact that because of sin our mastery is twisted, distorted and imperfect. But it is worth noting that it is *relativized*, not done away with – perhaps just as the image of God in us is marred, but not eliminated, so it is with our discovery and mastery of creation.

Psalm 139

Turning to Psalm 139, we see again the limits of human knowledge. Here, however, the focus is on the creation of the human person, the psalmist himself. The persistent theme of the psalm is that God knows everything about him, and has lovingly overseen the course of his whole life. *Time*: from before his birth until the number of his ordained days ends (v. 16). *Space*: from the loftiest heights of the world to the depths of the sea (v. 8), and to the secret place of the womb where God wove him together (v. 15). The critical statement comes in verse 6: 'Such knowledge is too wonderful[22] for me, too lofty[23] for me to attain', and the rest of the psalm drives this perhaps surprising

---

21. As a personal reflection on this point, I have long admired those skilled in photography. As a rank amateur, I am thoroughly perplexed by the complexity of aperture, exposure, film speed, and so on – and how these are all integrated simultaneously to create amazing pictures. Seeing beautiful photos, however, makes me want to discover and learn the art.

22. Heb. *pĕl'iâ* from *pālâ*, 'to be distinct, separated': cf. Judg. 13:18, 'beyond understanding'.

23. Heb. *niśgĕbâ*, from *śāgab*, 'to be too high, strong for, inaccessible'.

truth home: what is critical to the psalmist is not what he knows of God (although that is important), but what God knows of him (cf. vv. 1, 23).

This observation leads to an important implication: true knowledge does not arise from our being the all-knowing subject (as in modern epistemology), but *from being known by the all-knowing God*, a theme developed in the New Testament.[24] While this may seem initially odd (we are used to thinking about knowledge as a primarily *human* activity), it is actually a source of comfort and confidence. That we do not have all the answers is a good thing, because it gives us an oft-needed reality check: we are not God. Our perplexity thus leads to appropriate humility in our thinking and theology, and a willingness to listen to others with whom we may differ, knowing that we are not, nor do we have to be, the fount of all knowledge.

This awareness of our limits also gives us, then, the foundation of true knowledge. This is *God's* world. He knows how it works and how we work, because he is Lord. Thus we need to listen to what he tells us of how it works, and our place within his plans. Accordingly, though humility ought to characterize our theological reflection, we do not simply listen to other voices uncritically, but bring everything before the bar of Scripture, and test all other knowledge by its gospel-centred parameters (2 Cor. 10:3–5).

This aspect of perplexity also strengthens our doctrine of Scripture. The Bible does not tell us everything about life, ourselves or even God. It would, in fact, distort our understanding of the Bible if we were to claim that it does. But there is a good reason why this is the case: we are not told everything there is to know in Scripture, simply because we do not need to know everything. What we are told is everything we need; that is, for life, godliness and salvation (2 Pet. 1:3–4).

At this point we might be tempted to object that God is withholding knowledge from us we ought to have. But that is because

---

24. See further Brian S. Rosner, 'Known by God: C S Lewis and Dietrich Bonhoeffer', *EvQ* 77.4 (2005), pp. 343–352; '"Known by God": The Meaning and Value of a Neglected Biblical Concept', *TynB* 59.2 (2008), pp. 207–230.

to both modern and postmodern minds knowledge requires mastery; thus if it is not exhaustive, it cannot finally be legitimate. A right understanding of our limits under God frees us to say that our knowledge can be partial and perspectival, but still true. Not only so, but even though we can't know everything, we still know much and are directed to push further in our knowledge, especially of God's Word. And those who have delved into the Bible know that there is more than enough in its pages to occupy us for a lifetime![25]

Even more important than its description of *what* we can know, is the fact that the psalm grounds our epistemology in our relationship to God. The Hebrew verb 'to know' (*yāda'*) is primarily a word of relationship, even used of sexual activity (e.g. Gen. 4:1), and the relational nature of knowledge is the key concept in this psalm. To be known by God does not simply mean that he is aware of us, but that he has graciously established himself in right relationship to us as our Lord, so that our lives and salvation are ultimately in his hands, not our own. This is indeed good news when we recognize how frail, ignorant and sinful we actually are. If I had to depend on myself, I would be hopelessly doomed. There is true joy and hope in being safe in the hands of the God who knows everything. Most importantly, however, he knows *me*, and this is more wonderful than I could ever fully grasp. This is the psalmist's glorious message.

Our examinations of Psalms 8 and 139 show us that positive perplexity forms an important part of the foundation of a life of faith. Our limited knowledge drives us towards joyful trust in God, drawing assurance not from our own understanding and strength, but from his. This positive perplexity also sets the platform for the second strand of perplexity we see in the Psalms.

---

25. As Jerome put it, 'The Divine Word . . . [is] a river which is both shallow and deep: in which a lamb may wade and an elephant swim' (Cornelius á Lapide and T. W. Mossman, *The Great Commentary of Cornelius á Lapide* [London: John Hodges, 1891]; cited online at http://www. catholicapologetics.info/scripture/newtestament/generalpreface.htm, accessed 2 Nov. 2012).

'Negative' perplexity: Where is your former great love?

'Negative' perplexity is more apparent in the psalter, especially in the psalms of lament. There, perplexity comes when the current experience of persecution and suffering seems to contradict God's promises and goodness in the past. The resulting bewilderment drags probing questions out of the psalmist: 'How long, LORD, how long?' (Ps. 6:3), 'Why have you forsaken me?' (Ps. 22:1), and, ultimately behind all such cries, 'Where is your former great love, which in your faithfulness you swore to David?' (Ps. 89:49).

These two characteristics – love and faithfulness – cut to the heart of who God is. They are the characteristics God himself declares in the great revelation of his glory in Exodus 34:6–7; he is the God of *ḥesed wĕ'ĕmet* (steadfast/covenant love and truthfulness).[26] Negative perplexity thus has to do with the cognitive dissonance between the confession of God's *ḥesed wĕ'ĕmet* and their seeming absence in the present. In that vacuum perplexity rushes in and fills heart and mind with pain and frustration. I will focus on Psalm 73 as a test case, as it seems to be a key psalm within the book. Even more importantly, it has the full sweep of moving from perplexity to a renewed strength in Asaph's trust of God, in a manner that pushes us forwards strikingly to the gospel.

The psalm opens with a basic statement of God's goodness to Israel (v. 1), which is echoed near the end (v. 28). This suggests that the main subject of the psalm is the nature of God's goodness – in particular, how it is expressed and confirmed to his people. The problem comes in verses 2–12, as the psalmist observes the injustice of the wicked prospering and oppressing the righteous. The description reads almost like a nightmarish alternate reality, where the blessings of the covenant are present, but the recipients are the wicked, instead of the righteous. The wicked have no struggles

---

26. The characteristics often appear in the closely related pairs 'love and faithfulness', 'mercy and justice', 'grace and truth' or some combination of them. At this point, then, Brueggemann is correct to say that the critical subject in the Psalms as a whole is God's *ḥesed* in relation to his covenant people (W. Brueggemann, 'Bounded by Obedience and Praise: The Psalms as Canon', *JSOT* 50 [1991], pp. 63–92).

or trouble (vv. 4–5), are in authority (vv. 6–11) and are blessed materially (v. 12), while the righteous suffer at their hands.

The psalmist knows that God cannot approve of this. However, in verses 13–16 his bewilderment and frustration lead him almost to the point of giving up his trust in God. The language is reminiscent of Ecclesiastes: 'Surely in vain[27] I have kept my heart pure and have washed my hands in innocence' (v. 13); 'When I tried to understand all this, it troubled[28] me deeply' (v. 16). The point the psalmist makes in these verses is thus something like, 'If there is no *ḥesed* in God, then why should I keep *ḥesed* with him? If his promise is empty, then staying faithful to him is empty, pointless toil.'

Even as he says this, however, the psalmist acknowledges that to speak in this manner is neither true nor appropriate: 'If I had spoken out like that, I would have betrayed your children' (v. 15). How verse 15 fits in to the flow of the psalm is difficult, but at very least it indicates that even though this is an 'individual psalm', the psalmist is aware of the presence of the congregation, and speaks ultimately for their benefit. Indeed, in the light of verse 1 it would seem the psalmist recognized that he had a certain responsibility in leading God's people; to be faithless towards him was also to be faithless toward them. In this representative role there is at least an echo of the necessity of Jesus' being faithful to God, not only for his sake, but for ours as well (cf. Heb. 2 – 3).

The point here, however, is that the psalmist recognizes the inappropriateness of the thinking. In fact he has already hinted at this: 'Surely God is good to Israel ... *but* as for me, my feet had almost slipped' (vv. 1–2). The sustained understanding of the psalm is that the problem is not with God and his *ḥesed*; it is rather with our lack of understanding (vv. 21–22). Nonetheless, the striking thing is that he still gives full acknowledgment *both* to his frustration and bewilderment, *and* to his battle to keep trusting in God. In other

---

27. Heb. *rîq* (lit. 'emptiness') is slightly different from Ecclesiastes' characteristic *hebel*, 'breath, vapour, mist'. However, the idea in this regard is virtually identical.

28. Heb. *'āmāl* (toil); cf. Eccl. 1:3.

words, he considers that as giving full vent to feelings that run dangerously close to apostasy is completely *inappropriate*, and also at the same time (paradoxically) completely *appropriate*.

The Ecclesiastes-like language gives us a clue as to how to hold these together consistently. There is a clear awareness that this is God's world, still bearing the unmistakeable marks of his goodness, and yet all is not as it should be; it is fallen and frustrated, awaiting his liberation. Likewise, in the psalm there is a full expression of perplexity and the emotional state of the psalmist, but also it is set firmly in the assurance that God's *ḥesed wĕ'ĕmet* will be vindicated – there is no contradiction or abandoning of the creedal statement, but a recourse to it, even in the midst of his turmoil. Perplexity and assurance are placed side by side.

This has some immediate and powerful pastoral implications. We can be tempted to move people too quickly through grief and bewilderment, attempting to rush them into a superficial affirmation of orthodoxy for fear of getting things theologically 'wrong'. In reality, it may take a long time – months, even years – for someone to be reconciled to the circumstance they find themselves in, and affirming the legitimacy of their cries of pain and frustration, even towards God, may be the most appropriate and helpful service we can do them in the moment. On the other hand, we must all the while keep reminding them, gently but firmly, of the goodness and faithfulness of God revealed in the Scriptures, in order to help move people appropriately through dwelling on the mystery to trust and hope in God.

This hope is expressed in verse 17, the turning point in the psalm. The critical moment comes when the psalmist enters the sanctuary of God, and what he experiences or observes grants him a completely new perspective on his situation. Now he understands their destiny. The wicked *will* be judged by God as they should be, and the righteous vindicated. The key question that arises, then, is, 'What happened in the sanctuary to give him this absolute confidence?' Is it (as some commentators put it)[29] simply being near to God's

---

29. E.g. James Mays, *Psalms* (Louisville: John Knox, 1994), p. 243; Brueggemann and Miller, *Psalms and the Life of Faith*, p. 208.

presence? This is hard to deny, especially in the light of the end of
the psalm: 'As for me, it is good to be near God' (v. 28).

Perhaps, however, there is something more. The central significance of the sanctuary was that it was where the sacrifice for sins
took place. In other words, perhaps the psalmist is saying something
like, 'When you go into the sanctuary and see sacrifices being made,
you know there is a God who judges sin.'[30] If that is the case, the
ultimate question the psalm raises, then, is 'Where do we see God's
hesed wě'ĕmet come to pass'?[31] Where do his love and justice come
together in judgment and salvation? If the immediate answer of the
psalm is through the sacrifice made in the sanctuary, the ultimate
answer comes in the cross of Christ, where sin is judged and nearness
to God is opened up for us through his body (Heb. 10:19–22). While
the focus of this chapter is on the Psalms, I will make some brief
remarks on the theme in the New Testament and its application to
Christian life and ministry.

Perplexity in the New Testament

The gospel of perplexity

The thrust of the Scriptures is that the experience of the psalmist
is primarily the experience of Christ,[32] and this holds true with regard
to the theme of perplexity. Consider, for example, Jesus' ignorance
or distress at the details of the Father's plans (e.g. Mark 13:32; John
12:20–28), or, most prominently, the cry of dereliction 'My God,
my God, why have you forsaken me?' (Ps. 22:1). It is true that Old
Testament citations reflect the whole passage, not simply the quoted
part, and Psalm 22 does move on to resolution. However, this does
not evacuate the words of their truth or impact – Jesus was separated
in a real way from the Father on the cross that defies understanding;

---

30. Cf. Isa. 6:1–7, where the live coal from the altar (where the sacrifice was
    made) makes Isaiah fit for prophetic service through atoning for his sin.
31. In fact, this is the key question, whether or not one accepts what I have just
    suggested regarding sacrifice in the sanctuary.
32. See further the other contributions in this volume.

as Luther is reported to have said, 'Mystery of mysteries: God forsakes God!'[33]

The major stress in the New Testament, however, lies in the resolution to perplexity in the atonement. In the cross and resurrection of Jesus we see the ultimate revelation of God's *ḥesed wĕ'ĕmet*, graciously delivering his people and justly judging sin (John 1:14; Rom. 3:9–26). Moreover, this places our theme in its broader context of God's plan to reverse the curse of the Fall, for 'negative' perplexity is ultimately part and parcel of living under the shadow of death. In other words, perplexity arises because things in this world do not work as they should. Things do not work as they should because of the Fall, sin and death. Death, in particular, is the ultimate frustration of God's purposes for humanity, the clear sign that we do not rule over creation as we are meant to.

The resurrection therefore provides the critical resolution to the perplexity of living in a fallen world. Jesus has re-established humanity to our God-given place as rulers of creation, by sharing his victory over death with us (Heb. 2:5–18): both now, in the first fruits of new life in the Spirit and the assurance of God's all-conquering love (Rom. 8:5–39), and in his return, when victory is completed, and God 'will wipe every tear from their eyes' and there is 'no more death or mourning or crying or pain, for the old order of things has passed away' (Rev. 21:4).

Perplexity in Christian ministry and experience

That we continue to live in the overlap of the ages is critical in understanding Christian ministry, and so it should come as no surprise that the themes of perplexity raised in the Psalms – both 'positive' and 'negative' – should be echoed in significant ways in the New Testament.

---

33. This needs to be held together with orthodox affirmations of the unity of Father, Son and Spirit in the cross to avoid a serious distortion of the gospel. However, we must also avoid domesticating what is ultimately beyond our understanding, and so blunt the confronting truth of the Scriptures.

'Positive' perplexity in Christian ministry and experience

Whatever 'centre' one subscribes to, it is clear that Romans 11:33–36 is a climactic point in the epistle. Perhaps surprisingly, and a little humorously, 'positive' perplexity lies at the heart of the passage, in terms reminiscent of Psalms 8 and 139. For after giving perhaps his most developed exposition of the gospel in God's plan, encompassing sin, grace, assurance, predestination, the Law and the relationship and purpose of Jew and Gentile, in Romans 11:33–36 Paul, in effect, says, 'I still don't really get it!'

> Oh, the depth of the riches of the wisdom
>   and knowledge of God!
>   How unsearchable his judgments,
>   and his paths beyond tracing out!
> Who has known the mind of the Lord?
>   Or who has been his counsellor?
> Who has ever given to God,
>   that God should repay him?
> For from him and through him and to him
>   are all things,
>   To him the glory for ever! Amen
> (Rom. 11:33–36)

It is a most helpful example of humility and Godward wonder from which Christians can learn, not least those involved in ministry. Despite Paul's key role in God's plan (Gal. 1:11–24; Eph. 3:1–13; Col. 1:24–27), he remained ever aware that he was only a servant (2 Cor. 4:5), and a servant, moreover, to a master whose greatness so surpassed his own that even his insight and preaching were only scratching the surface of Christ's glory (see Eph. 2:6–7). If in Psalm 8 theology should lead to doxology and a right humility before God, then how much more for those who have seen the majesty of God's name in Christ? Christian teaching and pastoring, then, are not simply a matter of passing on information, nor of building oneself up to be a 'great one' in people's eyes. Instead, it is leading God's people, by word and example, to humble awe at his greatness, directing them to love and wonder at his glories, rather than our own.

'Negative' perplexity in Christian ministry and experience

In 2 Corinthians 4:8 Paul describes himself in his ministry as 'perplexed, but not in despair'. In the overlap of the ages, Christian experience is a nexus of both the victory of the age to come and the frustration of the present age. Paul continues, 'we always carry around in our body the death of Jesus, so that the life of Jesus may also be revealed in our body' (4:10). For Paul, then, there was a cognitive dissonance in his ministry that matched the nature of the gospel as hidden from human wisdom and power (1 Cor. 1 – 2). In other words, perplexity forms a significant aspect of Christian ministry. The pattern and expectation of the Scriptures is not that the right combination of theology and strategy will guarantee spiritually mature members, numerical growth and budgets in surplus. Rather, it is that Christian life and ministry will often involve bewilderment, frustration, and the failure of well-laid plans, as we walk with people through the muck of life in a fallen world, and feel its effects in ourselves and our ministry.[34]

Ministry in such situations, of course, will be as complex and context-driven as life is. Fundamentally, however, we must direct people to the fulfilment of God's *ḥesed wĕ'ĕmet* in the gospel, and to hope in Christ's return as the only place where the answers will finally become clear. As 1 Corinthians 13:12 says, 'now we see only a reflection as in a mirror; then we shall see face to face. Now I know in part; then I shall know fully . . .'. Even more important than knowing answers to the conundrums of life, however, is the final clause of the verse: 'even as I am fully known'. In line with Psalm 139 Paul's longing is that his knowledge of God will come fully in line with God's knowledge of him. The knowledge the Christian ultimately hopes for is not so much 'answers', as the full experience of the knowledge that really counts – knowledge of the deep and intimate love of God for us that surpasses knowledge (Eph. 3:19).

Another helpful perspective on perplexity comes in Revelation 6:10, where the martyrs cry out in echo of Psalm 94:3, 'How long?'

---

34. For a helpful perspective on 'success' in ministry in the light of this, see R. K. Hughes and B. Hughes, *Liberating Ministry from the Success Syndrome* (Wheaton: Crossway, 2008).

In response, they are given white robes (the colour symbolizing conquest, underscoring their ultimate victory over death in Christ), and told to wait a little longer, until their number is completed. This is significant, because it suggests that perhaps the major reason why this perplexing and painful world continues is so that God's elect, won (in part) through the faithful, suffering testimony of his people, might have more time to be saved (cf. 2 Pet. 3:8–9). Here there is encouragement for perseverance in Christian life and ministry; as stated previously, we do not need to know everything, but we do know as much of God's plan and purpose in this world as anyone (humanly speaking): God desires that his people be saved through the preaching of the gospel – the gospel of the suffering and glorified Christ, and his suffering and glorified people.

The preceding point raises one final doctrinal issue that undergirds the argument of this chapter, namely how it is legitimate, given that the words of the psalmist are primarily the words of Christ, to take the Psalms' words of perplexity as our own. The answer lies in our *union with Christ*; in particular, in his incarnation as one of us, and our incorporation into him. In terms of incarnation, Hebrews makes much of Jesus' fully sharing our humanity, including the experience of our weaknesses: 'we do not have a high priest who is unable to empathize with our weaknesses, but we have one who has been tempted in every way, just as we are – yet he did not sin' (Heb. 4:15; cf. 2:10–18). The incarnation included the common human experience of the frustrations of the fallen world. Jesus' experience was, of course, unique, in his representative and propitiatory role for us, and this is primarily what the Psalms testify to. However, inasmuch as he took on *our* sufferings (Matt. 8:17; cf. Isa. 53:4), there is then a derivative manner in which we may legitimately appropriate the sense of the psalmist's perplexity and his resolve to trust in God as our own, even though the specific situation is different.

Our incorporation into Christ also legitimates such a perspective. A major but sometimes neglected theme in the New Testament is our sharing in Christ's sufferings, as well as his glory. There is good reason for caution on this front, and historical surveys expose the distortions of the gospel that result from an overemphasis on Christ's work *in* us, rather than his work *for* us. The theme, however, is prominent, and we neglect it to our detriment: 'if we are children, then we are heirs – heirs of God and co-heirs with Christ, if indeed we share in his sufferings in order that we may also share in his glory' (Rom. 8:17; cf. 1 Pet. 4:12–13). Our suffering, of course, is not salvific, as his was. It is, rather, a 'fellowship' or 'sharing' (*koinōneō*) in them; derivative, but still, in a very real way *his*. It is therefore fitting that Christ should share his own cries of bewilderment (and his own trust in God through the darkness) with his people when bewilderment overtakes them.[35]

Conclusion

The Psalms demonstrate that perplexity and confidence go hand in hand; we need not pit one against the other. Rather, our perplexity gives us a significant opportunity to grow in our knowledge and assurance of God's great love for us. His creatures are led to wonder and marvel at his uncontainable greatness and glory, and draw humble assurance from the security of his perfect, loving knowledge of us, rather than our frail and flawed knowledge. His steadfast character and sovereignty, acknowledged by the psalmist and confirmed in the gospel, give his people secure parameters by which to navigate through the perplexing experience of living in a fallen world, and to hold fast to Christ until

> The throne of God and of the Lamb will be in the city, and his servants
> will serve him. They will see his face, and his name will be on their
> foreheads. There will be no more night. They will not need the light
> of a lamp or the light of the sun, for the Lord God will give them light.
> And they will reign for ever and ever. (Rev. 22:3–5)

---

35. A full exploration of the relationship between Christ's sufferings and those
    of his people is beyond the scope of this chapter. Besides Rom. 8 and
    1 Peter, the reader is directed to the discussion in C. R. Campbell, *Paul
    and Union with Christ: An Exegetical and Theological Study* (Grand Rapids:
    Zondervan, 2012), pp. 380–381.

11. THE POLITICS OF PRAISE: THE PSALMS AND CHRISTIAN SOCIAL ENGAGEMENT

Andrew Sloane

Introducing the politics of praise

At first glance this might seem an odd topic to address in a series of explorations on the Psalms. Surely the Psalms are primarily given to us to use in addressing God and shaping our lives together as God's people? Do not the Psalms aim at elevating us above the humdrum world of daily existence to the contemplation of God and his glory? Furthermore, if we were to be interested in the messy world of political discourse and public action, are there not more obvious places to go? The Torah and prophets, for instance, have a lot to say explicitly about the public and political life of God's people – and that of the nations (Deut. 17, 1 Sam. 18 and Amos 1 – 2 immediately come to mind). And, of course, much could be said (and has been said) about the politics of Jesus and of Paul (say, in relation to Matt. 5 – 7 or Rom. 13). So far so bad for the possibility of a 'politics of praise'.

Understandable as they may be, these are mistaken impressions. I aim to show that, contrary perhaps to first impressions, the book of Psalms has a lot to say that can helpfully shape our understanding of and engagement in the world – including the messy world of politics. I do not plan to articulate a particular political theology from the psalter; others are better placed to do that job, and I think that would be misguided anyway, as so much of what we might say needs to be carefully refracted through Jesus and the New Testament understanding of church and mission. Rather, I aim to look at the resources the psalter offers for shaping Christian hearts and minds, and how this shapes political theology and social engagement. I aim to examine this at two levels: first, a brief consideration of the shape of the psalter and its function and the way that informs our understanding of God, God's concern for human social arrangements and the role of God's people in enacting those concerns in society; secondly, a (somewhat) more in-depth look at some specific texts that ought to shape a politics of praise. But before I get to those substantive tasks, I think it best to do a little ground (or throat) clearing: first, a brief clarification of what I do and do not mean when I speak of politics and social engagement; then, a pre-emptive countering of a criticism of the enterprise as a whole.

Politics

Oliver O'Donovan has challenged us to think truly theologically about politics in the light of the gospel, suggesting that human political authority is limited to enacting judgment.[1] While politics describes both institutions and sets of practices, and involves ordering the priorities and distributing the resources of a particular community and/or state, I will be considering politics more broadly than just the role of government and the associated institutions, policies, laws, and so on, to include broader reflections on society and our common life – what Hunter calls the realm of the 'public'

---

1. Oliver O'Donovan, *The Desire of the Nations: Rediscovering the Roots of Political Theology* (Cambridge: Cambridge University Press, 1996); *Common Objects of Love: Moral Reflection and the Shaping of Community* (Grand Rapids: Eerdmans, 2002).

as opposed to the (narrowly) political.[2] Central to that will be an understanding of our common life and the institutions that shape it as being governed by a vision of human flourishing.[3] Political reflection, then, as I will use the term, will be oriented towards an analysis of the implicit or explicit vision of 'the good', or human flourishing, encoded in public life, and a critique of that vision and its achievement in our political life in the light of the gospel. It is also aimed at shaping our engagement in that common life and the way the Scriptures inform it by way of the vision of God, the world and human existence that captures our hearts and minds in the gospel.

By politics, then, I mean the criteria by which Christians ought to assess the functioning of political institutions, including the legitimate goals of human communities that a polity is meant to foster, and the kinds of influence that are appropriate for Christians to bring to bear on those institutions and for what kinds of ends. I will assume rather than argue for a general position that holds that it is appropriate for Christians, where the political realities allow for it, to function as a critical voice in their polity, reminding the 'world' of the true nature and goal of human community (the flourishing that political life is meant to enhance), and seeking to shape those communities in the direction of true human flourishing.[4] And where that polity fails, to lament this fact – understanding lament as a faithful expression of a holy dissatisfaction with the inequities

---

2. James Davison Hunter, *To Change the World: The Irony, Tragedy, and Possibility of Christianity in the Late Modern World* (Oxford: Oxford University Press, 2010).

3. Even a narrow reading of O'Donovan's notion of government-as-judgment requires this, for it depends on an understanding of what counts as justice that, in turn, requires a teleology of human flourishing. See Alasdair MacIntyre, *Whose Justice? Which Rationality?* (London: Duckworth, 1987).

4. Nicholas Wolterstorff, *Until Justice and Peace Embrace* (Grand Rapids: Eerdmans, 1983); *Justice: Rights and Wrongs* (Princeton: Princeton University Press, 2008); *Justice in Love* (Grand Rapids: Eerdmans, 2011); Hunter, *To Change the World*, esp. pp. 176–193, 197–286. So even Stanley Hauerwas, *After Christendom?* (Nashville: Abingdon, 1999), pp. 23–44.

and griefs of current reality articulated both to God and to those who have ears to hear in the human community.

Echoing Bauckham, the Psalms, of course, is not a book *of* politics, but it is a profoundly *political* book, inasmuch as it does shape particular understandings of God and God's rule, humanity and human agency, sin and the structures of human existence, history and the destiny of human life.[5] It shapes a political imagination, presenting a political vision through which we look at our political lives and structures. The Psalms do not, however, give us specific instructions as to which politician or party to vote for, or what our conclusions ought to be on current government policy on education, economics, asylum seekers or the environment. They are more general than that, functioning, so to speak, as a theological 'heads up display' through which we look at the world around us to discern its order and disorder. The primary function the Psalms play is in shaping the 'mind' and 'heart' we ought to bring to bear in our political engagement[6] – so the psalter operates at the 'general' level of the shaping of our vision, not the 'particular' level of the causes, parties or policies we ought to endorse. But a vision needs to be specific and oriented, and therefore should be open to address particular issues – to see, I suppose, how the vision informs practice. Indeed, to press the metaphor of a 'heads up display', we look *through* the Psalms at specific issues, policies and so on, to seek to discern how they do or do not fit the psalter's projected world.

Political engagement and the Psalms: what about Psalm 37?

That is all well and good, but it might be objected that the Psalms cannot or should not contribute to Christian social engagement. And some Psalms seem to give credence to the notion that this whole exercise is wrong-headed. Psalm 37 is an example of the kind

---

5. Richard Bauckham, *The Bible in Politics: How to Read the Bible Politically* (London: SPCK, 1989).

6. For the broader role of 'liturgy' in Christian formation, see James K. A. Smith, *Desiring the Kingdom: Worship, Worldview, and Cultural Formation* (Grand Rapids: Eerdmans, 2009).

of text that might be appealed to (via the Sermon on the Mount,
say, Matt. 5:5, 39) as a warrant for political quietism. If we are not
to fret in the face of wickedness (Ps. 37:1, 8), and indeed are not to
resist the evil-doer (Matt. 5:39), surely political engagement is
swallowed up in prayerful trust in God's sovereign action? Such a
view, however misreads both the psalter and this psalm. First, Psalm
37 addresses individuals who are tempted to anger in the face of the
success of the wicked, reminding them of the sovereign rule of
God, and of the value of relationship with God, calling them to
renounce the envy that fuels resentment.[7] Secondly, the kind of
suffering, persevering fidelity, of which the psalm – and Jesus –
speaks, is in fact a profoundly political act. If Jesus and Psalm 37
speak of inaction (which is open to question), this ought to be seen
as a withdrawal from the political process as an indictment of it. For
'fretting' or 'fuming'[8] (37:1, 7–8) suggests buying into the violence
of an intolerable political situation and its (currently) irremediable
injustice (note v. 8), rather than deferring to God's eschatological
judgment.

This broader perspective is evident in the psalm, in which the
future justice of God is the ground for current trust – trust that is
seen as *entrusting* our cause to God rather than seeking to enact our
own justice through our own power.[9] Furthermore, in the psalm
itself trust is seen neither as quietistic withdrawal from those social
processes that, if properly ordered, might bring about justice,
nor disengagement from commitments that embody justice. For
among those who 'shall inherit the land' are not only the meek
('*ănāwîm*, v. 11), but also those in the right (*tsaddîqîm*, v. 29); and
'righteousness' is a fundamentally *social* and *relational* notion in the
Old Testament, as seen in verse 30 in the fact that they 'speak
justice'. Patient perseverance in trust is contrasted with godless

---

7. John Goldingay, *Psalms 1–41* (Grand Rapids: Baker, 2006), pp. 533–535.

8. The hithpael of *ḥrâ*, 'become angry or indignant', is better translated 'fume',
   maintaining the sense of anger slowly burning, than 'fret', which speaks
   more of quiet irritation or anxiety at external affairs.

9. James C. McCann, 'Psalms', in Leander E. Keck (ed.), *The New Interpreter's
   Bible*, vol. 4 (Nashville: Abingdon, 1996), pp. 828–830; Craig G. Broyles,
   Psalms (Peabody: Hendrickson, 1999), pp. 178–184.

action aimed at achieving our own ends. However, this is not pietistic withdrawal from the social and political process in acquiescence to its current inequities, but a faithful witness to the justice of God in the face of human injustice, implicitly indicting and judging it in anticipation of Yahweh's public verdict in which all wrongs are rectified. Of this verdict the psalm is confident and the psalmist trusts in it.

The psalter and politics

We turn now to the psalter, its shape and function, to reflect on how that informs our political vision. As is now well known, the psalter has been deliberately shaped so as to function as a theological whole.[10] Within the psalter there are both 'cycles' and a clear progression. As Brueggemann notes, the book opens with a call to obedience and ends with a call to praise, but the journey that takes us from one to the other is rich, complex and fraught.[11] Psalms 1, 2 and 150 assume a theological and political order that undergirds human existence. God's rule is both affirmed in Psalm 1, and linked to the human exercise of power in Psalm 2. The final goal of the Psalms, the unfettered praise of Yahweh, entails an eschatological goal in which Yahweh's just rule is fully exemplified in the world, and in the world of human power (note the placement of Ps. 149, with its call to praise and aggressive action, prior to Ps. 150, with its call to unqualified, universal praise). Between these 'bookends' the dynamic cycles of praise, lament, confession, instruction and memory inform particular understandings of God and his rule, humanity and human agency, sin and the structures of human existence, history and the destiny of human life. They both inform our minds and capture our hearts, for as poetry (often dark and complex, but always powerful) the Psalms engage our hearts as much as they inform our heads.

---

10. See chapter 1 in this volume.
11. Walter Brueggemann, 'Bounded by Obedience and Praise: The Psalms as Canon', *JSOT* (1991), pp. 63–92.

This poetic function of psalms as a genre is worth considering in the light of speech-act theory.[12] We need to remember that words *do things*. One of those things is to assert (words have propositional force), but words also command, promise and warn – and thank and praise. The Psalms raise the question of what we are *doing* when we praise. Speaking narrowly for a moment of 'hymnic' praise, praise ascribes worth to God and validates certain qualities as ones for which God is rightly valued. It articulates a set of values and the (positive) emotions associated with them. But praise is also self-involving, both 'vertically' (involving us in the validating of these qualities of God) and horizontally (noting the way that this validates certain qualities as being worthy and worth imitating). The vertical self-involvement of praise requires that we perform the speech acts the poetry encodes: in this instance, expressing our valuing of God for these qualities and in so doing acknowledging the unique worth of God as the unique exemplar of those qualities. But it is also 'horizontally' self-involving, shaping our character and agency. For if we value those qualities, and God as the perfect exemplar of them, then we value them in all relevantly similar contexts, as seen in the condemnation of those who do not exhibit them (e.g. Ps. 82) and the commendation of those who do (e.g. the pairing of Ps. 112 with Ps. 111).[13] They are, then, not just qualities of the one we worship but qualities of the lives shaped by that worship and the God we worship. In the terms of older systematicians, praising God for certain of God's 'communicable' attributes serves to form them in us: doxology is an act of sanctification.

But the Psalms function as praises not just in a narrow but also in a broad sense: the book as a whole is *tĕhillîm*, 'praises'. And these praises include lament and other forms. It is in this sense of praise that I want to reflect further on the role of praise in shaping our political vision.

---

12. See especially Gordon J. Wenham, *Psalms as Torah: Reading Biblical Song Ethically* (Grand Rapids: Baker, 2012), pp. 57–76; and chapters 6 and 9 in this volume.

13. See Wenham, *Psalms as Torah*, pp. 158–166; David Starling, 'Meditations on a Slippery Citation: Paul's Use of Psalm 112:9 in 2 Corinthians 9:9', *JTI* 6 (2012), pp. 241–255.

Praise in the broader sense orients us rightly to God in relationship. This relationship includes the trusting recognition of the goodness of God and his governance of the world reflected in the hymns and other psalms of 'orientation', as well as the more complicated trust of lament and prayer and other psalms of 'disorientation' and 'reorientation' that engage with God and call him to act in ways that reflect his own character and sovereign purposes in response to the fractured nature of the world and society.[14] The trusting faith that lies at the heart of right relationship with God is, however, exemplified across a range of Psalms genres, and not just at the 'poles' of praise and lament.[15] Instruction, testimony, thanksgiving, the reminder of God's past acts of grace and power and of Israel's infidelity, as well as the thankful, trusting petition for divine blessing, all articulate this fundamental trust in God.[16] This right orientation to God, as both the one who acts justly and graciously in the world and on whom we depend in our need, chastens and contextualizes all political engagement as being subject to him, his scrutiny and judgment, and as aiming for the reflection of his glory in the world and the turning of the world to the praise he rightly deserves (cf. Ps. 67).

Praise, however, does not just function positively: the trust it expresses also serves to counter, even dismantle, the alternative systems of trust that we, like the psalmists, confront in our world. This functions, firstly, at the immanent 'human' level of historical systems and structures, for praise confronts us with the character of God and God's rule in the world and so calls us to a repentance that *changes things* and a faith that works. But it also functions at the transcendent 'spiritual' level of the non-human powers that operate

---

14. Walter Brueggemann, 'Psalms and the Life of Faith: A Suggested Typology of Function', in David J. A. Clines (ed.), *The Poetical Books: A Sheffield Reader* (Sheffield: Sheffield Academic Press, 1997), pp. 35–66; and its development in John Goldingay, 'The Dynamic Cycle of Praise and Prayer in the Psalms', pp. 67–72 in the same volume.

15. Claus Westermann, *Praise and Lament in the Psalms* (Atlanta: John Knox, 1981).

16. Walter Brueggemann, 'Praise and the Psalms: A Politics of Glad Abandonment (Part I)', *Hymn* 43.3 (1992), pp. 14–19.

in, over and through social and political systems. Praise exposes and dismantles idols – which in both the ancient Near East and our world entail the ideologies that generate and are 'legitimated' by the idols. Brueggemann states, 'Wherever this God is named, social possibility is envisioned ... The God of the Bible is relentlessly a political character whose presence delegitimates wrong power arrangements, whose purposes summon and authorize new power arrangements.'[17]

These observations stand despite questions that may be raised in the light of a Christological reading of the Psalms. The prominence of David in the psalter and the Psalms' role in the New Testament's proclamation of Jesus' identity and mission prompt the claim that they do not function primarily as our prayers, but as witnesses to the sufferings and faithfulness of the Christ.[18] While it is important to acknowledge their function as witnesses to Christ, a properly robust Christology allows us also to use them, derivatively, as our songs and prayers. Jesus is truly God and the true human, the one who embraces the realities of human existence and lives a truly faithful human life – he is *the* Son of Man, the representative human.[19] His appropriation of the psalter, then, is both *for us* and *with us*: it is an inclusive, not an exclusive use,[20] such that we are

17. Ibid., p. 17. This differs from O'Donovan's notion of idolatry and government (O'Donovan, *Common Objects*, esp. pp. 53–54, 70–71). The sinful distortion of politics is not because a focus on other *teloi* (ends) is an illegitimate goal for politics to engage in, but that illegitimate or distorted *teloi* are adopted in faithless social visions (see Smith, *Desiring the Kingdom*, pp. 75–130).

18. For the role of David in the Psalms and its connection with Christological readings of the psalter, see chapter 1 in this volume. For the stronger claim that a Christological reading makes Christian use of the Psalms in personal prayer and praise problematic, see chapter 2 in this volume.

19. See the helpful discussion (despite his problematic critique of Chalcedonian Christology) in Wolfhart Pannenberg, *Jesus: God and Man* (London: SCM, 1968), pp. 191–211.

20. This inclusive sense of the Christ's appropriation of (at least some of) the psalms is seen in the use Heb. 2 makes of Ps. 8. His glorification is not instead of ours, but is the means by which it is achieved, the guarantee that God's purposes in human creation will be ratified eschatologically, as demonstrated in the glorification of Jesus, the one who perfected the human calling to trusting obedience in his death.

invited to pray these powerful prayers and sing these powerful songs along with Jesus, our faithful high priest.[21]

Praise, then, in a number of ways across a range of genres and their associated functions, as well as at the level of the psalter as a whole, shapes our 'mind' (our view of the world, its fundamental realities and what counts in it and how they are prioritized) and our 'hearts' (our motivations, commitments and attachments – what we value, and how we feel about it), and so our engagement in the world. We turn, then, to some particular instances and see how praise shapes our view of and engagement with the world and aims at the proper ordering of both the internal affairs of the people of God and also the earth and the nations on it.[22]

Psalms and political vision – worked examples

Psalm 10 and dealing with a broken world

We begin with Psalm 10, a lament that articulates the brokenness of an (arrogantly) unjust world and the expectation of God's actions of justice.[23] Here we see the characteristic language of lament: a

---

21. That, in turn, means we can use these hymns and prayers in our address to God as well as to each other, as Eph. 5:19 and Col. 3:16 (not to mention the liturgical life of the church) would suggest we do.

22. Space limits discussion of other, obviously important, texts related to our topic. For reflections on Ps. 24 see Andrew Sloane, *At Home in a Strange Land: Using the Old Testament in Christian Ethics* (Peabody: Hendrickson; Grand Rapids: Baker, 2008), pp. 61–74. For the significance of Pss 72 and 146 for Christian use of power, see Andrew Sloane, 'Justifying Advocacy: A Biblical and Theological Rationale for Speaking the Truth to Power on Behalf of the Vulnerable', *ERT* 36 (2012), pp. 76–86. See also Denise Dombkowski Hopkins, 'Politics and Praise', *Christian Social Action* 17 (2004), pp. 3–4.

23. Concerning Ps. 10 and its relationship to Ps. 9 see, for instance, A. A. Anderson, *Psalms 1–72* (Grand Rapids: Eerdmans, 1972), pp. 104–119; Broyles, *Psalms*, pp. 74–78; Peter C. Craigie, *Psalms 1–50* (Waco: Word, 1983), pp. 113–128; Goldingay, *Psalms 1–41*, pp. 162–186; Geoffrey W. Grogan, *Psalms* (Grand Rapids: Eerdmans, 2008), pp. 54–56; James L. Mays, *Psalms* (Louisville: Westminster John Knox, 1994), pp. 70–75; McCann, 'Psalms', pp. 713–720; Artur Weiser, *The Psalms* (London: SCM, 1962), pp 146–154.

God who stands far off, hidden when most needed (v. 1). The wicked are those who forsake Yahweh (those who were or ought to have been in covenant relationship with God, v. 3), who treat God as ineffective ('there is no God', v. 4, makes a *functional* not an *ontological* claim – that is, no God who will act – hence v. 6 and their arrogant presumption of prosperity). They are violent, ruthless, covert in their actions, described in terms characteristic of the enemies of the laments as predators.[24] The oppressed are the poor, the helpless, the needy, those whose cause has been entrusted to Yahweh.

And Yahweh, the hidden and absent God, is the one who does see and who will act. Yahweh will dismantle the power of the powerful (breaking the arm of the evil-doers, v. 15) and the systems that sustain them (the nations will perish from *his* land, v. 16). Yahweh also upholds the weak and their cause (vv. 12–18). This is Yahweh's exercise of justice. Thus this song affirms key characteristics of God in ways that challenge the social (and theological) status quo and require that God acts so as to vindicate the claim that Yahweh *is* and *is enthroned* and *is enthroned as the king who enacts justice* (*lišpoṭ*, vv. 16–18). While a bold claim, this is typical of lament and, of course, coheres with Brueggemann's call to reclaim lament and its power.[25] Such a reclaiming of lament as a key element of our 'praises' has clear implications for social order, requiring, as it does, the voicing of the pain of injustice and a restless dissatisfaction with the status quo – a restlessness fuelled by the faith that articulates these painful words.[26]

This raises a number of issues for the 'politics of praise'. How does the very phenomenon of lament as (such) a (major) component of Israel's praises inform our political imagination? How does it enable us to articulate our awareness of the brokenness of the world, and of God's responsibility as Lord to act so as to restore its ruptured

---

While they are often read as a single psalm (so in the LXX), the differences in presumed speaker and the focus of the Psalms suggests it is legitimate to treat Ps. 10 as a psalm in its own right.

24. Goldingay, *Psalms 1–41*, pp. 179–182.

25. Walter Brueggemann, 'The Costly Loss of Lament', in David J. A. Clines (ed.), *The Poetical Books: A Sheffield Reader* (Sheffield: Sheffield Academic Press, 1997), pp. 85–97.

26. Ibid., pp. 90–93.

order? But this stance depends on our trusting affirmation of God as the one who is committed to the right ordering of the (social) world. How does this expectation that Yahweh is the guarantor of a just order in society inform our political imagination? In what ways does the realization that the ordering of the world depends not on our capacities but on a sovereign God fuel hope instead of despair, engagement rather than inertia? Given that there is a clear social order backed by the God addressed in such prayer, how does this psalm function as an implicit indictment of abusive (systems of) power? If our prayer 'God's kingdom come' entails a reordering of the world and its structures, does that not itself function as a criticism of that which needs to be reordered, a rejection in the name of the one in whose name we pray of all that is contrary to the will of the sovereign God? This necessitates identifying and countering abusive power and identifying and fostering the needs of the vulnerable – an active political imagination, if you will. It seems clear to me that the praise and prayer contained in psalms such as this, and the centrality in them of Yahweh's love of justice, must inform our political imagination. So, where are the songs of faith-filled pain, of hopeful discontent in our churches? Where are the songs that shape this restless political imagination? But the realities we address are more than political; our *social* struggle is not just against flesh and blood – as our next psalm makes plain.

Psalm 82 and the structures of power
This psalm demonstrates a fascinating ambiguity: does it refer to transcendent and 'spiritual' realities or immanent and 'human/political' ones? That is, are the rulers 'gods' or 'mortals'?[27] On the

---

27. For the ambiguity inherent in the psalm see Broyles, *Psalms*, pp. 335–338; Marvin E. Tate, *Psalms 51–100* (Dallas: Word, 1990), pp. 328–342. Most commentators see it as referring exclusively to divine beings in the heavenly court; so Kenneth M. Craig, Jr., 'Psalm 82', *Int* 49 (1995), pp. 281–284; John Goldingay, *Psalms 42–89* (Grand Rapids: Baker, 2007), pp. 558–570; McCann, 'Psalms', pp. 1005–1008; Mays, *Psalms*, pp. 268–271; Patrick D. Miller, 'When the Gods Meet: Psalm 82 and the Issue of Justice', *Journal for Preachers* 9 (1986), pp. 2–5; Weiser, *Psalms*, pp. 556–561. Grogan, *Psalms*, pp. 146–147, on the other hand, sees them as human figures.

one hand, they seem to be divine, called *'ĕlōhîm* twice in the psalm
(vv. 1 and 6), and in contexts that implicitly or explicitly contrast
them with mortals ('great assembly', 'sons of the Most High'). And
yet theirs is a clearly earthly and political function – their job, which
they manifestly fail to do, is to judge justly (using language that
echoes the Torah and the prophets, and from the Psalms).
Furthermore, they are described using language that elsewhere refers
to the ignorant and ungodly – those who know nothing, walking in
darkness.[28] Their ignorant incompetence threatens the very fabric
of created reality, so important is justice to the world God has made
and that he alone governs.[29] How does this work? It seems to me
that this refers to the complex phenomena of pagan worship-and-
culture systems and the interaction of idolatry and ideology and the
related cultic/religious and social/political systems we find so clearly
in Old Testament critique of the 'gods'. The gods are reflected –
even represented – in the social systems that reflect their rule
and the structures of divine life that are manifested in the ritual and
belief systems that constitute their service.[30]

These divine pretenders, then, are indicted on the basis of the
injustice of the social arrangements that reflect their rule and are
conducted in their name. God's response, as the one who rightly
owns the title of deity, is to judge them on the basis of this indictment, stripping them of the false power they have arrogated to
themselves and used in oppression or neglect of the poor. Their
end is the end of the social systems that pervert justice, along with
their religious systems that pervert true worship. The only one who
can rightly judge them is he who has authority over 'earth' and

---

28. This is reminiscent of Isaiah's indictment of Israel-under-judgment and
    idols and idol-makers, for which see G. K. Beale, *We Become What We
    Worship: A Biblical Theology of Idolatry* (Downers Grove: InterVarsity Press,
    2008). I think he misunderstands the role of the language of blindness
    and deafness in Isa. 6 and in the rhetoric of the book. Interestingly, his
    discussion of idolatry makes no reference to ideology of social systems,
    as illustrated by the absence of any citations of Ps. 82.

29. Broyles, *Psalms*, p. 337; Craig, 'Psalm 82', p. 283; McCann, 'Psalms', p. 1007;
    Miller, 'When the Gods Meet', pp. 4–5; Tate, *Psalms 51–100*, p. 337.

30. For more on this see Sloane, *At Home*, pp. 205–217.

'heaven' and who is characterized by justice, the appropriate exercise of power on behalf of the weak and the vulnerable. Hence the call for God to rise up and judge the earth, demonstrating the justice of true divine rule over the nations, and thereby claiming them as his own inheritance.

This, of course, has interesting implications for true worship and rightly formed social systems. For if the gods are judged on the basis of the social systems associated with their names (their worship and their character), then God has a responsibility to enact a social system that reflects the name Yahweh, the worship that calls on that exodus name and reflects the character of the one who bears it.[31] In terms of the worship that shapes the vision through which we look at political institutions, my question is this: Where are the songs that name the idols and call for their overthrow in the name of the one true Son of God? Where are the ones that name the 'powers' that blind and bind us?[32] And in terms of political vision, do we include in our political analysis a 'naming of the powers', a careful attempt to identify the 'gods' that lie behind the systems in which we have invested – and a repentance that enables us to turn from them to prayerful trust in the living God and to embrace the social

---

31. For similar observations see Goldingay, *Psalms 42–89*, pp. 569–570; Mays, *Psalms*, pp. 270–271. I think this sheds light on Jesus' use of this psalm in John 10:34. He not only defends his own claim to be the Son of God (one who, among other things, truly represents God's character and rule) but rejects his Jewish opponents' claim to speak for God, implying that the social and religious systems they endorse and represent are the systems we would expect from the so-called gods of the pagans: systems of oppression, injustice and illegitimate exclusion.

32. Such as market capitalism with its assumptions of infinite growth fuelled by the valorization of greed and planned obsolescence, or autonomous individualism and its implicit vision of the sovereignty of the nihilistic human will. See Terry Eagleton, *Reason, Faith, and Revolution: Reflections on the God Debate* (New Haven: Yale University Press, 2009); Graham Gordon, *What if You Got Involved? Taking a Stand Against Social Injustice* (Carlisle: Paternoster, 2003), pp. 57–69; David Bentley Hart, *Atheist Delusions: The Christian Revolution and Its Fashionable Enemies* (New Haven: Yale University Press, 2009), pp. 19–28.

values that reflect the character of the true God's rule?[33] This takes us nicely to Psalm 99.

Psalm 99 and the justice of God's rule, God's people and God's Torah

This is a clear instance of a hymn, one that celebrates Yahweh as king.[34] This rule is centred in Zion (and so Israel), but is universal in scope in both its exercise and the fitting response to it – all the nations are to tremble and praise Yahweh's great and terrifying name, the earth itself is to shake (vv. 1–3). This affirmation of Yahweh's rule, the recognition that Yahweh is holy, is self-involving: it entails praise, exaltation of Yahweh and doing obeisance before him, the holy and exalted king (vv. 3, 5, 9). Here we see once again the passionate, doxological character of theological reflection – at least on the Psalms. This psalm makes grand and important claims about God, claims that have significant implication for political engagement, but it does so in the context of doxology: our theology (including political theology) needs to arise out of and nourish a fundamental stance of praise.

Having begun, however, in verses 1–3 with general statements of Yahweh's worth as king and the way we ought to respond to it, the psalm moves on to give specific reasons to praise Yahweh, fundamental features of his character and action in the world, that are to be valued and that demonstrate that *Yahweh* is the divine king, worthy of obeisance and praise. Verses 4–5 call us to worship Yahweh as king of justice, the one who both loves it and works it out in the concrete life of the community of Jacob. This love of

---

33. James C. McCann, 'The Single Most Important Text in the Entire Bible: Toward a Theology of the Psalms', in Rolf A. Jacobson (ed.), *Soundings in the Theology of the Psalms* (Minneapolis: Fortress, 2011), pp. 63–75.

34. For issues relating to the kingship (or 'Enthronement') psalms, see Sigmund Mowinckel, *The Psalms in Israel's Worship*, vol. 1 (Oxford: Basil Blackwell, 1962), pp. 106–192; and the discussions of his work in J. Day, *Psalms* (Sheffield: JSOT, 1992), pp. 67–87; Ernest C. Lucas, *Exploring the Old Testament: A Guide to the Psalms and Wisdom Literature* (Downers Grove: InterVarsity Press, 2003), pp. 11–19.

justice is fundamental to Yahweh's claim to lordship,[35] as is the working out of this love in the world, establishing equity in Jacob. What legitimates Yahweh's claim to rule as king in Zion (in stark contrast to the fallen 'gods' of Ps. 82) is that his power is exemplified in the love of *mišpaṭ* (justice) and the way that love is seen in Yahweh's work in the world, establishing equity in Jacob.[36]

The question arises, of course, as to how this work of justice is seen in Jacob. Verses 6–9 tell us of God's acts in liberating Israel from bondage in Egypt, inviting and requiring the people to enact that freedom in the land, while living out a radical alternative social vision encoded in the Torah-instructions granted to them.[37] And so these verses recount for us Yahweh's responsive covenant engagement with key leaders in Israel, aimed at fostering a just community by way of the restoring forgiveness mediated through Israel's worship and the punishing of misdeeds evidenced in their history.[38] Yahweh loves justice – and his works of justice in, through and for Israel demonstrate that Yahweh is king.

Note, however, that this is not a restrictive view of divine justice in which only Israel's national life exemplifies it. Israel is called to be a paradigm of God's purposes for all humanity, a representative on the earth of God's will for all the earth, calling others to embrace

---

35. For discussions of the textual and translation issues in v. 4 see Broyles, *Psalms*, p. 385; John Goldingay, *Psalms 90–150* (Grand Rapids: Baker, 2008), pp. 128–129; Tate, *Psalms 51–100*, pp. 525–527. Most versions translate v. 4a along the lines of the NIV: 'The king is mighty, he loves justice', treating *'ōz* (might) as an adjective qualifying *melek* (king). Grammatically, however, *'ōz* is a noun in construct with *melek* so that 'king' functions adjectivally or as the qualifier of 'might'. Hence 'kingly might is loving justice', or 'the king's might is loving justice', which, I suggest, is a better translation.

36. Broyles, *Psalms*, pp. 384–385; Goldingay, *Psalms 90–150*, pp. 130–133; McCann, 'Psalms', pp. 1075–1076; Mays, *Psalms*, p. 315; Weiser, *Psalms*, pp. 642–644.

37. For Torah, moral formation and justice in the Psalms, see Wenham, *Psalms as Torah*, pp. 77–166, esp. pp. 115–118.

38. For this as an allusion to Exod. 34:6–7 see Goldingay, *Psalms 90–150*, p. 131; McCann, 'Psalms', p. 1076; Tate, *Psalms 51–100*, p. 530.

this God and his rule of justice.[39] The psalm itself suggests it, for the ones who are called to respond to the God whose might is shown in the outworking of justice include all the nations of the earth. If Yahweh's justice is to be reflected in social order, then while that right ordering is to be exemplified in Israel, it is exemplified there for the world. And so those who join with them in obedient praise (as the psalm expects all the earth to do) are to join with them in the obedience of praise in their political arrangements.

Here the worship of God both fosters a community of justice and is justified by it. The first is clear; but the second is worth thinking about. If the rule of God is reflected in the worshipping community whose common life is formed around the just rule of God, does our worship articulate that justice and shape us as communities who share God's own love for it? Does our common life together demonstrate our love of justice in our treatment of each other? Is power seen in our community as a trust to be directed towards the flourishing of the vulnerable or of our personal and theological interests? Are those who witness the patterns of our love prompted to say, 'So *that's* what God is like; *that's* what it means to be human'? If not, is ours legitimate worship?

Psalm 149 and shaping the goal of the life of (praise and) faith

Psalm 149 might seem an odd choice for our last psalm (and a puzzling inclusion at *this* point of the psalter). As Brueggemann says, 'This Psalm is exceedingly problematic, because, after a celebrative introduction (vv. 1–4), it combines "praise the Lord" with "pass the ammunition".'[40] First, we should be clear: while this is clearly exclusivist and particular – it is a psalm that speaks to Israel and the people of Zion as the praisers of God – it is not *ethnocentric*, for this is an Israel constituted by praise, honoured as the *humble* recipients of Yahweh's salvation (vv. 2–4).[41] Secondly, we should

---

39. Christopher J. H. Wright, *Old Testament Ethics for the People of God* (Leicester: Inter-Varsity Press, 2004); *The Mission of God: Unlocking the Bible's Grand Narrative* (Nottingham: Inter-Varsity Press, 2006).

40. Walter Brueggemann, 'Praise and the Psalms: A Politics of Glad Abandonment (Part II)', *Hymn* 43.4 (1992), p. 15.

41. AV, ESV rightly render *yĕšûʻâ* as 'salvation' rather than 'victory' (NRSV, NIV).

also be clear about the violence of this text. It speaks of a double-edged (well-constructed and ruthlessly efficient – literally, a two-mouthed) sword, of vengeance and punishment being inflicted on the nations, of the subjugation and bondage of kings and nobles.[42] Thirdly, it connects worship and this violence: not only are verses 6–9a set in the context of a praise psalm, but this section opens with praise (6a) and closes with their honour (9b), before rounding out the psalm with the now familiar *halĕlû yâ*. It seems fairly clear, then, that these acts of violence (or military force, if you will) are not only mandated by God but arise out of and contribute to the exaltation of Yahweh as Lord.

The key to that, I would suggest, is found in verse 9a: all of this is enacting the judgments inscribed for or against the nations,[43] written by the God of justice whose praise is thereby sung.[44] This, then, is not human violence being legitimated by the praise of God, but divine judgment being enacted by the praising community.[45] In this sense, worship issues in political action, action that uses force to rectify what is wrong in the world, including bringing into line those who stand against God and his purposes. Those who refuse the invitation issued in the Psalms to join the circle of praise in response to the mercies of God will nonetheless be included in the eschatological glorification of Yahweh by way of their unwilling submission to the rule of Yahweh exercised through those who are faithful to his call (*hăsîdâw*, faithful ones, v. 9).

What I think this shows is the complex of issues of particularity and universalism that run through both Old and New Testaments,

---

42. Joshua Berman, 'The "Sword of Mouths" (Jud. Iii 16; Ps. Cxlix 6; Prov. V 4): A Metaphor and Its Ancient Near Eastern Context', *VT* 52 (2002), pp. 291–303, suggests that the term deliberately evokes imagery of speech, thus connecting words (of praise) with weaponry and its use, thereby binding the two sections of the psalm together.

43. *La'ăśôt bāhem mišpāṭ kātûb.*

44. McCann, 'Psalms', pp. 1274–1277, sees it as referring ultimately to God's eschatological judgment (*pace* Goldingay).

45. Mays, *Psalms*, pp. 447–448.

something Bauckham has commented on to good effect.[46] This choice of Israel, even using them as agents of divine vengeance against rebellious nations, is for the benefit of the nations, to bring them within the circle of those who benefit from and sing praise in response to God's unsearchable mercies. To leave such rebellion alone would be to undermine the very goal of the psalter, the uninterrupted, unqualified praise of Yahweh. For how can it be that 'everything with breath' praises Yahweh when there are those who resist his will? Indeed, how can it be that Yahweh *deserves* such praise when injustice and rebellion hold out against him?

And so here we see that politics and praise are inextricably linked. The praise of God issues in what can be seen only as politically oriented action, and such political action issues in the reflex of the praise of Yahweh. To return to Brueggemann:

> The Psalm is a harsh one; it is nonetheless clear evidence, placed near the liturgical climax of the psalter, that praise is deeply and directly linked to serious and critical public policy and public practice. And if this Psalm turns out to be too dangerous to sing in our more bourgeois liturgies, then we may want to consider how such liturgy becomes innocuous and cuts God off from God's deeply rooted social intention.[47]

It is interesting, as a Christian, to think of how this informs the picture of the victorious Lamb in Revelation – from whose mouth comes a sword and whose name is the name of praise. It reminds us that the politics of praise is not quarantined to the Old Testament. It shows us, in fact, that the eschatological goal of universal praise can be accomplished only through the violence of judgment and the overthrow of all powers and structures – social/political and heavenly/demonic – that stand against the Ancient of Days

---

46. Richard Bauckham, *Bible and Mission: Christian Witness in a Postmodern World* (Grand Rapids: Baker, 2003). This is also evident in this section of the psalter and the interplay between particularity and universalism found in Pss 145 and 148, in comparison with Pss 147 and 149.

47. Brueggemann, 'Politics of Glad Abandonment (Part II)', p. 15.

and the Lamb who shares his throne. However, in contrast to Psalm 149, while the representatives of the people of God sit upon thrones to judge the nations, it is the slaughtered and raised Lamb who exercises judgment. Yes, as representative human, but also and uniquely as the one who inherits David's throne and shares God's. And he does so with the sword of his mouth (Rev. 19:15). Eschatological judgment on the nations is taken firmly into the hand of God, so that eschatological praise can be an unfettered gift from God to his people.[48]

This deferral to Yahweh's sovereign eschatological judgment coheres well, in fact, with the post-exilic context of the *book* of Psalms. For in that context Israel did not have the power Psalm 149 speaks of, and so this is a psalm sung in anticipation of and trust in God's action that enables the dismantling of oppressive earthly power. Here praise functions to shape an imagination that eagerly anticipates the final song of creation's praise and so recognizes that there are systems and structures and patterns of value and behaviour that are fundamentally inconsistent with the high praises of God, an imagination that awaits the action of the God who will tear them down in the building of his own kingdom, and so calls for action that mirrors the values and goals exemplified in our God's reign. This waiting is an act of indictment, judgment and resistance to the violent power of politics gone 'toxic', and a sign of trust in the one who will hold them to account (cf. Ps. 37).

What, then, does this say to us as we think about the politics of praise? It suggests that our praise needs to be open to that future which is God's gift, a future in which all tears will be wiped away, including the tears of those who cry out and struggle against injustice. But it also needs to acknowledge that every day in which we sing the high praises of God is not *that* day. And so our praises cannot and must not say, 'God is in his heaven; all is right with the world.' Rather, they must praise our Father in heaven both for the quality of his heavenly rule and in anticipation of God's so acting as to work out his rule on earth as it is in heaven.

---

48. Similarly, McCann, 'Psalms', p. 1277.

Concluding reflections: political doxology and doxological politics

As poetry that engages our hearts as well as instructing our minds, the Psalms shape a passionate political imagination of values and attitudes and desires as well as thoughts and purposes. It is, however, poetry that articulates a holy discontent with the status quo, and one that sees the world through the eyes of the vulnerable. As such, the psalms shape a politics that names and exposes the idolatrous ideologies enshrined in our systems and call us to sing and enact resistance to them in the name of Yahweh of hosts. They articulate a praise that joins with Jesus, our king and high priest and great faithful covenant partner in singing these songs, as we join our voices to his, trusting that his voice will carry ours when they falter in weakness of faith or failure of nerve. This praise will shape our life in community so as to reflect God's own action in exodus and resurrection, which recreate us as a people imaging God's own character and engaging in his world in his name. This politically realistic praise recognizes that structures of sin, evil and oppression will persist until Jesus slays them with the sword of his mouth and ushers in his perfected rule – but which thereby calls us to trusting, persevering fidelity as we witness to God's coming kingdom and strive to see it realized in this broken world.

But Psalms' politics of praise also present us with a challenge: To what extent does the worship life of the contemporary (evangelical) church allow them to do their work? Using the Psalms in worship entails an active commitment to the ethics we thereby affirm. They play a key role in the pedagogy of desire, the reshaping of our hearts and minds, our values, passions and lifestyle that ought to take place in the common life of the Christian worshipping community that aims at our embodying, proclaiming and enacting God's kingly rule in the world.[49] As Wenham states, 'To pray a psalm is to address God and fellow worshipers . . . Liturgy does not simply invite assent, it demands it.'[50] To what extent do contemporary

---

49. Smith, *Desiring the Kingdom*, pp. 133–214.
50. Wenham, *Psalms as Torah*, p. 205.

'praise songs' used in churches articulate this vision and shape this imagination? In what other ways can our worship practices – our liturgies, if you like – shape a community of political doxology and doxological politics?

In the end, however, praise is not an instrumentality of our political purposes. It is not a means to that, or any other, end, however laudable that end might be. It is an end itself, indeed, the chief end of human existence. It is, in one sense, a pointless and useless activity that aims at and achieves nothing.[51] The goal of praise is also its content: the glory of the sovereign Lord. So while praise is a profoundly political activity and needs to be reshaped to form us rightly as political agents, we are to praise, not because it fits with our agenda or suits our enlightened political consciences, but because it is a form of faithfulness. It is one of the facets of that gloriously useless activity that is our chief end as rescued creatures of the living God.

---

51. Brueggemann, 'Politics of Glad Abandonment (Part II)', p. 19.

12. PRAISE AS MISSION: PROCLAMATION AND THE NATIONS IN PSALMS

Greg Anderson

John Piper's aphorism that 'mission exists because worship doesn't' has become a commonplace in many missionary circles.[1] But we might turn the question around and ask, 'Where worship does exist – as it obviously does in the Psalms – where is mission'? The purpose of this chapter is to investigate the place of proclamation of God and his saving purposes within the Psalms, focusing particularly on what they might show us about this proclamation among the nations.

The core of Christian mission is the proclamation of God's saving acts in Jesus Christ, calling on people to submit to him in repentance, obedience and love and receive his mercy and blessing.[2]

---

1. John Piper, *Let the Nations Be Glad: The Supremacy of God in Mission*, 3rd ed. (Grand Rapids: Baker, 2010), pp. 15, 35.
2. The definition of mission is one of the many contested areas of missiology. Gospel proclamation is emphasized by Andreas J. Köstenberger and Peter T. O'Brien, *Salvation to the Ends of the Earth: A Biblical Theology of Mission*, NSBT 11 (Leicester: Apollos, 2001), p. 21. Dickson, similarly, places proclamation as central in mission, although he also wants open space for

If we think of Old Testament mission as similarly proclaiming or speaking out God's saving acts, and his character of holiness and faithfulness that leads to those acts, we find both as prominent themes in the psalter.

As we might expect, the speaking out of God's works happens most frequently in the psalter within the context of the holy nation. It is not proclamation seeking to win outsiders so much as celebrating and reinforcing what God has done for Israel in order that they might love him and continue in obedience to his covenant with them.[3] Although God's work in creation and providence is proclaimed in many psalms (e.g. Pss 8; 19; and perhaps 29; 33; 65; 104; 148), the main focus is on the saving work that he has undertaken for his people as a whole (e.g. Pss 46; 87; 98; 111; 145), but also his rescue for the individual psalmist (e.g. Ps. 61). Typically, the way the proclamation of God and his salvation is framed, both across the psalter and within each of its five books, is as a telling-forth within the nation of Israel, particularly the nation as an assembled body. In Book 1 we see, for example, 'I will declare your name to my people; / in the assembly I will praise you (Ps. 22:22) and 'From you comes the theme of my praise in the great assembly; / before

_____

'non-proclaimers' to *promote the gospel* in various ways (John Dickson, *The Best Kept Secret of Christian Mission: Promoting the Gospel with More Than Our Lips* [Grand Rapids: Zondervan, 2010], p. 23). Christopher J. H. Wright, *The Mission of God: Unlocking the Bible's Grand Narrative* (Nottingham: Inter-Varsity Press, 2006), p. 67, refocuses the definition so that it centres on the *missio Dei*, but also includes 'the committed *participation* of God's people in the purposes of God for the redemption of the whole creation' (italics original), which might include more than just proclamation. H. Peskett and V. Ramachandra, *The Message of Mission: The Glory of Christ in All Time and Space* (Leicester: Inter-Varsity Press, 2003), p. 29, similarly speak of human participation in the divine mission, which will include acting out God's restoration of creation by working for justice as well as engaging in proclamation.

3. S. B. Bevans and R. P. Schroeder, *Constants in Context: A Theology of Mission for Today*, American Society of Missiology Series 30 (Maryknoll: Orbis, 2004), p. 174, point out that in the early use of the word *mission* for Christian activity (in the sixteenth century) it applied both to outreach to pagans and to fortifying the faithful.

those who fear you I will fulfil my vows' (Ps. 22:25). Similarly, the call for people to praise God and to recognize his rule is found most often as a call to his chosen people:

> You who fear the LORD, praise him!
> All you descendants of Jacob, honour him!
> Revere him, all you descendants of Israel!
> (Ps. 22:23)

In Book 2 we have 'Praise God in the great congregation; / praise the LORD in the assembly of Israel' (Ps. 68:26). In Book 3 belonging to the people of God is expressed in temple language: 'Blessed are those who dwell in your house; / they are ever praising you' (Ps. 84:4). An example in Book 4 is expressed from within the community in the first person:

> Come, let us bow down in worship,
>   let us kneel before the LORD, our Maker;
> for he is our God
>   and we are the people of his pasture,
>   the flock under his care.
> (Ps. 95:6–7)

In Book 5, we have

> What shall I return to the LORD
>   for all his goodness to me?
> I will lift up the cup of salvation
>   and call on the name of the LORD.
> . . .
> I will fulfil my vows to the LORD
>   in the presence of all his people,
> in the courts of the house of the LORD –
>   in your midst, Jerusalem.
> (Ps. 116:12–13, 18–19)

It is hardly surprising that this proclamation within Israel forms a central core of the nation's liturgical and devotional life.

Mission and the nations

What seems more surprising is that the hymnbook of the nation has so much to say about other nations. There are over one hundred references in the Psalms to outsiders: the peoples, the nations, the islands/ coastlands, the earth, the Gentiles, sometimes specific nations: Egypt, Babylon, Philistia, Tyre (Ps. 87:4), Moab and Edom (Ps. 60:8). Moreover, these references are spread throughout the five books of the psalter.

During most of the times when individual psalms were composed, and in the time when the whole collection as we have it today was finally edited, Israel's relationship with the nations was troubled, to say the least. Given this, it is hardly surprising that hostility from, and towards, enemies is the frequent cry of the psalmist, as representative or king of Israel. While in many cases the enemies are not specified, poetic parallelism strongly suggests that on the whole, and unless otherwise specified, it is legitimate to equate them with the nations around Israel (see e.g. Ps. 18:47–48). This hostility is sometimes focused on God's anointed king, and often leads the psalmist either to an invocation of God's vengeance on the enemies or a declaration of God's judgment on them (such as in Ps. 9:5, 'You have rebuked the nations and destroyed the wicked', or v. 19, 'Arise, LORD, do not let mortals triumph; / let the nations be judged in your presence. / Strike them with terror, LORD; / let the nations know they are only mortal'). The whole of Psalm 83 is given over to Israel's invoking God's action against the threat of the surrounding peoples. This theme is crystallized in the final stanzas:

> Make them like tumbleweed, my God,
>   like chaff before the wind.
> As fire consumes the forest
>   or a flame sets the mountains ablaze,
> so pursue them with your tempest,
>   and terrify them with your storm.
> Cover their faces with shame, LORD,
>   so that they will seek your name.
>
> May they ever be ashamed and dismayed;
>   may they perish in disgrace.

> Let them know that you, whose name is the LORD –
>> that you alone are the Most High over all the earth.
>
> (Ps. 83:13–18)

This last verse seems threatening rather than conciliatory: knowing that God is the Most High is their acknowledgment of defeat, rather than repentance. But we must also note in the last clause of verse 16 that the knowledge of God's greatness can be a prelude to this repentance.

The nations and worship

While the frequent testimony of the psalter, then, is of hostility to the nations, this alternative note in Psalm 86:16b signifies that there is also a more positive development, which can be traced through four steps.

First, in a surprising extension of the declaration of God's praises within Israel, God's glory will be declared (presumably by the Israelites) among the nations. This is seen, for example, in Psalm 57:9, 'I will praise you, Lord, among the nations; / I will sing of you among the peoples', and Psalm 96:3, 'Declare his glory among the nations, / his marvellous deeds among all peoples.'

Secondly, the nations are invited themselves to join in the praise of God. This is exemplified in Psalm 47:1, 'Clap your hands, all you nations, / shout to God with cries of joy,' and Psalm 148:7a, 11, 'Praise the LORD from the earth . . . kings of the earth and all nations, / you princes and all rulers on earth.'

Thirdly, and we might see this as a development of the invitation, the nations will come and worship God. This is seen in Psalm 22:27, 'All the ends of the earth / will remember and turn to the LORD, / and all the families of the nations / will bow down before him,' and Psalm 86:9, 'All the nations you have made / will come and worship before you, Lord; / they will bring glory to your name.'

Fourthly, and most surprising of all, some among the nations would be ingrafted into Israel. The Moabite ancestry of David's great-grandmother exemplifies this hope – a hope expressed somewhat obliquely in Psalm 87:4:

> I will record Rahab [Egypt] and Babylon
> among those who acknowledge me –
> Philistia too, and Tyre, along with Cush –
> and will say, 'This one was born in Zion.'

This ingrafting is one of the possible trajectories of the fact that the nations are the gift of God to Israel, designated as her inheritance. More specifically, they are the Messiah's inheritance, as expressed in Psalm 18:43, 'You have delivered me from the attacks of the people; / you have made me the head of nations'; Psalm 68:29, 31, 'Because of your temple at Jerusalem / kings will bring you gifts . . . Envoys will come from Egypt; / Cush will submit herself to God'; and Psalm 111:6, 'He has shown his people the power of his works, / giving them the lands of other nations.'

In the wider context of the psalter, with its recurrent theme of mutual hostility between Israel and the nations, it must be seen as an act of grace that this engagement with the nations would happen at all. Further, whether the submission of the nations is voluntary or forced, there is blessing for them as they submit, as the Messianic Psalm 72 indicates.

The shape of proclamation in the arrangement of the psalter

It is one thing to point out a selection of verses in support of the argument that mission among the nations can be recognized as a significant theme, but we can go further by showing that a number of features of the canonical arrangement of the psalter also provide evidence for this proposition. The first and last psalms can be seen as clearly marking both the key points and the overall trajectory of the framework. Some of the aspects of the proclamation theme are quite evenly spread through the psalter; others are more clustered (or less present) among the five books.

Psalms 1 and 2: introduction of proclamation themes

Psalms 1 and 2 belong together, as indicated by the *inclusio* of Psalms 1:1 and 2:12b, among other features. On the positive side, they introduce the key themes of God's sovereignty over all, including over all the nations; the blessings that flow to his faithful people; and the installation of his king. On the negative side, they introduce God's enemies, depicted as the nations who rebel against God and his king, and against whom God's judgment is coming. It is important to note that the nations and their rulers are not guaranteed to experience destruction, but are invited to submit to God in the person of his king (Ps. 2:10–12), since they are in fact his eventual proper inheritance (Ps. 2:8).

Psalm 149: the destruction of God's enemies as the context of praise

At the other end of the psalter, the subtext of the extravagant celebration of God is his vindication of his people and the destruction of his enemies. This is seen in Psalm 149:

> May the praise of God be in their mouths
> > and a double-edged sword in their hands,
> to inflict vengeance on the nations
> > and punishment on the peoples,
> to bind their kings with fetters,
> > their nobles with shackles of iron,
> to carry out the sentence written against them –
> > this is the glory of all his faithful people.
> (Ps. 149:6–9)

The call for all to praise God – indeed, not only the nations, but all living things – reaches its climax in the final verse of the psalter: 'Let everything that has breath praise the LORD' (Ps. 150:6).

Trajectories within the psalter

The intervening psalms continue to express the rights God has over the nations as both king and judge. The kingship of God over the nations is expressed explicitly throughout the psalter, except in Book 3 (see Pss 22:27–30; 24:1; 47:2, 7; 95:3; 99:2; 113:4; 135:5). The theme that God will judge the nations is also quite widely distributed, being found in Books 1, 4 and 5 (see Pss 7:8; 9:19; 98:9; 110:5–6).

The psalms that focus on the evil the nations have done are concentrated in the first three books of the psalter (see particularly Pss 2; 9:15, 17; 46:6), but particularly Book 3. This is hardly surprising if its focus is the challenge of the exile to Jewish identity, as James Hely Hutchinson argues.[4] We have, for example, Psalm 79:

> O God, the nations have invaded your inheritance;
>> they have defiled your holy temple,
>> they have reduced Jerusalem to rubble.
> They have left the dead bodies of your servants
>> as food for the birds of the sky,
>> the flesh of your own people for the animals of the wild.
> They have poured out blood like water
>> all around Jerusalem,
>> and there is no one to bury the dead.
> We are objects of contempt to our neighbours,
>> of scorn and derision to those around us.
>
> (Ps. 79:1–4)

The counterpoint to the hostility between Israel and the nations is the invitation to the nations to submit to God and his king, and to join in Israel's praise of him. As we have seen, this is effected through the declaration of the praises of God by Israel among the nations (e.g. Ps. 18:49, 'I will give you thanks among the Gentiles'; cf. 9:11; 57:9; 96:3; 105:1). Testimony to this declaration is absent from Books 3 and 5. The nations are specifically called on to join in the praise of God (e.g. Ps. 33:8, 'Let all the earth fear the LORD, / Let all the people of the world revere him'; and Ps. 47:1, 'Clap your hands all you peoples'). Such calls are absent from Book 3, but relatively frequent in Book 4, which is not surprising if this is the book that tracks biblical theology – the Abrahamic covenant was always with a view to the blessing of the nations. Thus we have, for example, Psalm 96:1b, 'Sing to the LORD all the earth' (cf. 97:1, 7; 98:2; 99:1; 100:1; 117:1; 148:11–13). The polarities of

---

4. Chapter 1 in this volume.

hostility and invitation are blurred by the possibility that, in seeing God's faithfulness to his people, some among the nations are drawn to accept God's rule through his king – as they are called to do in Psalm 2 – and that they are fully drawn into the community of God's people, while others will decline the invitation and remain under judgment.

The desired outcome of this praise, that the nations will express their subjection to God and his human king, is also distributed throughout the Psalms, including all five books. In Book 1, for example, we have Psalm 22:27:

> All the ends of the earth
>   will remember and turn to the LORD,
> and all the families of the nations
>   will bow down before him.

In Book 2 there is the specific reference of Psalm 45:12: 'The city of Tyre will come with a gift, / people of wealth will seek your favour,' and the more general reference of Psalm 66:4:

> All the earth bows down to you;
>   they sing praise to you,
>   they sing the praises of your name.

In Book 3 we see, for example, Psalm 86:9:

> All the nations you have made
>   will come and worship before you, Lord;
>   they will bring glory to your name.

In Book 4 an example is Psalm 102:15, 22:

> The nations will fear the name of the LORD,
>   all the kings of the earth will revere your glory. . . .
> when the peoples and the kingdoms
>   assemble to worship the LORD.

In Book 5 we see Psalm 138:4–5:

May all the kings of the earth praise you, LORD,
> when they hear what you have decreed.
May they sing of the ways of the LORD.

The fairly even distribution of these passages indicates the significance of this concept in the Psalms.

The last psalm in Book 2 (Ps. 72) has an important role before the greater darkness of Book 3, in celebrating the blessing to all nations that flows from the Davidic king. Whether the verbs in verses 8–11 are jussives or futures, the beneficent rule of the Messiah for the nations is in focus, as we see, for example, in verse 8, 'May he rule [or, He will rule] from sea to sea / and from the River to the ends of the earth,' and in verse 17b, 'Then all nations will be blessed through him'.

As the psalter reaches its conclusion, the focus on blessing beyond the nation of Israel continues. In Psalm 145:9 God's blessing is seen in its full extent:

The LORD is good to all;
> he has compassion on all he has made.

But in verses 18 and 20, in a concept reminiscent of Psalm 2:12, there is particular mention of God's goodness to those who call on him truly, and who love him:

The LORD is near to all who call on him,
> to all who call on him in truth. . . .
The LORD watches over all who love him,
> but all the wicked he will destroy.

These trajectories of proclamation are summarized in the table below. The goal of universal praise is present throughout, but the assertion of God's kingship is briefly interrupted in Book 3, as the actions of the nations against God's people and the apparent failure of the covenant (Ps. 89) are focused on. A renewed call to the nations to praise God in Book 4 sees the goal of universal praise achieved by the final book of the psalter.

Table 12.1 Trajectories of praise through the psalter

Book	God is king over the nations	Evil done by the nations	Call to nations to praise God	Nations will worship God
Psalms 1 – 2: God is king over the nations: call to submit to him				
1	+	+/–	+	+
2	+	+/–	+	+
Psalm 72: All nations to be blessed through David's rule				
3		++		+
4	+		++	+
5	+			+
Psalms 149 – 150: God judges the nations: all earth praises him				

Praise and mission

We might summarize all this by saying that as the people of God engage in praising God, as his people proclaim his kingship, his judgment and his faithfulness – not just within Israel, but in the whole world – they are undertaking mission. Bound up with God's kingship is the expression of his universal rule in the person of the Davidic king whose home is among the covenant people, but who will exercise dominion over all the nations (as is spelled out most clearly in Ps. 72). Thus, for the nations to join with Israel in praising God as king, they must submit to God's Messiah as king.

Miller accordingly describes praise as both the *goal* and *instrument* of mission. His words are worth quoting at some length:

> That is the purpose of praise – to respond to the experience of God's grace and power, to exalt the one who is seen and known to be gracious and powerful, and to bear witness to all who hear that God is God. In that sense the praise of God in the Old Testament is always devotion that tells about God, that is, *theology* [my emphasis], and proclamation that seeks to draw others into the circle of those who worship this God, that is, *testimony for conversion* [my emphasis]. Indeed no aspect of the Old Testament serves as a vehicle for getting at the biblical notion of God in so full and extended a fashion as do the songs of praise and thanks – and

this in part because they point back to the supplications and God's way
with the human creature as well as forward to God's intention for the
whole creation. Perhaps less clear in the minds of many readers of the
Old Testament is the fact that the praise of God is the most prominent
and extended formulation of the *universal* and *conversionary* [emphases
original] dimension of the theology of the Old Testament.[5]

With this in mind, we can look at proclamation in the psalter through
a slightly different lens – thinking not so much of the nations
in particular, but the place of praise as mission. The first step in
mission, from this point of view, is the praise of God's sovereignty
as creator and sustainer, both within and outside Israel. It is particularly noteworthy that so-called gods or 'sons of heaven' are called
on to join in this praise of God (e.g. Ps. 29) – their own imagined
authority is subverted when they recognize the power of God and
his voice. The praise of God here includes not just addressing him,
but recalling to others, including the peoples, what God has done
in creation and providence. The recording of praise *to* God, however,
also acts as a model for all those who respond to the invitation to
praise. Thus the vertical and horizontal dimensions of praise –
speaking to God himself of his greatness, and speaking to others
of God's character and actions – belong together and are mutually
reinforcing.

The second step in mission, from this perspective, is praise for
God's character, particularly as the one who is faithful to his covenant
and righteous in his judging. Miller points to a threefold theme of
God as king, warrior and judge.[6] This praise is most at home in
Israel, as the people of God remember the specific examples of
God's dealings with them, whether that is corporately or individually,
particularly in saving them from their enemies. To establish with
praise that God is true to himself, however, is a great recommenda-
tion to all people to trust him, since his integrity and reliability are
assured. This is the case even when testifying to God's determination

---

5. Patrick Miller, '"Enthroned on the Praises of Israel": The Praise of God in
   Old Testament Theology', *Int* 13.1 (1985), p. 9.
6. Ibid., p. 17.

to punish his enemies since his trustworthiness and covenant commitment are enhanced – hence the number of psalms where God's actions are recorded as arising from his faithfulness. In some ways, even the psalms of lament can be seen as testimonies to God's steadfast love: first of all, because the psalmist knows that God is the one to whom to cry out, but also because so many of the lament psalms conclude with a word of praise or recollection of what God has done to rescue his people in the past. God is depicted as the one who is able to turn sadness to joy and oppression to freedom.

The third step in mission is calling on others to join in the praise of God for who he is as sovereign and what he has done as saviour. This is what Miller calls 'testimony for conversion'.[7]

The biblical-theological framework of mission in the psalter

The final perspective to be considered with regard to the missional praise of the psalter is the undergirding biblical-theological framework, which itself finds expression in many of the psalms. We could say that the psalter mirrors and focuses the story of salvation history. Although some parts of the framework are more obviously missional than others, the whole schema hangs together to explain and justify the significance of mission for God's people in the world. The logic of the framework rests on the uniqueness and universality of God's rule.

God as creator
As the single creator (e.g. Pss 8; 19; 148), Yahweh is owed allegiance not just by Israel but by the whole world. The Psalms celebrate not only his creation, but also his sustenance of all that he has made (e.g. Pss 104; 147:8–9).

God as supreme sovereign
Yahweh is superior to all the other spiritual and physical forces. His superiority means that he is God of all gods (e.g. Ps. 136:2, 'Give

---

7. Ibid., p. 9.

thanks to the God of gods'), and therefore that he overrides any authority they claim (e.g. Ps. 82:1, 'God presides in the great assembly; / he renders judgment among the "gods"'). Because of this, he is the only one worthy of trust (e.g. Ps. 146:3).

The covenants with Israel

As ruler of the whole world (Ps. 24:1), God has made a covenant with the nation of Israel (Pss 135:4; 147:19–20), which in the sequence of Psalms 105 and 106 is clearly in continuity with the Abrahamic covenant. This covenant has stipulations, and although Israel has not kept them (Pss 50; 78), God will not forget his covenant (Ps. 111:5–9). In partial fulfilment of the promises to Abraham, God has installed Israel in the land he promised.

As God's chosen people among the nations, they are to be a kingdom of priests, mediating the knowledge of God in the world. This is the basis of their proclamation and praise among the nations.

God's covenant with David, implied in Psalm 2, which cannot be broken (Ps. 89), ensures that there will be a remnant within Israel that God will not forsake, and indeed an eternal king.[8]

The place of the nations

Since Israel's arrival in the Promised Land has displaced its original inhabitants, and since other nations also desire to claim this land, the nations have become Israel's enemies (Pss 44:2; 45:5; 79; 111:6; 136:21; 137). However, the Abrahamic covenant was always to bring blessing to all the nations, again providing a basis for Israel's engagement with them in proclamation and praise of God.

The victory and justice of God's king

In their present struggles Israel calls on God to save them (Pss 79:5–6; 80:2), recognizing that their troubles are in some cases God's just punishment for their sin (Ps. 79:8). In the end God will triumph over his enemies and vindicate his people. His righteous character

---

8. Gordon Wenham, 'The Nations in the Psalms', *Encounter* 33 (2010), p. 7, lists the divine choice of David as one of the prominent missional themes through the psalter.

means also that he will engage in judging the world with justice (Ps. 96:13). The enemies or nations will finally be defeated by or submit to the king in David's line (Ps. 2), who will rule over all the nations.

As Christians, we see the Lord Jesus as this eschatological Davidic king who has come once to inaugurate the kingdom and will come again to establish it in its fullness. Because of this, we may conclude with some reflections about what might be learnt by Christians from the missional praise of the psalms.

Praise as mission: lessons for Christians

Vertical and horizontal praise

Praising God is the major note of the psalms. The interface between Israel and the nations includes praise – Israel will praise Yahweh among the nations, the nations are called on to praise Yahweh, and this call will be fulfilled at least to some extent. But there has been discussion in Christian circles as to whether praise is fundamentally vertical – addressed to God, or horizontal – declaring God's goodness to others.[9] From the numerous references (both in Psalms and other parts of the Old Testament) to praising or singing to God,[10] it appears that there is certainly a vertical dimension. There are also, however, many places where the vertical is in parallel with the horizontal (e.g. Ps. 9:1, 'I will give thanks to you, LORD, with all my heart; / I will tell of all your wonderful deeds'; Ps. 9:11, 'Sing the praises of the LORD, enthroned in Zion; / proclaim among the nations what he has done'), and others where the horizontal comes more to the fore (e.g. Ps. 108:3, 'I will praise you, LORD, among the nations; / I will sing of you among the peoples';

---

9. See e.g. Tony Payne, 'Confessions of a Teenage Praise Junkie' <http://matthiasmedia.com/briefing/1996/02/confessions-of-a-teenage-praise-junkie>, accessed 8 Sept. 2012.

10. E.g. Ps. 66:1–2, 'Shout with joy to God, all the earth! / Sing the glory of his name; / make his praise glorious. / Say to God, "How awesome are your deeds!"'; 68:4, 'Sing to God, sing in praise of his name'; and 95:1; 96:1; 98:1, 4–5; cf. 2 Sam. 22:50; Isa. 12:5.

Ps. 111:1, 'I will extol the LORD with all my heart / in the council of the upright and in the assembly'; Ps. 138:1, 'I will praise you, LORD, with all my heart; / before the "gods" I will sing your praise'). We can conclude that both dimensions are included in what it means to praise God.

The objects of praise
The character of God
The first object of praise is God's character. His compassion, greatness, holiness and righteousness are frequently mentioned. God's righteous character means also that he will engage in judging the world with justice (Ps. 96:13). The final outcome of God's rule through his king is that representatives of the nations will submit to him (Ps. 72) and in so doing will experience blessing, which will flow to the whole creation. For this, the whole creation will praise God, and all are called on to anticipate this by praising God in the present (Ps. 96:7–10). For the Christian, the character of God is seen in Jesus Christ (John 14:9–10).

The saving work of God
The psalms praise God for what he has done in the past (Pss 105; 106; 136), in the present (Pss 9:4; 118:10–14) and for what he will do in the future. As he has brought salvation in the past, so he will make his people, through their king, finally victorious (Pss 18:47; 72). God's faithfulness to his covenant and his people demonstrates his character, which his people celebrate, both within their own nation (Pss 118; 135:19–20), but also among the peoples of the earth (Ps. 117). Indeed, the whole created order will participate in this celebration (Ps. 148). The Christian knows of the fulfilment of God's saving work in Christ and can praise God accordingly.

Using the psalms in Christian mission today
The psalms teach us and model for us something about the nature and practice of proclamation about God. But we might also ask whether the psalms are just our teacher in this regard, or whether they might themselves be used in our proclamation in the form in which they come to us. Are the psalms as such useful for proclamation of the gospel?

The praising community

It seems within the realms of probability that the early church would not have been averse to using psalms in this way. The Colossians and Ephesians are told to sing psalms, and we may presume that they did this when they met together. It is clear from 1 Corinthians 14 that Christian meetings were not closed to outsiders, and what outsiders heard at church could lead them to repent. The context of the injunction to sing in Ephesians 5 includes the prior exhortations to live as light, and to make the most of every opportunity, both of which seem to have an evangelistic component (cf. Col. 4:5 and Matt. 5:16). We might draw the conclusion that attending the gathering of Christians, with all that this involved, including the teaching of the apostolic message and the singing of psalms and other songs, was one way in which proclamation happened. The fact that the psalms speak so clearly about God's love and providence, his saving king, the personal struggles of life, about God's attitude to the world, to his people, to justice and injustice, and the fact that they call on the nations to join in the worship of God means that they are well suited to serving in this way. Wu asserts that hymnic materials in the early church were devised for evangelism among other things[11] – if they were used in this way, it seems likely that psalms were also. Of course it will not be the psalms alone that will constitute the proclamation of the message of God, but neglecting them, given their immediacy, conciseness and emotional resonance, seems something of a loss.

The poetic community

A dimension of the psalms that might be highlighted with regard to their use in gospel proclamation is the *poetic form* in which they come to us – indeed, poetry which is likely to have been set to music for congregational use. Although the poetry and music were specific to their own local culture, it is worth mentioning that for many of the world's cultures, including Western culture, song and poetry have been the repository for some of the most deeply held beliefs, for daily wisdom and for the expression of the culture's values. Whether

---

11. J. L. Wu, 'Liturgical Elements', in *DPHL*, pp. 557–560.

it is the Homeric epics, the song lines of Aboriginal Australia, or songs of sexual desire or unrequited love on the Top 40, there is something about using an art form, rather than merely a prose statement, that seems to connect with the most profound aspects of the human condition. A number of cross-cultural mission movements in recent years have sought to explore the possibilities that might emerge from expressing Christian proclamation in the song and poetry forms of various cultures, contextualizing the approach that the psalter takes. This *ethnodoxology* is worth exploring further, both in Western and Southern contexts.[12] It assumes that truth comes wrapped up with emotional expressions and commitments, and that the truth is best conveyed in this manner. By translating the psalter from Hebrew into vernaculars, whether using a formal equivalence or making use of local poetic forms, and perhaps setting it to locally appropriate music, it may be that the style of proclamation enables deeper engagement with the text.[13]

Conclusion

We have seen that the psalter is in some ways a school for world mission. As the people of God praise God in their own community for who he is and what he has done in creation and redemption, they inevitably proclaim God outside their own community, drawing attention particularly to the judgment that arises from God's holiness, and the blessings that flow from submitting to his anointed king. God is the God of the whole earth. This is a vital theme in the Psalms, and spurs us on in our witness to the one God and the one Lord Jesus Christ in the world.

---

12. See e.g. the website of the International Council of Ethnodoxologists <http://www.worldofworship.org>, accessed 21 May 2013.
13. See chapter 6 in this volume.

INDEX OF SCRIPTURE REFERENCES